D1555519

LITHUANIAN HASIDISM

LITHUANIAN HASIDISM

WOLF ZEEV RABINOWITSCH

foreword by **SIMON DUBNOW**

SCHOCKEN BOOKS · NEW YORK

Published in U.S.A. in 1971 by
Schocken Books Inc.
67 Park Avenue, New York, N.Y. 10016

Library of Congress Catalog Card No. 72-148840

It gives me pleasure to express my grateful appreciation to
Mr. M. B. Dagut, Lecturer in English at the University
College of Haifa, for the care and scholarship which he has
devoted to the translation of this book.

The Hebrew original of this work, החסידות הליטאית
was published by Mosad Bialik, Jerusalem.

Translated from the Hebrew by

M. B. DAGUT

The author gratefully acknowledges the assistance of a research grant from
the Memorial Foundation for Jewish Culture.

First published in Great Britain 1970
by Vallentine, Mitchell & Co., Ltd.
18 Cursitor Street, London, E.C.4.

ISBN : 0 853 03021 9

Printed in Great Britain by Lewis Reprints Limited
London and Tonbridge

TO MY WIFE AND HELPMATE

THE TRANSLITERATION of Hebrew names and words in this volume follows the Sephardi pronunciation, and is based on the phonetic method employed in scholarly works. Special note should be taken of the following conventions:

Hebrew *beth* with *dagesh* is represented by *b*.

  „   *beth* without *dagesh* is represented by *v*
                                        (e.g., *Avraham*).

  „   *heth* is represented by *h* (e.g., *hasiduth*).

  „   *kaf* without *dagesh* is represented by *kh*
                                          (e.g., *Barukh*).

  „   *peh* without *dagesh* is represented by *f*
                                          (e.g., *sefer*).

  „   *tav* with *dagesh* is represented by *t* (e.g., *toledoth*).

  „   *tav* without *dagesh* is represented by *th*
                                          (e.g., *toledoth*).

  „   *tsaddi* is represented by *ts* (e.g., *tsaddik*).

The *dagesh forte* is represented by a doubled letter (except in the words *mithnaged, mithnagdim*).

The *sheva mobile* is represented by *e*.

Proper names from the Old Testament have been written as spelt in the Revised Standard Version of the English Bible.

Russian place names appear in the text according to their usual Jewish pronunciation. The Russian form of the names has been added in the Index. Both these place names and the names of Russian writers, books and articles have been transliterated phonetically for the convenience of the reader. Note should be taken of the following ligatures:

kh as in Scottish *loch* (e.g., La*kh*ovich).

ch „ „ *church* (e.g., Lakhovi*ch*).

sh „ „ *bush* (e.g., *Sh*neur).

zh „ „ *pleasure* (e.g., *Zh*itomir).

The titles of books and articles written in Hebrew, Yiddish and Russian appear in the text only in transliteration. A translation has been added in the Bibliography.

The author's explanatory additions to the text of original documents and to Hebrew terms have been placed in square brackets, thus [ ]. Additions or variants forming part of the original text appear in ordinary brackets, thus ( ).

vi

CONTENTS

ILLUSTRATIONS

FOREWORD

THERE WAS a period in Jewish historiography when hasidism was written about with partisan passion, the question debated being whether the movement was beneficial or harmful to the development of Judaism. Scholars were divided into an anti-hasidic and pro-hasidic school, and even in our time some writers have tried to continue this controversy. Today, however, we have reached the point at which dogmatism is giving way to a historical approach, and partisan argumentation is being replaced by objective scientific research into the nature and interconnection of the events.

Now that we possess a general history of hasidism in the period of its origin and growth, the time has come for more detailed individual studies on this topic—monographs on various schools of thought within hasidism and their founders, or on dynasties of *Tsaddikim* which had an effect on the Jewish masses in various countries.

One excellent monograph of this kind that has come to my notice is Dr. Zeev Rabinowitsch's book on the Karlin hasidic dynasty. The very great importance of this family of *Tsaddikim* lies not so much in the extent of its influence, as in the fact that its origins go back to the first period of the hasidic movement—to the period of the Great *Maggid*, whose disciple, R. Aharon 'the Great' of Karlin, founded the first 'sect' of hasidim in Lithuania, and thereby set off the first polemical attack on hasidism by the *Gaon*, R. Eliyahu of Vilna. By discovering new source-material relating to this important chapter of history or new combinations of old material, the author has succeeded in presenting us with a complete history of the dynasty from its beginnings to the present day. For this he has earned the gratitude of all lovers of Jewish history, including myself.

Berlin, *Nisan.*   SIMON DUBNOW.

AUTHOR'S NOTE

When I found the 'holy writings' in the 'court' of the Karlin dynasty in Stolin, i.e., 'The Stolin *genizah*,' and made this collection the basis of my research into Karlin hasidism, the cradle of the whole Lithuanian movement, I sent the manuscript to the distinguished Jewish historian, Simon Dubnow, who was at that time writing his book *Toledoth ha-Hasiduth* (The History of Hasidism). It was Dubnow that urged me to publish my research, and he was even good enough to write a foreword to it. Subsequently, I came into possession of further material on the history of hasidism in Lithuania, and expanded this book to include all the branches of Lithuanian hasidism.

PREFACE

THE HISTORY and teachings of Lithuanian hasidism, and its place in the general history of the hasidic movement, have not, up to now, been adequately studied. It is true that Dubnow, the leading historian of hasidism, stresses that as early as the first days of the movement a clandestine group of hasidim was established in Karlin, a suburb of the 'principal community' of Pinsk.[1] He further mentions that Karlin, and afterwards Amdur, close to the 'principal community' of Grodno, were the scenes of the bitter sectarian struggle waged between the hasidim and the mithnagdim (or *misnagdim*, as they were popularly called) for a period of more than thirty years.[2] It is also true that Horodezki, and many other students of hasidic doctrine, give a separate, detailed description of the spiritual character of the founder of Karlin hasidism,[3] and quote examples of his teachings and those of his descendants and disciples (Buber and others). But, in spite of all this, no light has really been thrown on the historical development of Lithuanian hasidism and on the part played by its leaders, those pioneers of hasidism who established a centre for the movement in the northern part of the Pale of Settlement—in the heart of rabbinic Lithuania —corresponding to the centre at Mezerich in the south. Their vicissitudes and struggles during the persecutions and bans [*herem*] to which they were subjected in Lithuania, their spiritual importance, and their relations with the other branches of hasidism have all remained a blank in our knowledge, as has the subsequent development of Lithuanian hasidism in the nineteenth century.

In both the earliest and latest source—material—from the first polemical writings of the mithnagdim in the year 1772[4] and the memoirs of eye-witnesses from the earliest days of hasidism,[5] through the documents of the Russian Senate from the years 1800-1801,[6] down to the popular Jewish parlance of the nineteenth century,[7] the name 'Karliner' is found as a designation of all the hasidim. The struggle between the mithnagdim and the hasidim in the years 1796- 1801 has been investigated by Dubnow[8] and Hessen,[9] but they were interested only in the light thrown by this struggle on the general history of hasidism, and therefore did not give due weight to the part played in it by the Lithuanian hasidim.

In the present study of the history, offshoots, and teachings of Lithuanian hasidism, I have made use of both written and oral sources. The former include 'the holy writings' which I found in the archives of the 'court' of the Karlin dynasty in Stolin ('the Stolin *genizah*'), the historically reliable information contained in the hasidic literature, the 'teachings' of the *Tsaddikim* of the various dynasties that arose in Lithuania, the polemical writings of the mithnagdim, official documents of the Russian government, and historical material concerning the cultural, political and economic conditions of the Jews in Polesia,[10] the region in which Lithuanian hasidism originated. The oral sources include information communicated to me verbally by the last *Tsaddikim* of the Karlin and Libeshei dynasties and by individual descendants of the other dynasties, as well as stories and legends about persons and events connected with Lithuanian hasidism, a careful distinction being made, of course, between fact and fiction.

From a study of all this material, it emerges that Lithuanian hasidism had three main branches. The first and most important of these, to which the great majority of Lithuanian hasidim belonged, comprised the 'Karlin dynasty' and the dynasties of the Karlin *heder* [school] formed by generations of its disciples. Secondly, there was Amdur hasidism. And thirdly there were the dynasties which originated in Volhynia and subsequently established themselves in Lithuania.

NOTES TO PREFACE

[1] S. Dubnow, *Toledoth ha-Hasiduth,* pp. 111, 146, 271, Tel Aviv 1932 ; see also Graetz, *Geschichte der Juden,* Vol. XI, pp. 107, 557, Leipzig 1900.

[2] Dubnow, *op. cit.,* pp. 111, 145, 157, 221, 364, 367-370.

[3] S. A. Horodezki, *Ha-Hasiduth ve-ha-Hasidim,* Vol. II, p. 113-121, Tel Aviv 1951. M. Buber, *Tales of the Hasidim, Early Masters,* 195-202, 273-285 ; Idem, *Tales of the Hasidim, Later Masters,* pp. 153-173, New York 1966. M. Buber made a collection of the finest teachings and legends contained in the extensive hasidic literature. In this work he presents sayings attributed to the Lithuanian *Tsaddikim,* R. Aharon and R. Shelomo of Karlin, R. Mordekhai of Lakhovich and two of his descendants, and R. Moshe of Kobrin. In his penetrating introductions to the volume, Buber paints a hasidically inspired portrait of the spiritual character of these *Tsaddikim,* as reflected in these writings.

[4] '*Zemir Aritsim ve-Harvoth Tsurim,*' published by Dubnow, in *Chassidiana,* supplement to *He-Avar,* Vol. II, p. 25, Petrograd 1918.

[5] *Salomon Maimons Lebensgeschichte,* ed. by J. Fromer, p. 188, Muenchen 1911. Two abridged English versions have now been published under the titles. *Solomon Maimon, An Autobiography,* ed. by M. Hadas, New York 1947, and *The Autobiography of Solomon Maimon* with an Essay by Hugo Bergman, London 1954. Se also Grégoire, *Histoire des sectes religieuses,* Vol. III, p. 322, quoted by Graetz, *op. cit.,* Vol. XI, p. 557. V. infr. Chap. 2.

[6] Published by Dubnow in *Yevreyskaya Starina,* Vol. III, pp. 257-280, St. Petersburg 1910.

[7] A. Friedkin, *A. B. Gottlober un Sayn Epokhe,* p. 75, Vilna 1925 ; S. Y. Fuen, *Kiryah Neemanah,* p. 275, Vilna 1860 ; M. Lipson, *Mi-Dor Le-Dor, Vol.* III, p. 210, Nr. 2368, Tel Aviv 1929-1938. Cf., the well-known popular saying: 'If you don't become a Karliner [i.e., a hasid] you'll become a Berliner [i.e., an "enlightened" Jew].'

[8] Dubnow, *Toledoth ha-Hasiduth,* pp, 242-278 ; Idem, *Yevreyskaya Starina,* Vol. III, pp. 84-109, 253-282.

[9] J. Hessen, *Yevreyi v Rossiyi,* p. 143 ff., St. Petersburg 1906.

[10] The name 'Polesia' denotes the region in the western part of Russia around the Pripet Marshes, with the town of Pinsk in its centre, and stretching westwards almost to the town of Brest-Litovsk, eastwards to the town of Mozyr, and northwards to the approaches of Minsk, while to the south it includes the northern portion of Volhynia. See the map of Polesia in the volume: *Toyzend Yor Pinsk,* ed., Dr. B. Hofman, p. 291 New York 1941.

Chapter I

The Beginnings of Hasidism in Lithuania (to 1760)

HASIDISM HAD ITS cradle in the southern provinces, in Podolia and Volhynia. It was here, in an atmosphere of blood-libels and Cossack massacres, that the voice of hasidism, with its joyous affirmation of life, its fervour and faith, first made itself heard ; and it was from here that it spread to become a mass-movement in almost all the Jewish settlements in Eastern Europe. In Podolia the founder of the movement, Rabbi Yisrael *Baal Shem Tov* (the Besht), 'revealed himself' ; and in nearby Volhynia his disciple and successor, R. Dov-Baer, 'the Great *Maggid*' of Mezerich, lived and taught. The political and social conditions of the time made the southern provinces particularly favourable soil for the growth of the hasidic movement. Politically, the seventeenth and eighteenth centuries were in this region a time of lawlessness bordering on complete anarchy, with frequent peasant riots and Cossack revolts, civil wars, and anti-Jewish pogroms. The breakdown of political stability undermined the economic status of the Jews, who lived mainly in the villages and small towns and thus suffered most from the general collapse of law and order. As there were hardly any large centres of Jewish culture in this region, the confused political situation brought about a spiritual weakening of the Jewish communities and a decline in the authority of the organs of Jewish autonomy. In the general neglect of Jewish learning, the masses sought consolation for their hardships in mysticism and fantasy.

The few rabbinical scholars that there were treated the 'ignorant' masses with contempt, until the two classes came to be divided by an antagonism so deep that they ceased to understand each other's language. The rabbis, for example, could not understand that the ordinary Jew was forced by the difficulties of his daily life to relax his observance of the *mitsvoth* [practical commandments], and they therefore

1

never ceased reproaching and upbraiding him for his sins. This attitude on the part of the rabbis greatly lowered their prestige among the simple masses. Thus to the political chaos and economic distress there was added a spiritual crisis. The Jews of Podolia and Volhynia not knowing where to turn in their great need, were overwhelmed by a sense of helpless despair. It is therefore no wonder that it was in these southern provinces that there arose a wave of passionate yearning for both national and individual redemption. And indeed, we find that almost all the pseudo-messianic movements (Hayyim Malakh, Yehudah Hasid, Yaakov Frank) took hold and spread mainly in these southern provinces.

The situation in the northern provinces, particularly in Lithuania, was quite different. The ' Vaad [Council] of the Principal Communities of the Province of Lithuania ' functioned actively in the five 'principal communities' of Lithuania (Grodno, Brest-Litovsk, Pinsk, Vilna and Slutsk) from 1623 to 1761.[1] In the cities and larger settlements, the Lithuanian Jews enjoyed a certain degree of internal autonomy. Apart from the 'Council of the Province,' every city had its own well-organised kahal [communal committee] which managed all the communal institutions and administered the payment of taxes to the secular authorities and the Jesuits. The Jews of neighbouring White Russia (Reissen —the provinces of Mohilev, Vitebsk, and part of the province of Minsk) and of Zamut (Zhemud, roughly the boundaries of the province of Kovno), who were culturally closely related to Lithuanian Jewry, for a long time also came under the control of the 'Council of the Province of Lithuania': Reissen belonged to the kahal of Brest-Litovsk and Zamut to the kahal of Grodno.

The Jews of Lithuania suffered very little from the Cossack uprising ;[2] and since they lived mainly in large concentrations, their economic situation was sounder than that of the Jews in the south. In the region of Pinsk, in the province of Polesia (which is particularly important for the present study), very many Jews, as testified by the Vilna documents,[3] earned their living as land-stewards and innkeepers (arendators) ; and half of the documents connected with

Pinsk and its surroundings concern land-stewardship and the like. Culturally, too, the condition of Lithuanian Jewry was far better than that of their fellow-Jews in the south. Most of the rabbis and leading scholars of Eastern Europe, and some of Western Europe, were the products of the Lithuanian *yeshivoth*. Even the cultural level of the ordinary people was higher here.[4] The *Kabbalah* was also studied in Lithuania, as is explicitly related by Solomon Maimon.[5] Lithuania was the home of the saintly R. Tsevi-Hirsh of Koidanov (the author of *Kav ha-Yashar*), of R. Betsalel of Kobrin (the author of *Amudeha Shivah*), of R. Naftali of Minsk (the author of *Nethiv ha-Yashar*), and other famous scholars. The *Gaon* of Vilna, too, the greatest talmudic authority of Lithuanian Jewry, is also known to have studied the *Kabbalah*. But in Lithuania interest in the *Kabbalah* remained a purely individual matter.[6] The pseudo-messianic movements had no large following here. The Jewish community's cultural institutions and its whole spiritual life were jointly directed by the *kahal* and the rabbis.

The difference between the political, social and spiritual conditions of the Jews in the southern provinces and of those in Lithuania resulted in hasidim being given a very different reception in Lithuania from that accorded it in Podolia and Volhynia. The whole essence of hasidism was a dual protest: against absolute domination of communal life by the *talmid hakham* [rabbinical scholar], and against the attempts by the masses to find redemption in the fantasies of the pseudo-messiahs. One of the main tenets of hasidism was that true piety consists not in great learning or in the rigorous formalistic observance of the *mitsvoth*, but in prayer. The love of God is not to be attained by intellectual power or learning, but by the outpouring of the soul in prayer: 'Prayer is not simply a standing *in* God's presence ; praying is itself a revelation *of* God's presence . . . since we find God through prayer.' By prayer every Jew actually comes closer to his heavenly Father. And not only by prayer: every pure thought and every good deed also brings the individual Jew nearer to his Creator. Hasidism, which concerned itself not only with the future coming of the

3

Messiah, but also with the amelioration of the individual Jew's lot on this earth, aspired to bring some joy into the lives of the suffering Jewish masses. The Besht is reported to have said that his teaching was based on three loves: the love of God, the love of Israel, and the love of the *Torah*. Hasidism was an offshoot of the *Kabbalah* ; but, unlike the *Kabbalah*, it rejected withdrawal from life as one of the ways of worshipping God and strove, on the contrary, to imbue its adherents with a spirit of joyful optimism, since ' the Father would rather see His children happy than sad.' Joyfulness thus became one of the central tenets of the new movement. The element of religious pantheism in hasidism, and the movement's ethical and educational content, were noticed only by a small minority. To the ordinary Jew, hasidism was simply something that gave him back his belief in the meaningfulness of his own life, and restored his social self-respect.

Small wonder, then, that in such circumstances the teaching of the Besht was received with great enthusiasm by the Jews of Podolia and Volhynia, but quite otherwise in Lithuania. Setting prayer above study, criticising established religious customs and traditions, changing over to the Sephardi version of the prayers—all this seemed to Lithuanian Jewry to constitute a grave defiance of accepted religious authority. Even the minor reforms introduced by hasidism into the order of the prayers aroused in the Lithuanian rabbis apprehensions of another pseudo-messianic movement, originating once again in the southern provinces. The realistically minded Lithuanian Jews were also alarmed by the fact that the Besht, and his disciples after him, were not content with being spiritual leaders, but also set themselves up as wonder-workers, predictors of future events, healers of the sick, and the like.

The Besht ' revealed himself ' in the middle of the thirties of the eighteenth century. At the time of his death in 1760 his followers are estimated to have numbered about 10,000, all of them Jews from Podolia, Volhynia, and Galicia. On only one occasion did the Besht venture into Lithuania, on a visit which is described in both hasidic[7] and mithnaged[8] sources. Two of the arendators of Prince Radziwil[9] built a

4

house in the Lithuanian town of Slutsk (according to the mithnaged source, in Visoki, close to Brest-Litovsk) and invited the Besht, who had a reputation for being able to predict the future, to come to them. The hasidim relate that, during his stay in Slutsk, the Besht was subjected to a spate of abuse by the mithnagdim.[10] According to the version of the story traditionally told by the mithnagdim, they forcibly ejected the Besht from the city. This implies that the Besht's name was already known in Lithuania and White Russia during his lifetime. Indeed, among his disciples were R. Mendel of Vitebsk and R. Pinhas of Korets, the latter of whom came from Shklov, the heart of the Jewish aristocracy and the metropolis of White Russia. According to hasidic sources, Lithuanian Jews used to travel to listen to the Besht's teaching of his doctrine.[11] Nevertheless, in the Besht's lifetime there were still no organised groups of hasidim in Lithuania. In none of our sources is there any indication that the Besht's emissaries visited Lithuania to spread the teachings of hasidism there. His followers among the Lithuanian Jews used to come to him in Podolia, while he himself did not venture to go to them and preach his doctrine publicly in Lithuania. Official Lithuanian Jewry did not react at first to the Besht's movement and to the pilgrimages made to him by individual Lithuanian Jews. The first open protest against hasidism was made by a Polish rabbi, R. Shelomo of Helm, in 1751.[12]

To the Lithuanian rabbis there did not seem to be anything serious or dangerous in the Besht's appearance, because of his lack of talmudic learning. Characteristic of this contemptuous attitude is the popular tale to the effect that the rabbis examined the Besht on the contents of the prayer-book, to see if he was really conversant with the laws governing prayer. The piety of the Lithuanian rabbis and the piety of the Besht derived from such completely different sources that they were unable to find a common language. At that time the rabbis could not have imagined that, within about fifty years, the Besht's doctrine would be accepted by the majority of East-European Jewry. There is no historical foundation to the hasidic story that the Besht's influence in Lithuania even in his lifetime was so great that he was able, as early as 1746, to have R. Yehiel Margalith appointed Rav in Grodno.[13] Nor is there any historical truth in the declaration allegedly made by the Besht and his disciples against the supposed Shklov *herem* in 1757. What is true is that Besht's son, R. Tsevi, as related by popular tradition, lived in Pinsk and that he is buried in the old cemetery there. The devout hasidim of Pinsk—so the story goes—made a practice of removing their shoes when visiting the old cemetery, out of respect for the saintly men buried there, and as they did so they would also mention the name of ' Hershele [= Tsevi], the son of the *Baal Shem*.' Although the Besht's son lived in Pinsk during the persecutions of the hasidim, the details of his life there are unknown. Indeed, as is well known he plays no part in the hasidic movement. He was not a *Tsaddik* ; and according to the mithnagdim, he lived his whole life in Pinsk in the house of his father-in-law (R. Shemuel Hasid) and being supported by him. He died in Pinsk before 1810.[14]

NOTES TO CHAPTER I

[1] *Pinkas Medinath Lita*, ed. Dubnow, Preface, Berlin 1925. The geographical division which was in a certain sense purely Jewish in origin, is also found in later Russian and Polish Documents. Cf., *Akty Isdavayemyye Vilenskoyu Kommissiyeyu dla Razbora Drevnikh Aktov*, Vol. XXIX, Nos. 155, 163, 194, 195, etc., Vilna 1902.

[2] Except for individual incidents. Cf., The Vilna Documents, Vol. XXIX, passim.

[3] *Ibid.*, Vol. XXVIII, Vilna 1901, and Vol. XXIX, passim ; Nadav, 'Kehillath Pinsk bi-Thkufah she-mi-Gezeroth Tah-Tat ad Shalom Andruszov (1648-1667),' *Zion*, 21st year, p. 185 ff., Jerusalem 1966 ; Idem, *Toledoth Kehillath Pinsk*, passim, in ms.

[4] On the difference between the scholars and the masses even in Lithuania, see *Maimons Lebensgeschichte*, p. 69 ff.

[5] Maimon, *op. cit.*, p. 151 ; Cf., I. Tishby, 'Ha-Rayon ha-Meshihi ve-ha-Megammoth ha-Meshihiyoth bi-Tsmihath ha-Hasiduth,' *Zion*, 32nd year, p. 16 ff, Jerusalem, 1967.

[6] V. infr., the dialogue between the Vilna Gaon R. Eliyahu and the Pinsk *Av Beth-Din* R. Rafael Hacohen, Chap. 2. Cf., A. Lourié, 'Di Tsavoe fun a Pinsker Baal-ha-Bayith fun Onheib Neinzenten Yorundert,' *YIVO Bletter*, Vol. XII, pp. 390-427, New York 1938. The funeral instructions given by the writer of the above-mentioned will, R. Shaul Karliner—who was also one of the leaders of the Karlin community—show how great was the influence of kabbalistic doctrine on the belief and way of thinking of one of Lithuanian Jewry's greatest representatives in the first quarter of the nineteenth century.

[7] *Shivhei ha-Besht*, ed. Horodezki, p. 87, Berlin 1922 ; *Adath Tsaddikim*, p. 32, Lemberg 1865.

[8] *Zoth Torath ha-Kanauth*, cited by Graetz, *op. cit.*, Vol. XI, p. 552 ; M. L. Wilensky, 'The Polemic of Rabbi David of Makov against Hasidism,' Proceedings of American Academy for Jewish Research, Vol. XXV, pp. 137-156, New York 1956.

[9] Mentioned in *Maimons Lebensgeschichte*, p. 73.

[10] *Shivhei ha-Besht*, ed. Horodezki, pp. 87, 88.

[11] *Ibid.*, p. 84.

[12] Shelomo mi-Helmo, *Mirkeveth ha-Mishne*, Preface, Frankfurt on the Oder 1951.

[13] *Shivhei ha-Besht*, p. 73 ; S. E. Friedenstein, *Ir Gibborim*, p. 50, Vilna 1880.

[14] S. M. Rabinowitsch, 'Al Pinsk-Karlin ve-Yoshveihen,' *Talpiyoth*, Pt. *Kehilloth Yaakov*, p. 14, Berdichev 1895. The author quotes an entry in the records of the Pinsk *Hevra Kaddisha* [burial society] to the effect that the new cemetery was used for burial starting from the 28th *Av*, 1810. He writes that R. Tsevi was buried in the old cemetery ; A. Valden, *Shem ha-Gedolim he-Hadash, Maarekheth Gedolim*, p. 39, s.v.: *Tsevi ben . . . ha-Besht*, Warsaw 1880. According to hasidic tradition, R. Tsevi died in 1780. Many eye-witnesses report that the old cemetery was destroyed by the Soviet authorities who turned the site into a park.

Chapter II

Karlin Hasidism

A.   R. Aharon the Great (1765-1772)

AFTER THE DEATH of the Besht, his disciple and successor, R. Dov-Baer, the Great *Maggid,* established a new centre for the movement in the small town of Mezerich, in Volhynia. From Volhynia, which lay to the north of Podolia, R. Baer was able to extend his influence over Lithuania and White Russia. The personality of the Great *Maggid,* his efforts to base hasidism on the historical tradition of Judaism, and apparently also his organisational talents, compelled the *Rabbanim,* particularly in Lithuania, to pay serious attention to the new movement. For Lithuania, we have two different pieces of information on this subject, one from hasidic sources and the other of mithnaged provenance ; and, in addition there is the testimony of Solomon Maimon.

In the well-known collection of mithnaged writings, *Zimrath Am ha-Arets,*[1] there is a letter from the mithnaged preacher, R. David of Makov, to R. Shelomo-Zalman, the *Av Beth-Din* [Head of the Rabbinical Court] of the community of Nashelsk. In this letter it is stated that the *Rosh Yeshivah* [Head of the Talmudic School] and the *Av Beth-Din* in Pinsk, R. Rafael Hacohen, paid a visit to the Great *Maggid* of Mezerich, in order to become acquainted with both the man and his doctrine.[2] On his return, he made a report to the *Gaon* of Vilna. To the *Gaon's* question 'Is he [sc. R. Baer] a scholar ?' R. Rafael answered 'No.' When the *Gaon* asked R. Rafael about R. Baer's knowledge of *Kabbalah,* he replied : 'I do not know, since I myself am not conversant with this lore. I can only judge his knowledge of hidden doctrine from his knowledge of revealed teaching [i.e., *Gemara*].' Further on in his letter, R. David of Makov writes that in the year 1765-1766 R. Baer became widely known in the Jewish world, and *Rabbanim* and

8

talmudic scholars began flocking to him to study hasidic doctrine under his instruction. Hence, it may be assumed that in this year (1765-1766) the penetration of hasidism into Lithuania was already in process. Among R. Baer's disciples we find the kabbalist and talmudic scholar, R. Pinhas Horowitz (the author of the work *Haflaah*), who was at that time a *Rav* in the small Lithuanian town of Lakhovich. In the introduction to the book *Maggid Devarav le-Yaakov* by 'R. Dov-Baer . . . of the holy community of Mezerich,' mention is made of 'the learned, pious and humble aged *Rav*, our teacher R. Zeev-Wolf of the holy community of Greater Horodno [Grodno] in the Province of Lithuania.' This R. Zeev-Wolf was a disciple of the Great *Maggid,* and wrote down his master's teachings. R. Baer's great success is also attributed to the emissaries whom he sent out to every Jewish community, including those in Lithuania.

Solomon Maimon, himself a Lithuanian Jew—from Nesvizh, near Slutsk—has the following to say about these emissaries in his autobiography[3]: 'Its leaders [sc. of hasidism] sent emissaries to every place to preach the new doctrine and gain adherents to it. . . . It once happened that a young man, who had already joined this society and had had the privilege of speaking in person to its leaders, passed through the town where I was living. . . . His words so fired my imagination that I was completely carried away. Seized by an overwhelming desire to attain to true happiness by becoming a member of this noble society of men, I resolved to go to the town of M. [ezerich] where the Rebbe B. [aer] was living.' The events described here belong to the middle of the 1760s, and there must no doubt have been many young Lithuanian Jews who at that time made their way to Mezerich, like Solomon Maimon, to hear 'the new doctrine' there. Among them was the future founder of the Karlin branch of hasidism, R. Aharon, known to the hasidim as 'R. Aharon the Great,' who became one of the Great *Maggid's* most distinguished disciples.

R. Aharon of Karlin was born in 1736.[4] His father, R. Yaakov, was a native of the small town of Yanovo (close to Pinsk) who earned a meagre livelihood as the *shamash* [caretaker and usher] of a *beth midrash* [house of prayer and

study].[5] At about the same time as the Pinsk *Av Beth-Din,*
R. Rafael Hacohen, returned disappointed from Mezerich,
the young man from the Pinsk suburb of Karlin was so
attracted to R. Baer's doctrine that he became not only the
Maggid's devoted disciple, but also one of the main propagators of his teachings. He travelled regularly through the
small Lithuanian towns preaching hasidism, as he later
wrote of himself in his will: 'He used to admonish the
masses with a sternness that concealed an inner love, in
order to bring all Jews closer to their heavenly Father.'
Hence he came to be popularly known as 'the admonisher.'[6]
R. Aharon was the one and only hasidic Rebbe in Lithuania
at that time. R. Mendel of Vitebsk and R. Yisrael of Polotsk
were mainly active in White Russia, even though the town
of Minsk where R. Mendel then lived was within the borders
of 'the Province of Lithuania'; and R. Shneur-Zalman does
not appear on the scene until about 1781. R. Aharon was
thus the pioneer of hasidism in Lithuania.

So it was that Karlin became the centre of the hasidic
movement in Lithuania, particularly in that part of it known
as 'Polesia.' In the years 1770-1772 there were Karlin
hasidim in Vilna and the other Lithuanian towns,[7] as we
know from several contemporary references to their
existence. Thus, for example, Solomon Maimon writes in
his autobiography: 'These people [sc. the hasidim] used
to make pilgrimages to K. [arlin], M. [ezerich], and other
" holy " places where the leaders, teachers, and great lights
of this sect lived. Young men would leave their parents,
wives, and small children and travel in groups to visit these
great " Rebbes " and to receive instruction from them in the
new doctrine.'[8] Karlin is also described as a hasidic centre
by Grégoire.[9] The full extent of R. Aharon's influence, not
only in Karlin, but also in the whole surrounding district,
can be inferred from two postscripts added by him in the
communal *pinkas* of Nesvizh, which was found among the
'holy writings' of the Karlin *Tsaddikim.*[10] Preserved in these
Karlin hasidic archives (the Stolin *genizah*) are several pages
from the above *pinkas,* containing the resolutions passed
by the heads of the *kahal* in the matter of communal taxes.
Appended to the resolutions are two postscripts by R.

Aharon, indicating his assent to the resolutions passed. From internal evidence it is clear that both the resolutions and the postscripts belong to the year 1769.[11]

The resolutions in the Nesvizh *pinkas* are worded as follows:

'These are the ordinances which were enacted . . . by the drafting committee chosen . . . together with the leaders of the assembly, on Friday . . . 10th *Adar* I, 1769.

'In the ordinances concerning the meat tax [*korobka*] which were drawn up in the year 1765 there are several seeming iniquities to be put right. Moreover, there is even a contradiction, and this must be corrected. But it is not expressly stated that the heads of the *kahal* are empowered to amend the meat-tax ordinances. Therefore, we have confined ourselves to making only this amendment—that in future neither the heads of the *kahal* nor the leaders of the assembly may impose a double meat-tax, but only a single one. If the money [raised does not] suffice for the needs of the community, then everything shall be done [in conformity with the amendment] and with the ordinances mentioned below, which the heads of the *kahal* will have to make in addition to the meat-tax of 1765, but without doubling it.'

The drafters of the enactments then go on to explain how the communal tax was to be collected. This was apparently a joint property-and-income tax which all the Jews had to pay. After the signatures of the *Rabbanim* of Kletsk and Slutsk [?], we find the following two postscripts by R. Aharon:

I. 'After I have beheld the poverty of our Jewish people, how can I hold my peace, when I have seen the bitter plight of the poor of Israel and heard the cry which they utter in their great pain, and I am concerned that the leaders of the community should not go astray (Heaven forbid!) in this bitter iniquity of robbing the poor? Wherefore an assembly was convened and chose some of its number to draw up enactments to deliver the oppressed poor, and they apparently formulated these enactments according to their own opinion. The whole assembly then solemnly undertook to confirm and observe every detail of

11

the enactments. . . . I therefore decree that whosoever shall nullify these enactments and infringe the rights of the poor shall be utterly excommunicated and accursed. Seeing that I am authorised by our teacher . . . the learned Sage of the whole *golah* [diaspora], the *Maggid* of the holy community of Mezerich, to remove any stumbling block from the path of the children of Israel as far as my power extends, even to the proclaiming of a *herem* [ban]. Wherefore my advice is not to breach the fence [erected round the Law] by the Sages, so as not to be caught (Heaven forbid!) in the trap [of sin]. He that hearkens [to this decree] will be blessed with every good. Such are the words of Aharon, the son of our Teacher R. Yaakov (of blessed memory) of Karlin.'

II. 'I hereby require that it be recorded as my solemn decree that, on pain of excommunication, no meat-tax shall be collected from *melammedim* [children's teachers], i.e., deducted from their tuition fees. Moreover, I hereby decree, under pain of excommunication, that no one shall lease double the meat-tax of the year [5]525—[= 1765] as registered there, without the agreement of the drafters of the enactments whose signatures appear on the previous page, p. 160, or of all the inhabitants of the city, all the poor and penniless listed in the meat-tax register. Even a single one of the taxpayers can prevent [a double meat-tax]. If someone should innocently ask the reason for the enactment [not to permit a double meat-tax], the answer is that, according to the law of our sacred Torah, no meat-tax at all is permitted. Those who ask questions like this in order to strip the poor of Israel of their last penny are most certainly of the seed of the Gibeonites. . . . Whosoever shall seek to nullify the enactments signed on the foregoing page is hereby placed under the ban and excommunicated from all the communities of Israel. But he that hearkens unto them shall be blessed with every good, for whoever is merciful to his fellow-creatures shall receive mercy from Heaven. Such are the words of Aharon of Karlin.'

The strong wording of R. Aharon's postscripts testifies to the powerfulness of his position and to his profound concern for the poor. At this time, the *kahal's* jurisdiction over the Jewish community was still legally recognised by the secular power, and there was bitter antagonism between the leaders of the *kahal* and the masses, even to the extent of open conflict. R. Aharon, as we see from the postscripts, fearlessly takes the side of the poorer classes and in doing so evidently acts as an influential leader. Apparently then, by about 1769 the hasidic movement had already gained support in Lithuania, too. The first clash with the mithnagdim (1772) had not yet occurred, otherwise R. Aharon would not have been bold enough or strong enough to write in the *pinkas* of another Lithuanian town his own opinions and instructions about the resolutions passed by an assembly of *Rabbanim* and *kahal* leaders. R. Aharon's assertion, 'I am authorised by our Teacher . . . the learned Sage of the whole *golah*, the *Maggid* of the holy community of Mezerich,' shows that R. Baer was not only well known but was also apparently recognised as an authority even by the Jews of Lithuania.

This was the period of the hasidic movement's taking root and first flowering in Lithuania. However, on account of R. Aharon's untimely death, and as a result of the persecutions of the hasidim which began at that time (1772), the importance of Karlin for hasidism in those years was forgotten.

Karlin's sister town, Pinsk, was a strong hold of rabbinism. It was in here that the first shots in the war against hasidism were fired, and they were aimed principally at R. Aharon. This much is evident from the following letter, found in the Stolin *genizah*, from R. Baer of Mezerich to R. Eliezer Halevi, a *Moreh-Tsedek* [rabbinical judge] in Pinsk and author of several homiletical works,[12] and to R. Hayyim, also of Pinsk. The text runs as follows:[13]

'Greetings to my dear friend, the learned and venerable *Rav* Eliezer Halevi, and to his compeer the learned and renowned *Rav*, the Teacher R. Hayyim. I write to urge you to live together in peace and to work in partnership and harmony with our distinguished and renowned friend, R. Aharon. It is well known that his guidance is pleasing to God (?). Why, then, should you turn away [from him] ? What wrong, Heaven forbid, has been found [in his conduct] that provides any ground for doubt ? Set aside evil thoughts,

that there may be no schism between you (Heaven forbid!).
Let the previous good relations be restored, and let not this
matter be unimportant to you. Then you will be granted
peace from the Lord of peace, and from me, your friend
and well-wisher, Dov-Baer, the son of R. Avraham of
blessed memory.
'These words are also addressed to the learned scholar,
the Teacher R. Shelomo, that he should strive in his wisdom
to establish peace in your camp.'

The letter bears no date, but it was most probably written
between 1769 and 1772 and is thus evidence of the first
persecutions of the Karlin hasidim led by R. Aharon. It also
shows that R. Baer, who here takes his disciple, R. Aharon,
under his protection, was well known in Lithuania and felt
sufficiently sure of his own authority to intervene with a
Moreh-Tsedek in Pinsk. The R. Shelomo mentioned in this
letter is R. Shelomo of Karlin, one of the outstanding
disciples of the Great *Maggid,* a disciple and associate of
R. Aharon and subsequently his successor as Rebbe.
R. Shelomo was at that time living with R. Aharon in Karlin
and was his chief aide in the campaign to propagate the
hasidic doctrine among the Jewish masses.

According to hasidic sources, at this same time another
of R. Baer of Mezerich's outstanding disciples, R. Levi-
Yitshak (later known as R. Levi-Yitshak of Berdichev) was
officiating as *Rav* in Pinsk. These sources state that, in 1771,
R. Levi-Yitshak was elected the *Av Beth-Din* and *Rosh
Yeshivah* of Pinsk.[14] However, from his written approvals
to the volumes *Hovath ha-Levavoth* (1772) and *Erkhei
ha-Kinnuyim* (1775) we learn that, in those years, R. Levi-
Yitshak was in fact still officiating as *Rav* in Zhelikhov.[15]
Nor does hasidic literature contain any historical material,
or even legendary traditions, about the relations between
R. Aharon and R. Levi-Yitshak in Karlin or Pinsk. We do
know that a bitter dispute broke out between R. Levi-
Yitshak and the mithnaged population of Pinsk, which
resulted in R. Levi-Yitshak's deposition from the office of
Rav and his expulsion from Pinsk. But this event occurred
after the death of R. Aharon.[16]
While in Lithuania the attacks on hasidism were being

directed against individual adherents of the movement,[17] the first assembly of the communal representatives and *Rabbanim* of neighbouring White Russia was convened in the Shklov, in White Russia. This assembly issued the first public anti-hasidic proclamation drawing the attention of the communal leaders, and in particular of the *Gaon* of Vilna, to the danger in the new movement.[18] From a letter written by R. Shneur-Zalman of Ladi to R. Avraham of Kalisk (Kolishki, in White Russia) we learn that this assembly took place in the winter of 1771-1772.[19] It was called primarily on account of the strange conduct of R. Avraham of Kalisk, on his return home from the *beth midrash* of Mezerich. His strange antics while praying ('turning repeated somersaults,' and the like) and his contemptuous and abusive attitude to talmudic scholars outraged not only the *Rabbanim* but even the Great *Maggid* himself. R. Avraham and his followers were popularly known as the *Talk* [= 530] hasidim, with reference the year 5530 [= 1769-1770], when they first made their appearance in Kalisk. The above-mentioned letter by R. Shneur-Zalman goes on to state that in the ensuing public debate between the communal leaders and the *Maggid's* disciples, R. Avraham of Kalisk was obliged to apologise. The Shklov assembly of 1771 decided to persecute the hasidim, and appealed to the *Gaon* of Vilna for his support.[20]

In spite of the persecutions and the general atmosphere of hatred all around them, the Karlin hasidim, led by R. Aharon, continued their vigorous propagation of hasidic doctrine among the Jews of Lithuania. The collection of anti-hasidic writings known as *Zemir Aritsim ve-Harvoth Tsurim,* published in 1772, gives us a picture of contemporary hasidism as seen by the mithnagdim. In his volume the hasidim are referred to as ' Karliners ': ' Lament for the hasidim of this time who are called Mezerichers and Karliners.'[21] The hasidim in Vilna were also called ' Karliners ':' It was resolved to drive out and scatter forthwith the Karliner *minyan* [in Vilna].'[22] We also read that ' in these times we have heard to our sore amazement of the flourishing of the wicked in the Province of Lithuania, how they have multiplied and become very strong. . . . And

15

C

because of our many transgressions the plague has spread to every province, and to every city.'[23] The hasidim formed their own *minyanim* [prayer quorums], so as to be able to follow the Sefardi form of prayer and to pray with their customary noisy fervour. They distributed large numbers of broadsheets containing the tenets of hasidism, and perhaps also propaganda letters from R. Aharon who was not permitted to preach the hasidic doctrine publicly and freely, like his comrades in the south. These sheets, however, have not been preserved, since the mithnagdim, as is clear from their own broadsheets, used to burn all hasidic writings that they could lay hands on.[24]

It was already the custom, in those early days, for a hasidic leader to wear white garments on Sabbaths and Festivals.[25] His disciples would assemble in his home—so hasidic tradition relates—for the ' third meal ' [eaten on the Sabbath in the late afternoon] and the *melavveh malkah* [gathering of hasidim on the Sabbath night to eat and to sing liturgical songs together]. Then the Rebbe would deliver a discourse, and his assembled followers would sing *zemiroth* [liturgical poems]. According to the tradition of the Karlin hasidim, these customs were already practised by R. Aharon the Great. These, then, would be the first signs of tsaddikism. However, in the actual writings of R. Aharon the Great—his letters and will—there is no allusion to any such cult in the *Tsaddik*.

The tendency of the hasidim to segregate themselves from the rest of the community greatly alarmed the Lithuanian communal leaders and *Rabbanim,* who feared the appearance of a new messianic movement. The hasidic demand that ritual slaughtering be performed with ' polished knives ' also aroused great indignation. In the larger cities—Vilna, Minsk and Shklov—the hasidim began to be severely harassed. R. Mendel of Vitebsk, who was then living in Minsk, travelled to Vilna in an attempt to see the *Gaon,* R. Eliyahu, but was not received by him.[26] Karlin is not mentioned in contemporary documents, even though in Karlin R. Aharon had his own house of prayer and hasidic community, and his followers flocked to him from the whole surrounding district.[27] His most important disciples in those days were his friend and future successor, R. Shelomo of Karlin and R. Hayyim-Heikel of Amdur.[28] They were both drawn to hasidism through the influence of R. Aharon and subsequently became disciples of the Great *Maggid*.

The increasing success of hasidism in Lithuania brought home to the leaders of Lithuanian Jewry the alarming realisation that what they were confronted with was not just a series of isolated incidents, but a large-scale popular movement. After the Passover Festival in 1772 the first *herem* against the hasidim was proclaimed, on the authority of the *Gaon* of Vilna, in every *beth midrash* and synagogue in Vilna. The prayer-houses of the hasidim were forcibly closed, their preachers assaulted, and their writings burnt.[29] Moreover, the formation of new hasidic groups was proclaimed unlawful. The Vilna community further published a manifesto, signed by the *Gaon*, calling on the four other principal Lithuanian communities (Pinsk, Grodno, Brest-Litovsk, Slutsk) and on those of White Russia (Shklov and Minsk) to outlaw the hasidim, as the Vilna community had done, and to persecute them relentlessly.[30]

At the very time when the Vilna hasidim were being subjected to persecution and excommunication,[31] there occurred in Karlin an event which was to have a great effect on the future development of Karlin hasidism and of Lithuanian hasidism in general. On the fourth intermediate day of Passover, 19th *Nisan*, 1772, R. Aharon the Great died suddenly in Karlin, at the early age of thirty-six. The Karlin hasidim thus found themselves bereft of their Teacher and Rebbe, while the hasidic movement as a whole lost one of its most important leaders and the Great *Maggid* one his most loyal and active disciples. 'The *Tsaddik*, R. Aharon the Great, was devoured by the flame of piety that burnt in him,' said the hasidim to one another.[32]

R. Aharon the Great's personality is revealed in his 'Exhortations,' his letter and his will,[33] as well as in sayings and thoughts attributed to him and legends told about him.[34] The Besht, as already stated, had based his doctrine on three loves. Every one of his disciples subsequently concentrated all his efforts and aspirations on one of these three: to R. Levi-Yitshak of Berdichev the most important principle

17

was the love of Israel ; for R. Shneur-Zalman of Ladi, the founder of the *Habad* school of hasidism, it was love of the *Torah* ; and for R. Aharon the Great it was the love of the Creator—'bringing Israel closer to their heavenly Father,' as he wrote in his will. R. Aharon's strong sense of religious awe transported him into a state of constant spiritual devotion and mystical ecstasy. According to hasidic tradition, R. Shneur-Zalman of Ladi said of him: 'R. Aharon's fear of the Holy One Blessed Be He was like the fear of a condemned man who stands bound to the stake while a soldier in front of him aims the arrow at him, and he sees the head of the arrow leaving the bow and speeding towards him. Such was his fear in small matters. In great matters, it was beyond all conceiving.' Hasidic legend further relates that, whenever R. Aharon recited the Song of Songs, there would be a commotion in Heaven and the angels would cease singing their pæans of praise to the Holy One Blessed Be He and gather together to listen to R. Aharon's holy melody. The ecstatic fervour which is still seen to this day in the praying of the Karlin hasidim is said by the hasidim themselves to take its origin from R. Aharon the Great.

R. Aharon demanded that every one of his disciples should 'shut himself up in solitude in a special room for one day of every week and spend the time in fasting, repentance, and study of the *Torah*. . . . And if possible, he should shut himself up alone every day. Even without fasting let him take care to withdraw for not less than an hour, and let him make confession to his Creator and entreat His forgiveness.'[35] This shows that R. Aharon did not completely shake off the kabbalistic tendency to asceticism. He himself used to fast frequently, though he would warn his disciples against excessive fasting. In a letter to one of his disciples he writes: 'Frequent fasts, ascetic practices, and ritual immersions are a device of the evil impulse to distract you from your study and prayer, to make you pray with a weakened body and a confused mind.'[36] To his advice to his disciples to study the volume *Reshith Hokhmah* he adds: 'You shall carry out all that is written in it, except the self-mortifications and fasts prescribed in it, and then it will be well with you.'[37]

18

R. Aharon also required of his disciples that they should study the *Aggadah*, a demand that was also alien to the Lithuanian Jew who was primarily interested in the *Halakhah*. In his 'Exhortations' R. Aharon writes: 'Beware of pride and anger even in the performance of a *mitsvah*, still more of dissension (Heaven forbid!), and be particularly careful in this even with one's own family.'[38] '"Know Him in all your ways" means that eating, drinking, sleeping, and sexual intercourse are all to be directed only to the worship of the Creator, blessed be His Name.'[39]

R. Aharon the Great was the author of the lyrical Sabbath song 'Yah Ekhsof Noam Shabbath' ['Lord, I yearn for the Sabbath's delight'], a poem filled with spiritual love and religious longings.

This liturgical poem was sung by the adherents of Karlin hasidism and its offshoots—Lakhovich, Koidanov, Kobrin, Slonim and others—privately in their own homes, or all together on the Sabbath eve and at 'the third meal.'[40] The Karlin hasidim have about twenty different tunes for this song[41] which is called by them simply *Ha-Zemer* ['*the* liturgical poem']. One of these tunes has become widely known as *Ha-Niggun ha-Kadosh* ['the holy tune']. There are also hasidic stories about R. Aharon's special customs on *Simhath Torah*.[42]

In hasidic tradition R. Aharon is described as possessing a keen capacity to distinguish 'between pure and impure.' He could also discern lofty souls in simple Jews and, on the contrary, lay bare the true character of hypocrites. This is why the Great *Maggid* used frequently to send him out 'to purge away impurity.'[43] The apocryphal hasidic literature contains various sayings and ideas attributed to R. Aharon the Great[44] which, though of doubtful authenticity, combine to give us a picture of his character and his influence on his adherents down the generations. Thus, he is reported to have said that melancholy is not a sin, but that it dulls the heart more than the gravest sin. 'And what is actually the source of melancholy? It is when I feel I am entitled to something or lack something, physical or spiritual. But all this is my own good. And what of it, if I lack something? What really matters is that God should not be deprived of His due.'

19

R. Aharon distinguishes between 'melancholy, which is a bad quality, and bitterness which is really wilfulness, because I have not made a start on doing good deeds. For nothing in the world, no matter how minute, can be achieved without devotion. And since I had no devotion, I have done nothing, and therefore I do not deserve anything; so that I cannot maintain that I lack anything. Nevertheless, I breathe God's air and have what I require. This in itself should make us happy. Hence bitterness is good.' R. Aharon expatiates on this point: 'There are some young scholars that think they are bitter, when in fact they are simply melancholy. A man must know how to distinguish between these two conditions. After the soul-searching that comes from melancholy, a man goes to sleep, being unable to bear himself, much less his friend, and seething with anger. But after the soul-searching that comes from bitterness, a man cannot sleep. For what actually is bitterness ? The recognition that you have not begun to do good deeds. So you forthwith make haste and set yourself to study and prayer. Now you feel that you are a Jew. You enjoy seeing another Jew. Nevertheless, you must know that only a hair's breadth separates bitterness from melancholy. The most spiritual bitterness touches on melancholy, while even the coarsest joy springs from holiness.'[45] In another place, the following words are attributed to him: 'When we speak of the value of joyfulness, we do not mean the joy that comes from the performance of a *mitsvah*, since this joy is already a higher degree which not every Jew can be required to attain to. What we mean is the denial of melancholy. Quite simply, a Jew who is not happy with his lot as a Jew is ungrateful to God. It shows that he has never once heard the blessing, " That hast not made me a Gentile." But when he examines himself to see if he is a hasid or not, that is pride. What does it matter if he is a hasid or not ? He is a Jew.' [46]

R. Aharon's humility and self-effacement are illustrated by the following story. On one occasion, one of the disciples of the Great *Maggid* happened to pass through Karlin on his way home from a visit to his master in Mezerich. His desire to see R. Aharon was so great that he decided to call

on him, even though it was the middle of the night. So he
went and knocked on the window of R. Aharon's house and
called: 'Aharon, open the door to me!' When R. Aharon
asked who was there, the other answered simply, 'I,' because
he was sure that R. Aharon would recognise him by his
voice. But R. Aharon did not reply, and did not open the
door. Again the disciple knocked, and again R. Aharon
made no response. Then the disciple asked: 'Aharon, why
do you not want to open the door to me ?' To this R. Aharon
replied: 'Who is it that arrogantly calls himself "I," an
appellation fitting and proper only to the Holy One Blessed
Be He ?' 'In that case,' said the disciple to himself, 'I have
not yet learnt anything from my Teacher,' and he at once
returned to Mezerich.[47]

Hasidic doctrine has its own special definition of humility.
Man is merely dust and ashes, and must therefore never
forget his own imperfection in comparison with the perfection of the Creator ; yet, at the same time, he must also
know that he is the son of a King. True humility consists
in the proper synthesis of these two perceptions. This was
the kind of modesty possessed by R. Aharon the Great. In
his will he calls himself 'the greatest of sinners and worst
of offenders' ; but, at the same time, he enjoins 'that my
place of rest shall have a clear space, four cubits wide, left
all around it—that is to say, that no one shall be buried
within four cubits of my grave, unless it be someone whom
you know I would certainly have wanted as my close
neighbour. If anyone wishes to transgress this injunction
and to bury there someone whom it is known I certainly
would not have agreed to have as a close neighbour, let
him know that, just as in my life in this world I zealously
punished any who sinned against the Creator, so will he
be punished by the zealous God of vengeance. . . . I further
enjoin that no words of praise shall be spoken of me. Whoever wishes to speak ill of me may do so, and I hereby give
him leave ; but let him know full well that, if he utters any
falsehood, he will be judged for it in the court of heaven. . . .
Only the true disciples of our Teacher and Master
[sc. R. Baer], the God-fearing and perfect ones, may speak
such praises of me as they know for a certainty to be true

and may intercede [sc. with God] on my behalf. But they, too, must be extremely careful in any matter wherein they are not certain of what was my real intention. The best would be for them not to speak at all. . . . Immediately after the seven days [of mourning], a memorial stone shall be erected on my grave, but no honorific titles shall be inscribed on it. Only the following shall be engraved on the stone: Here lies so and so, who was himself vouchsafed Divine grace and was several times granted to obtain it for others, devotedly sacrificing himself for this purpose,[48] according to his own understanding, in order to obtain Divine grace for the many ; and who used to admonish the masses with a sternness that concealed an inner love, in order to bring all Jews closer to their heavenly Father and join them to Him in a perfect union.'[49]

To his disciples he addressed the following last wish: ' All those that have ever learnt from me a single letter of Divine worship, I do most solemnly and earnestly request them, as if I were actually standing in person in their presence . . . every day for a whole year [after my death] to study at least two or three lines of *Aggadah*.'

B.   R. *Shelomo of Karlin* (1772-1792)

The year 1772 was a hard year for the hasidic movement as a whole, and in particular for Karlin hasidism. After the Passover Festival of that year, the first *herem* against the hasidim was proclaimed in Vilna. Three weeks after the proclamation of the *herem,* the Vilna community sent letters to the Brisk [Brest-Litovsk] community[50] and to the other communities in Lithuania and White Russia[51] informing them of the step taken. At the instigation of the Vilna community, a *herem* was now also proclaimed in Brody. The Pinsk community, too, must undoubtedly have received the broadsheet announcing the excommunication of the hasidim, for in the protocol found in the Vilna communal archives we read: ' The leaders of the five principal communities in Lithuania have already taken measures to put a stop to this aberration, in the year[5]532—[= 1772].'[52] At the same time, the collection of anti-hasidic writings, *Zemir*

22

Aritsim ve-Harvoth Tsurim, was circulated among Lithuanian Jewry. The Lithuanian communities were now divided by a spirit of bitter factional strife. In the hasidic camp the worst sufferers were the Karlin hasidim who lost their leader, R. Aharon the Great, just at that time when the Vilna *kahal* forcibly dispersed the 'Karlin *minyan.*'

At the end of 1772, in the month of *Kislev,* the hasidic movement suffered a further blow with the death of its teacher and leader, the Great *Maggid* of Mezerich. The same year saw the first partition of Poland, which resulted in the severance of White Russia from Lithuania. In consequence of this great political change the Karlin hasidim were largely deprived of the spiritual and organisational support which they had been receiving from the hasidim in neighbouring White Russia led by R. Mendel of Vitebsk and R. Yisrael of Polotsk. The new political frontier did not, it is true, cut off the Jews on either side of it from all communication with each other. Thus, for example, the decisions on religious questions and on points of Mosaic law handed down by the *Beth-Din* of the Brisk or Vilna community[53] were still binding on all the Jewish communities. Similarly, the relations between the Lithuanian hasidim and their counterparts in White Russia continued uninterrupted. But since the main attack on hasidism was launched in Lithuania, the Karlin hasidim suffered more than those in White Russia. It was not until after the second and third partitions of Poland, in 1793 and 1795, that the two regions were once again united under Russian rule.

The war against the hasidim was jointly waged by the *Rabbanim* and the heads of the *kahal,* which continued to be recognised by the secular authorities even after the abolition of the *Vaad ha-Medinah* (1761).[54] Thus, for example, the anti-hasidic broadsheets were signed not only by the *Rabbanim,* but also by communal leaders,[55] and sometimes—as in the case of the broadsheets of 1781—even by the latter alone.[56] The sheets were sent from one town to another addressed to both the *Rabbanim* and the *kahal.*[57] The participation of the leaders of the *kahal* in these anti-hasidic activities provoked the hasidim into a deliberate attempt to shake off the *kahal's* jurisdiction, a struggle in

23

which they were considerably helped by the general dissatisfaction of the masses with the rule of the *kahal*. The fight against the *kahal* was begun by the Karlin hasidim and ended in their complete emancipation from its control (1793), but only after a long and bitter struggle.

Prompted by the 'bans' of 1772, the mithnagdim proceeded to hound the hasidim, spying on them, boycotting them socially, and refusing to intermarry with them. The *kahal* forcibly closed their prayer-houses, and the hasidim were compelled to say their prayers and hold their meetings clandestinely. In this critical period, the heavy task of the physical and spiritual leadership of the hasidim was assumed by R. Aharon the Great's most devoted disciple, R. Shelomo, to whom the Karlin hasidim turned for protection. He headed the Karlin movement throughout these troubled years (1772-1792). After a life full of suffering he was driven out of his native town, Karlin, and died a martyr's death in his place of banishment, Ludmir [Vladimir-Volhynsk].

R. Shelomo, the son of R. Meir Halevi of Karlin, was born, according to hasidic tradition, in 1738.[58] Of his birthplace and childhood nothing certain is known. Even hasidic records on these points are very scanty.[59] Like his teacher, R. Aharon the Great, R. Shelomo was also one of the Great *Maggid's* chief disciples, and he is mentioned by the *Maggid* in the latter's letter to the Pinsk *Moreh-Tsedek*, R. Eliezer Halevi.[60] When R. Aharon set up his *beth midrash* in Karlin R. Shelomo became one of his most devoted disciples,[61] and used to travel together with him to Mezerich. And when, after R. Aharon's death, R. Shelomo took over the leadership of the Karlin hasidim, he made himself responsible for the upbringing of R. Aharon's son, R. Asher, who was to be the next *Tsaddik* in the Karlin dynasty founded by his father.

At this very same time (1772-1773), another of the Great *Maggid's* disciples, R. Hayyim-Heikel, who was also a disciple of R. Aharon's and had in his youth been a *hazzan* [synagogue cantor] in Karlin, established another hasidic centre in Lithuania—in the small town of Amdur [Indura, near Grodno]. R. Hayyim-Heikel's extreme and uncompromising anti-rabbinism still further exacerbated the relations between *Rabbanim* and hasidim in Lithuania.[62] Karlin and

Amdur were the two main strongholds of Lithuanian hasidism in those critical days. In the other parts of Lithuania, especially in Vilna and the region of Polesia, the hasidim were few in number. This difficult period in the history of Lithuanian hasidism is well summed up in Solomon Maimon's statement: 'All that now remained of this sect was a few isolated and scattered remnants.'[63]

In White Russia at this time were living R. Mendel of Vitebsk, R. Yisrael of Polotsk, R. Avraham of Kalisk, and R. Shneur-Zalman of Ladi, then still a young man. The main hasidic leader in this region was R. Baer's elderly disciple, R. Mendel of Vitebsk, who was also known as R. Mendel of Minsk and, later, R. Mendel of Horodok. Still in the Great *Maggid's* lifetime, R. Mendel had taken up residence in Minsk in the ' Province of Lithuania,' and made it his centre for the propagation of hasidic doctrine. In the small volume *Zemir Aritsim ve-Harvoth Tsurim,* published in 1772, we read the following: '. . . the holy community of Minsk where dwells the symbol of bigotry . . . in whose company there is a band of wicked men, like R. Mendel of Minsk. On this R. Mendel we have the testimony of two and more witnesses [that he has done] disgraceful and ugly deeds such as are fobidden in Israel. . . .' From a deposition made by a mithnaged in the year 1772, we learn that Minsk was then a hasidic pilgrimage centre: 'R. Hirsch the son of R. Iser of Horodno [Grodno] wrote down all the names [of the men] . . . who wanted to travel to Minsk, and [the mithnagdim] prevented them from going.' The 'house of the hasidim' in Minsk, which served as a refuge for the persecuted adherents of the movement, is also mentioned by R. David of Makov.[64] It is quite possible that R. Mendel's presence and activities in Minsk were among the factors that decided the Minsk *kahal* to intensify its attacks on the hasidim just at that time. R. Mendel was forced by the harassment of the mithnagdim to leave Minsk and take up residence in the small town of Horodok (close to Vitebsk). R. Mendel's forced departure from Minsk took place about ten years before R. Shelomo's banishment from Karlin and R. Levi-Yitshak's expulsion from Pinsk.

In c. 1775 R. Mendel of Vitebsk and R. Shneur-Zalman

25

went to Vilna in an attempt to explain the tenets of hasidism to the *Gaon* and to make peace between the two warring factions. But the *Gaon* refused to see them. They then tried to meet the mithnagdim of Shklov for the same purpose, but there, too, they were rebuffed.[65] As a result of this hostile attitude on the part of the mithnagdim, the leaders of the hasidim in White Russia, with the sole exception of R. Shneur-Zalman, decided in 1777 to emigrate to Palestine. Since R. Shneur-Zalman maintained that he was not yet fit to be their Rebbe, the hasidim of White Russia were left without a leader and used to address their enquiries to R. Mendel of Vitebsk in faraway Palestine.[66] In this interregnum (1777-1781)— 'between one king and the next,' to use the hasidic expression—R. Shelomo of Karlin began to extend his influence into White Russia, and many hasidim there chose him as their Rebbe.[67]

Preserved among the hasidic writings is a letter of farewell from R. Shelomo to the hasidim of Shklov in White Russia. He writes as a *Tsaddik* and leader to his followers: 'I beseech the Lord that they [sc. the hasidim living in Shklov] may be granted grace through me and no one else.'[68] This provides further evidence that the links between the Jews in the two northern provinces of Lithuania and Reissen were not broken by the political partition of Poland: R. Mendel of Vitebsk and R. Shneur-Zalman travel to the Vilna *Gaon* to debate the doctrines of hasidism with him, and conversely R. Shelomo of Karlin's influence penetrates from Lithuania, across the frontiers of Poland, into White Russia.

Found amongst the 'holy writings' in the Stolin *genizah* is the following letter from R. Shelomo of Karlin to R. Aharon of Vitebsk:

'Greetings to my very dear friend, the learned and renowned hasid . . . R. Aharon Segal, may his light shine out!

'Now . . . about the matter that has occurred in your province I have much to say to your honour, only it is not possible to explain everything in writing, but only face to face. However, the truth is with us, for God performs wonders unaided, even against the laws of nature . . . in all places and at all times. Fare you well. From him who prays that the love of the Creator shall be shown to Israel, Shelomo, the son of . . . R. Meir Segal of blessed memory. ' I request you to send me two glass bottles.'

The letter bears no date nor does R. Shelomo specify what he means by ' the matter that has occurred in your province [sc. Reissen: Vitebsk].' But possibly this letter, which is addressed to one of R. Shelomo's followers or supporters, belongs to the period under discussion.[69]

As is well known, it early became one of the most important principles of hasidism for every hasidic group to be headed by a leader and teacher. Hence it was inconceivable for any such group to exist without a Rebbe, i.e., without a *Tsaddik*. The anti-hasidic broadsheets of 1781 show us how significant the role of the *Tsaddik* was even in those early days.[70] Hence the great importance of R. Shelomo of Karlin for the now leaderless hasidim of White Russia. The conditions of the time made it impossible for R. Shelomo to extend the influence of the hasidic movement ; and indeed any such attempt would have been foreign to his wholly pacific temperament. His task was the more modest one of holding together and strengthening the already existing groups of hasidim in White Russia, by becoming their Rebbe after their own *Tsaddikim* had left them to fend for themselves.

In these same years—up to 1781—Karlin hasidism gradually began to provide itself with a proper internal organisation. During a lull in the attacks of the mithnagdim, R. Shelomo was able to devote himself to the task of giving Karlin hasidism its own distinctive form. He placed special emphasis on two principles. The first of these was the manner of praying that he had taken over from his own teacher, R. Aharon—with the maximum of intellectual intensity [*kavvanah*], emotional fervour, and spiritual devotion. ' For he used to move mountains with the power of his prayer, since he devoted his whole soul to the Almighty.' Hasidic tradition relates that, when a friend once invited R. Shelomo for the following day, he replied: ' You

27

stupid man! This evening I must say the evening prayer
and read the *Shema*, which means devoting my spirit to
God. Then comes sleep, and the next day I must pray again,
and in prayer there are several worlds till the reading of
the *Shema* is reached. And then there is prostration in
prayer, which is also a devoting of the spirit to God, and it
is still uncertain whether the Almighty will grant my wish
[sc. to remain alive]. Yet you want me to promise you that
I shall come to your house tomorrow!' A similar story is
also told of R. Uri of Strelisk, a devoted disciple of R.
Shelomo of Karlin. It is related that, before going to say the
morning prayer, he used every day to take a fond farewell of
his wife and children and tell them his last wishes, in case
he should depart this life while praying, as a result of the
intensity of his devotion to God [*devekuth*]. To illustrate
the intensity of R. Shelomo's belief in the power of prayer,
particularly of his own prayers, the hasidim relate that, once
it was charged in the Court of Heaven that the children of
Israel were no longer praying with true *kavvanah*. A certain
king therefore determined to forbid all prayer. In the commotion that ensued, the *Tsaddikim* in Heaven were first
asked if they agreed to the decree. Then R. Shelomo of
Karlin was asked. He prayed with such fervour that, when
he passionately declared that he undertook to pray for all
Israel, the decree was forthwith annulled.

These and similar stories, as well as various teachings
attributed to R. Shelomo, show that the 'Karlin manner of
prayer' was his creation. From his correspondence with
R. Shneur-Zalman we learn that R. Shelomo 'used to despise
the natural piety [i.e, the non-ecstatic prayer]' of the
mithnagdim all around him. R. Aharon the Great, the
thinker, taught that every act performed by man on earth
should be a kind of Divine worship or prayer. R. Shelomo
on the other hand, the man of feeling, is said to have taught
that all other acts are only ways leading to the true worship
of the Creator which is prayer, and prayer is therefore of
greater importance than anything else. He is reported to
have said that the greatest miracle is to teach a single Jew
to pour out his heart to the Almighty.

The second main principle developed by R. Shelomo in

Karlin hasidism was the concept of tsaddikism. The essence of this idea was that the *Tsaddik* is not merely a spiritual leader and teacher, but also has the power to help his followers in worldly affairs. From being a spiritual leader, he thus becomes a wonder-working saint. Hasidic tradition, which refers to R. Shelomo as ' the little *Baal Shem*,' reports him as saying: ' In Heaven a measure is kept of the fields and woods traversed by the hasid on his journeys to the *Tsaddik*.' In its conception of the *Tsaddik*, Karlin hasidism differs considerably from *Habad* hasidism and is closer to the southern branch of the movement in Volhynia and Podolia. R. Shelomo's doctrine with regard to the importance and power of the *Tsaddik* was still further developed by R. Asher, his successor as head of the Karlin dynasty, and reached its climax in the time of R. Asher's son, R. Aharon the Second. R. Shelomo's teaching was also propagated after his death by his two most important disciples, besides R. Asher: R. Mordekhai of Lakhovich, and R. Uri of Strelisk, ' the Seraph.'[71]

There was originally nothing at all conceited or vainglorious in this exaggerated conception of the *Tsaddik's* importance. On the contrary, it was accompanied by a profound awareness of the value of every individual Jew, even the most insignificant. The following parable of R. Shelomo, which R. Aharon the Second of Karlin was in the habit of quoting, testifies to this remarkable awareness of the great individual worth of every single Jew in the sum total of the whole Jewish nation: ' All Israel together are a single edifice, and every individual Jew is needed to make this edifice complete. It is like a man who has to get something lying in a very high place and who hasn't a ladder to reach that place. What does he do ? He stands many men on each others backs, from the floor up to the place where the object he wants is lying. Can it be said that a single one of these men, even the smallest of them, is superfluous ? If a single one of them moves, they will all fall down. So it is with the whole people of Israel. Every single Jew completes the edifice, each according to his own size and worth, small and great alike, and all together they can ennoble this world and raise it to ever greater spiritual heights.'

At this same time, the well-known *Tsaddik* R. Levi-Yitshak (of Berdichev) was *Av Beth-Din* and *Rosh Yeshivah* in Pinsk. This R. Levi-Yitshak was remarkable, not only for his own individual interpretation of hasidic doctrine,[72] but also for his talmudic scholarship. He was elected *Rav* in Pinsk in 1775 or 1776, during the lull in the mithnaged attacks on the hasidim. The only information that has come down to us about his pro-hasidic activities consists of a few popular legends, according to which the leaders of the *kahal* were displeased with him for devoting most of his time to prayer and the like, instead of dispensing halakhic rulings. It was evidently the lull in the hostilities between mithnagdim and hasidim in the latter 1770s that made it possible for a *Tsaddik* like R. Levi-Yitshak, who aspired to putting hasidic doctrine into practice in his daily life, to be elected *Av Beth-Din* in Pinsk.[73]

However, the wrath of the Lithuanian mithnagdim was soon aroused again by a combination of factors—the great success of hasidism in the south, the stubborn resistance of the hasidim in the north, and the hasidic attack on the rabbinical method of talmudic study and on the whole rabbinical philosophy of life. The leaders of this attack were R. Shelomo of Karlin (as we learn from his correspondence with R. Shneur-Zalman), and also the second Lithuanian *Tsaddik* of that period, R. Hayyim-Heikel of Amdur, and others. Especially infuriating to the mithnagdim was the publication of the first hasidic book, *Toledoth Yaakov Yosef*, by R. Yaakov-Yosef of Polonnoye (1780), without the consent of the *Rabbanim*. The renewed conflict which now (1781) broke out was even bitterer than that of 1772 and the Karlin hasidim were now persecuted even more severely.

In the summer of 1781, the Lithuanian communities for the second time proclaimed a *herem* on the hasidim. At about the same time, R. Levi-Yitshak defended hasidism in a public debate in Warsaw with the *Rav* of Brisk, R. Avraham Katzenellenbogen. On the 20th *Av*, 1781, the *herem* was read out in all synagogues and *batei midrash* in Vilna. Four days later the Vilna community sent a letter to all the other Lithuanian communities, calling on them, too, to impose the *herem* on the hasidim and to boycott them.

Two emissaries were sent for this purpose to the Lithuanian fair at Zelva (near Grodno), where all the heads of the Lithuanian communities had gathered together. At the instigation of these emissaries, and on the authority of the Vilna *herem,* a ban on the hasidim was now proclaimed in Zelva, too (1st *Elul*).[74] The communal leaders informed their communities in writing that the hasidim were to be placed under the ban and persecuted relentlessly. The representatives of the Grodno community, headed by their *Av Beth-Din,* wrote to their members to this effect on the self-same day.[75] On the next day, the *Av Beth-Din* of Brisk, the well-known adversary of hasidism, R. Avraham Katzenellenbogen, who was also present at the Zelva fair, drew up a public proclamation containing a bitter, vengeful denunciation of the hasidim. Similar action was taken by the representatives of Pinsk[76] and Slutsk.[77] On the return of the emissaries to Vilna (13th *Elul*), the *herem* was again proclaimed in that city, this time with the solemn ritual of blasts on the *shofar,* lighting of black candles, and so on.

The letter drawn up by the representatives of the Pinsk community and sent from Zelva to Pinsk is important for our study, because of the proximity of the latter town to Karlin. The text of the letter reads as follows:

'On the occasion of our being here in the community of Zelva on the day of the market, the Lord willed that we should meet . . . a great and esteemed member of the holy community of Vilna, the learned scholar . . . David *Moreh-Tsedek* . . . and his compeer, the renowned scholar . . . Zelig. They showed us a letter . . . which the Lord prompted . . . the leaders of the holy community of Vilna [to write], together with the *Rav* of Vilna and also our Master the pious *Gaon* [sc. R. Eliyahu], who . . . girded up their strength to fight zealously for the Lord of Hosts and built a fence to repair the breached edifice [of the *Torah*] . . . as was explained at length. . . . They were surely right in all that they said, that there should be one *Torah* for them all, joined together and united in a lasting bond. . . . Therefore we, too, do fully and firmly endorse . . . all the words . . . of the leaders of the above-mentioned holy community [of Vilna] together with the above-mentioned *Gaon,* as written . . . in their aforementioned letter. It is fitting and proper for God-fearing men of perfect faith to strengthen and support each other and restore the crown [sc. the *Torah*] to its former glory, that they should not be separated from each other, but should be joined together like one man, as of old. We have agreed to the enforcement of the great *herem* proclaimed in the . . . glorious community of Vilna and of the words uttered and heard in the holy community of Zelva on the day of the market. All that hear this . . . shall cease to be . . . separated from the community of the Lord . . . and [shall cease] to reject the authority of the early Sages, who from of old have followed their thoughts which are based on . . . the truth. . . .

'In confirmation whereof we, the leaders and officers of the Pinsk community, gathered here in Zelva on the day of the market, do herewith sign our names, on the sixth day of the week, the 3rd *Elul*, [5]541[= 1781].

'Signed: Nahman, the son of Eliezer Segal;
Yaakov, the son of Avraham;
Yehudah-Leib, the son of Elhanan;
Menahem-Nahum, the son of R. Meir;
David, the son of . . . Feivel;
Shalom, the son of Eliyahu;
Tsevi-Hirsch, the son of Dov-Baer.'

Unlike the public proclamation issued by the heads of the Grodno and Brisk communities, which was also signed by the *Av Beth-Din* of the town, the call of the Pinsk leaders does not bear the signature of the *Av Beth-Din*, since in this particular year this office in Pinsk was held by R. Levi-Yitshak.

The letters from the Vilna *kahal* and from the *Rav* of Brisk, R. Avraham Katzenellenbogen, are particularly strongly worded. Realising that the weapons employed against the hasidim in 1772—the closure of hasidic prayer-houses, the forcible breaking up of hasidic groups and the like—had been completely ineffective, the *Rabbanim* this time decided to ban the hasidim from all social contact with the Jewish community and therefore decreed that no one should eat at their table or have any dealings with them at all. This new wave of bans and boycotts that swept through the towns of Lithuania must have constricted R. Shelomo of Karlin's sphere of influence again and confined it to Karlin which, together with Amdur, once more became the refuge of Lithuanian hasidism.

In this desperately critical time for the hasidic movement, a new figure came to the fore—the youngest and most spiritually gifted of the Great *Maggid's* disciples, R. Shneur-Zalman. The main centre of R. Shneur-Zalman's influence was in White Russia and he was, in fact, the founder of hasidism in these northern districts. He gave this hasidism a distinctive character of its own, which marked it off both from the hasidism of Karlin and from that of Volhynia and Podolia.

R. Shneur-Zalman, known for short as ' the *Rav*,' was born and educated in White Russia. He acquired an erudite knowledge of both revealed teaching [*Gemara*] and hidden lore [*Kabbalah*]. At the age of twenty (in 1768) he went to the Great *Maggid* in Mezerich and became one of his most devoted disciples. It was the *Maggid* that assigned him the task of compiling a *Shulhan Arukh* [codification of halakhic law] in the spirit of hasidism (the so-called *Shulhan Arukh shel ha-Rav*). In the course of two years R. Shneur-Zalman compiled the main sections of this work. After the Great *Maggid's* death, R. Shneur-Zalman did not seek to become a *Tsaddik,* like most of his Teacher's disciples, but, together with the *Maggid's* son, R. Avraham Hamalakh, he continued his study of *Gemara* and *Kabbalah*. Eventually, he became one of the close associates of R. Mendel of Vitebsk, whom he accompanied on his journeys to Vilna (c. 1775) and Shklov to take part in debates on hasidism. When, as described above, the leaders of the White Russian hasidim emigrated in 1777 to Palestine, R. Shneur-Zalman— apparently at R. Mendel's request—settled in White Russia. According to hasidic tradition, R. Mendel designated him his successor. Nevertheless, R. Shneur-Zalman refused to take over the leadership of the hasidim at once. It was not till three years later that he agreed to accept this responsibility. During these years, as already stated, White Russia came under the influence of R. Shelomo of Karlin. Also living in this region at this time were R. Yisrael of Polotsk (who had returned from Palestine) and R. Yissakhar-Baer of Lubavich with their own hasidic groups of followers.

In c. 1781 R. Shneur-Zalman assumed the leadership of the hasidim in White Russia and created what came to be known as the *Habad* brand of hasidism [an acronym of the Hebrew words *hokhmah* = wisdom, *binah* = understanding, *daath* = knowledge]. He introduced into hasidism something of the spirit and character of the talmudic 'Lithuanian' Jews of the northern provinces. He also enriched hasidic literature with his work on the philosophy of hasidism, *Likkutei Amarim*, better known as *Tanya*. In connection with the polemical debate between the mithnagdim and the hasidim, it is especially important to note that R. Shneur-Zalman did not regard hasidism as a protest against rabbinism, but rather as its complement; just as he did not consider the head of a hasidic community to be a wonder-working *Tsaddik*, but merely a spiritual guide and leader. A Jew needed to study hasidism just as much as he needed to study the *Talmud*, and vice versa; and therefore the religious opinions and way of life of talmudic scholars were not to be despised. The essence and spirit of Judaism were to be learnt from all the available sources; and every form of prayer—not necessarily or solely that of hasidism—brought the Jew closer to his heavenly Father.

R. Shneur-Zalman's name rapidly became widely known. His influence was not restricted to White Russia (Vitobsk, Mohilev, Shklov, etc.), but spread also to a section of the Lithuanian hasidim, especially those in nearby Vilna where the hasidim were being particularly violently persecuted and had no *Tsaddik* or spiritual guide. The Vilna hasidim were called 'Karliners' already in the time of the Great *Maggid*, [78] and the name continued to be applied to them still later (1800),[79] even though they had never actually been followers especially of the Karlin Rebbe. We hear nothing about any relations between R. Aharon the Great and the two propagators of hasidism who were then in Vilna—R. Hayyim and R. Iser—or indeed about R. Aharon's whole attitude to the Vilna hasidim. Hence, when R. Shneur-Zalman appeared on the historical scene, most of the hasidim in Vilna regarded him as their leader and Rebbe, though the mithnagdim continued to refer to them as 'Karliners,' a name which had for them become synonymous with 'hasidim.' The hasidim of White Russia, some of whom had from 1777 to 1781 looked to R. Shelomo of Karlin as their leader, now also went over to R. Shneur-Zalman. The sphere of influence of Karlin hasidim within the territory of Polesia was thus little by little reduced at the beginning of the 1780s.

Under the pressure of the mithnaged attacks from outside and of the contraction of his influence from within, R. Shelomo was forced to abandon the old home of hasidism, Karlin, and seek another shelter for himself and his *beth midrash*. According to hasidic tradition, he had originally intended to withdraw to the small White Russian town of Beshenkovich (in the province of Vitebsk), where several of his followers lived. But, in the meantime, R. Shneur-Zalman's influence had become predominant there and R. Shelomo found himself obliged to ask his consent to the move.[80] R. Shneur-Zalman is said to have made his consent conditional upon R. Shelomo's undertaking not to show contempt for talmudic scholars and scholarship, not to dismiss as worthless the performance of *mitsvoth* even without *kavvanah* [true devotion], and not to teach that the *Tsaddik* has the power to help his followers in everything—that 'the *Tsaddik* carries the whole flock.' R. Shelomo accepted the first two demands, but rejected the third, and was therefore compelled to give up the idea of settling in White Russia. This hasidic tradition is evidence of the difference of opinion between these two hasidic teachers on the place and function of the *Tsaddik* in the life of the hasidic community. It further confirms that, in Karlin hasidic circles just as in other branches of the hasidic movement (R. Yaakov-Yosef of Polonnoye, R. Hayyim-Heikel of Amdur, R. Avraham of Kalisk, and others), the orthodoxy of the mithnagdim was contemptuously dismissed as a purely formalistic observance, and their method of talmudic study was likewise treated with scorn. From the written approval by R. Shelomo prefaced to the volume *Kether Shem Tov*, we learn that in 1784—the year of the book's publication—he was already in Ludmir. He signs the approval as follows: 'Shelomo of Karlin, at present in the holy community of Ludmir.'[81]

From what is known of R. Aharon Segal of Vitebsk, to whom the above-quoted letter from R. Shelomo was addressed, it may be assumed that R. Shelomo's words— 'about the matter that has occurred in your province I have much to say to your honour, only it is not possible to explain everything in writing. . . . However, the truth is with us '— refer to differences of opinion, perhaps even to a dispute about their respective authorities 'in your province' (i.e., White Russia), between R. Shelomo and R. Shneur-Zalman. R. Aharon Segal of Vitebsk was originally a loyal adherent of R. Shneur-Zalman, and the latter refers to him in one of his letters (apparently from the early 1780s) as 'the renowned *Rav* and hasid.' Subsequently however, he became one of R. Shneur-Zalman's opponents. R. Avraham of Kalisk was obliged to come to his defence in a letter which he wrote to R. Shneur-Zalman: '. . . Let the wise man hearken and learn to be reconciled with the friend of the Lord, the aged and venerable *Rav*, the Teacher R. Aharon Halevi of Vitebsk; for it is to his honour to support him and to esteem him as formerly. . . . There is no greater profanation of the Divine Name than to humiliate such a man.' In one of his later letters—after 1805—R. Shneur-Zalman writes disparagingly of R. Aharon Segal: 'It is my duty to warn our followers . . . to keep far away from the band of agitators and seducers who travel with the letter of the Rebbe of ·Tiberias [sc. R. Avraham of Kalisk], led by the well-known old man from beyond the river of Vitebsk.' R. Shneur-Zalman here refers to R. Aharon Segal as the 'old man" (the appellation used by R. Avraham of Kalisk), without explicitly naming him. R. Shelomo of Karlin and R. Aharon of Vitebsk joined forces in opposing R. Shneur-Zalman. It is to the ferment created in hasidic circles as a result of this joint opposition that R. Shelomo is referring in his above-quoted letter to R. Aharon.

Just as R. Shelomo had been forced by the pressure of the mithnagdim to leave Karlin before 1784, so R. Levi-Yitshak was in 1785 driven out of Pinsk by the local population. On the 18th *Tammuz*, 1785, he was still a *Rav* in Pinsk: that is

the date on which he wrote his approval of the book
Halakhah Pesukah (Shklov, 1787) by R. Shelomo Katz of
Pinsk. But on the 25th *Tammuz*, 1785, when he wrote his
approval of the book *Kanfei Yonah*, by R. Menahem-
Azaryah (Korets, 1786), he signed it 'here in the community
of Berdichev.' It follows then, that in the week between the
18th and 25th *Tammuz*, 1785, R. Levi-Yitshak must have
moved from Pinsk to Berdichev. According to the hasidic
sources, physical force was used to expel him and his family
from Pinsk. This indignity was no doubt brought about by
the violently - worded letter from the heads of the Vilna
kahal, led by the *Gaon* R. Eliyahu and the *Rav* R. Shemuel,
to 'the leaders of . . . the holy community of Pinsk.'[82] Here
is the text of the letter:

'May the righteous flourish . . . the leaders . . . and sages
. . . of the holy community of Pinsk. . . .

'We have received your appeal . . . couched in words of
truth and good will to come to your aid . . . against the man
who has been set up in your community as a Teacher and
Gaon, yet supports doers of iniquity that throw off the yoke
of the *Torah* and *mitsvoth* and have introduced new manners
and practices unthought of by our holy forefathers. They
are the sect of the suspect, the self-styled *hasidim* [i.e., pious
ones]. . . . The leaders and officers of the principal communities, together with the *Rabbanim* and *Geonim*, after giving
great thought to the matter, have firmly resolved to fight
zealously for the Lord of Hosts . . . to root out the thorns . . .
and to disperse those wicked bands of men and drive them
far away from their confines, and to put an end to their
practices which are different from, and opposed to, the
religion of our holy *Torah*. It is the Lord's will that they
[sc. the leaders] have successfully stood firm in the breach
. . . to subdue them and make them like the dust of the
earth, so as firmly to establish the true faith. . . . However,
Satan is still at work among us . . . for the above-mentioned
sect have spread . . . their uncleanness . . . so far that even
the leaders of your community are till now members of the
sect, and . . . follow the new practices . . . which they have
introduced. . . . We warned them in letters, informing them
of the bans and excommunications . . . proclaimed by . . .

the leaders . . . together with the *Rabbanim* and *Geonim*, against the above-mentioned sect and against those that support them. . . . But the members of your community did not incline their ears and shut tight their eyes, even though there have always been in your community renowned and God-fearing men. Being oppressed by the supporters of the above-mentioned sect, they longed [to shake off the oppression] but had not the strength, until they could endure no more and determined to requite their adversaries. Whereupon the leaders of your community arose and took the courage . . . to lift up the stumbling-block and remove the stones from the highway, and they gave instructions to the *Gaon* in your community. . . . It was desireable that you should take away the crown from the *Rav* and *Gaon*. But after we saw that you agreed not to dismiss him . . . we, too, confirmed your agreement, in the hope that he might turn back from his misguided way and no longer lead the people astray. But if he obstinately refuses . . . we have already admonished you in our letter and do so now again. . . . We order you, according to the resolution of the province [sc. Lithuania], to remove the crown from the above-mentioned *Rav*, the *Av Beth-Din* of your community. . . . He shall neither teach, nor judge . . . but shall be utterly expelled. As for their [sc. the sect's] fabrication that the true *Gaon* . . . R. Eliyahu (may his light shine out!), has changed his mind and that we, too, have had second thoughts about the bans . . . imposed till now, this is a lie and another crooked invention of theirs. On the contrary, every day their shame is publicly made known according to the books of the above-mentioned men [sc. of the sect]. . . . We have always supported all the bans, that you should take care to observe what our whole province [sc. Lithuania] has undertaken to do—that the above-mentioned sect be neither seen nor found in our province— and should proclaim . . . in your community [sc. Pinsk] and the community of Karlin and the district which are under your jurisdiction, that, under pain of utter excommunication, no one shall perform . . . the abominations of that sect. And as for those that support and assist them . . . you shall draw up a list of their names and deeds, for they are a root from which

poison grows and spreads. They that call their leader
'Rebbe,' and he is the chief of sinners, in your community
and in the holy community of Karlin and in the other communities under your jurisdiction, those men must be rooted
out. Be strong . . . in zealously fighting the battle of the
Lord of Hosts . . . and do not rest. We are confident that you
will give heed to these our words and assert your authority in
the land . . . to drive out the sinners . . . from the bounds
of your holy land, to harass and pursue [the members of
the sect] to the utmost of your power, and to utterly wipe
out this filth. Such is our just request.

'Written by the heads . . . of the holy community of
Vilna . . . together with our Master, the Teacher and *Rav*,
the great and renowned *Gaon*, the *Av Beth-Din* of the
community of Vilna and also the great, pious and famed
Gaon, Eliyahu (may his light shine forth!). In witness
whereof we have signed our names on this fourth day of
the week, the 6th *Tammuz*, [5]544[= 1784].

'Shemuel, *Rav* of the above-mentioned holy community,
and Eliyahu, the son of R. Shelomo-Zalman of
blessed memory.'

This letter is dated 'Wednesday, the 6th *Tammuz*,
5544 [= 1784].' No names are mentioned in the letter
and there is an error—as Dubnow pointed out—in one
detail of the date, since in the year 5544 the 6th *Tammuz*
fell on a Friday, not a Wednesday. Nevertheless, there
is no doubt that the following passages—'the man who
has been set up in your community as a Teacher
and *Gaon*, yet supports doers of iniquity . . . to remove the
crown from the above-mentioned *Rav*, the *Av Beth-Din* of
your community. . . . He shall neither teach nor judge '—
must refer to R. Levi-Yitshak, since these appellations do
not fit R. Shelomo of Karlin. The letter also throws some
light on the sequence of events in Pinsk and on the attitude
of the Pinsk community to R. Levi-Yitshak before his
expulsion from the town. The Jews of Pinsk 'did not incline
their ears and shut tight their eyes' to the warnings of the
Vilna *kahal*, 'being oppressed by the supporter of the above-
mentioned sect.' Even though 'the leaders of your community [sc. Pinsk] arose and took the courage . . . to lift up

the stumbling-block and remove the stones from the highway,' and 'it was desirable that you should take away the crown from the *Rav* and *Gaon*,' nevertheless 'you agreed not to dismiss him . . . we, too [sc. the Vilna *kahal*], confirmed your agreement, in the hope that he might turn back from his misguided way.' From another sentence in the letter—'As for their [sc. the sect's] fabrication that the true *Gaon*, the pious *Rav* R. Eliyahu . . . has changed his mind and that we, too, have second thoughts about the bans'— we learn that, even at that time, the hasidim were already trying to spread it abroad that the *Gaon* of Vilna had revised his hostile opinion about them, a step which he did not actually take, as we know, until ten years later.

At this very time—according to one document, on the 8th *Tammuz*, 1784—R. Levi-Yitshak was violently attacked by the *Rav* of Brest-Litovsk, R. Avraham Katzenellenbogen, in a bitterly-worded open letter.[83] The 'officers of the *kahal*' in Pinsk this time acceded to the demand of the leaders of the Vilna *kahal* that 'he shall be utterly expelled.' R. Levi-Yitshak would appear to have continued to feel an attachment to Pinsk and to have hoped to return there one day, since he signed his approval of the work *Meir Nethivim* by R. Meir Margolioth (Polonnoye 1791), dated the 4th *Iyyar*, 1791, as follows: 'Av *Beth-Din* and *Rav* of the holy community of Pinsk and the district, at present *Av Beth-Din* of the holy community of Berdichev.' This is exactly the same formula as that used by R. Shelomo of Karlin, when he signed his approval of the book *Kether Shem Tov*: 'Shelomo of Karlin, at present in the holy community of Ludmir.' But the two men never returned to their respective towns.

Karlin was thus left without a *Tsaddik*. Of R. Shelomo's life in Ludmir very little is known, and we have to rely on hasidic oral traditions. His authority as a disciple of the Great *Maggid* and of R. Aharon the Great must have helped him in rapidly gathering a new circle of disciples and followers. His adherents in Polesia, who remained faithful to him, must also have visited him regularly in his place of exile. His loyal disciples, R. Asher (the son of R. Aharon the Great) and R. Mordekhai of Lakhovich, accompanied their Rebbe to Ludmir; and there he was apparently joined by a third disciple, R. Uri of Strelisk. R. Shelomo left no written works, unlike others of the Great *Maggid's* disciples, but teachings attributed to him and legends about him can be found in the following works by his own disciples: *Imrei Kadosh ha-Shalem* by R. Uri of Strelisk (Lvov, no date of publication), and *Beth Aharon* by R. Aharon (the Second) of Karlin (Brody, 1875).[84] All his life he was known as 'R. Shelomo of Karlin,' and that is the name by which he is referred to in hasidic writings down to the present day.

R. Shelomo died a martyr's death during the wars between Russia and Poland, on the 22nd *Tammuz,* 1792. Many legends have grown up around his death. One of them, which is true to his spiritual nature, runs as follows: During the war between Russia and Poland, the Russian commander gave his troops permission to do as they pleased with the Jews of Ludmir for two hours. This was on the Sabbath eve, when almost all the Jews of the town had taken refuge in the synagogue in which R. Shelomo of Karlin was in the habit of praying. R. Shelomo was standing by the table and saying the *kiddush* [blessing over the wine] with his usual intense devotion. Just then, a lame Cossack passed by the synagogue and aimed his rifle at R. Shelomo. R. Shelomo's small grandson, who was standing next to him, saw what was happening and tugged at R. Shelomo's robe to rouse him from his trance. At that same moment the Cossack fired at him and wounded him. R. Shelomo said that if his grandson had not roused him from his trance of devotion, the Cossack would not have had the power to harm him. The hasidim wanted to take R. Shelomo out of the synagogue, but he refused to move until he had finished sanctifying the Sabbath. When he had finished his prayer, they laid him on a bed, and while they were dressing his wound he asked for the *Zohar* to be brought to him. The volume remained open in front of him till his soul departed.

The hasidic legend adds that the lame Cossack was actually Armilus who, according to the *Midrash,* is to kill the Messiah, the son of Joseph [the Messiah of suffering who was to precede the Messiah, the son of David]. R. Shelomo himself used to say: 'I am ready to be the Messiah, the son of Joseph, provided that the Messiah the son of David comes at last.' The hasidim believe that every generation has its Messiah the son of Joseph, who by his sufferings and devotion brings nearer the final redemption, and R. Shelomo was this Messiah in his generation. His nameless grave was dug in Ludmir. Over it there is an *ohel* [structure over the grave] containing a large stone with two holes in which written requests can be placed, and a narrow opening for the lighting of a *ner tamid* [perpetual light]. The hasidim used reverently to point out the place where R. Shelomo, for twenty years the leader of Karlin hasidism, was laid to rest after a life full of trials and tribulations.

In addition to his role as Rebbe and spiritual guide in a period of crisis, R. Shelomo's other great claim to a place of honour in the history of Lithuanian hasidism was that he provided it with its future leaders. After his death, the ' Karliners ' overcame the opposition of the mithnagdim and achieved equal and independent status in communal affairs. By the 1790s Karlin hasidism was already enjoying its second heyday, which R. Shelomo had not been spared to see. Two of his disciples, R. Asher and R. Mordekhai, returned to Polesia and established hasidic centres there. What R. Shelomo himself had been unable to do was achieved by his disciples and their successors, who at the end of the eighteenth century and throughout the nineteenth, succeeded in propagating the doctrine of hasidism not only in Lithuania and White Russia (R. Asher of Stolin, R. Mordekhai and R. Noah of Lakhovich, R. Shelomo-Hayyim of Koidanov, R. Moshe of Kobrin, R. Avraham of Slonim), but also in Volhynia (R. Moshe, the son of R. Shelomo, and his descendants) and Galicia (R. Uri of Strelisk, R. Yehudah-Tsevi of Stretin).

C. *The Second Ascendancy of Karlin Hasidism* (1792-1794)

After R. Shelomo left Karlin and moved to Ludmir (before 1784), his followers in Karlin remained faithful to their Rebbe and his teachings. The hasidic way of life and mutual loyalty instilled into the Karlin hasidim by R. Aharon the Great proved strong enough to withstand the mithnaged excommunications and persecutions (in the period 1772-1781), just as the hasidism of neighbouring White Russia withstood the decrees passed by the mithnaged assemblies in Shklov and Mohilev (1784). Although the mithnagdim impeded the spread of hasidism in Lithuania, and undoubtedly slowed the pace of its development, they could not check it entirely. The number of Karlin hasidim in the second half of the 1780s, and particularly in the first half of the 1790s, steadily increased, until by 1793 they were strong enough to advance from passive to active resistance. Characteristically enough, the Karlin hasidim began their fight in the small towns, most of whose inhabitants were already hasidim, directing their offensive against the mithnaged community of Pinsk and, more particularly, its *Rav*, R. Avigdor, who was also *Rav* of the entire district.

R. Avigdor the son of R. Yosef-Hayyim—in Russian documents 'Haimovich'—had formerly been *Rav* of the little town of Lesli in Poland, and was probably called to the Rabbinate of Pinsk and its district in 1785. This date can be inferred from the petition presented by him to the Russian government in 1800, in which he writes that the hasidim 'drew out the matter for almost six more years,' in addition to the one year that had passed after his deposition. It follows, then, that R. Avigdor was removed from the position of *Rav* in Pinsk seven years before he presented his petition—that is, in 1793. In another place R. Avigdor writes that he paid a large sum to obtain the post of *Rav* in Pinsk for a period of ten years, and that he lent money without interest to the Pinsk community for the same period of time. He then adds: 'This sect . . . expelled me with great ignominy two years before my appointed time,' i.e., after he had served as *Rav* of Pinsk for eight years. From this it would follow that R. Avigdor was appointed *Rav* of Pinsk in 1785. This inference accords with the conclusion reached above concerning the year of R. Levi Yitshak's expulsion from Pinsk and his withdrawal to Berdichev, for hasidic sources assume that it was R. Avigdor that was responsible for this expulsion.[85] R. Avigdor's approval of R. Eliezer the son of R. Meir Halevi's book *Siah ha-Sadeh* (Shklov 1787) is dated 1787, and his approval of the work

Reiah ha-Sadeh by the same author (Shklov 1795) is dated
1791, both of them being signed by him in his capacity as
the Pinsk *Av Beth-Din.* It will be remembered that Rabbi
Eliezer son of R. Meir Halevi, ' the *Rav* of the synagogue
and *Moreh-Tsedek* of the holy community of Pinsk,' was
one of the first persecutors of the hasidim in Pinsk, as early
as the time of R. Aharon the Great, and, as has been
described above, it was to him that the Great *Maggid* of
Mezerich appealed concerning these persecutions. The
joint opposition to hasidism of the *Moreh-Tsedek* and of
the *Av Beth-Din,* of the author of the two volumes and the
writer of the approvals to them, apparently brought the two
men closer together.

Chronological considerations apart, the date of R.
Avigdor's appointment as *Rav* in Pinsk cannot be placed any
earlier, since the description of contemporary events given
in his petition does not accord with the difficult plight of
Karlin hasidism during the period of the first and second
bans pronounced against them (1772-1781), nor with the
time of R. Shelomo's departure from Karlin (c. 1784). The
fact that R. Avigdor occupied the Pinsk rabbinical office
which a short time before had been occupied by the *Rav*
R. Rafael Hacohen Hamburger, and also the fact that he
was asked to give his approval of books, is evidence that
he was widely known as a great talmudic scholar and
halakhic authority.

R. Avigdor's petition (in Russian to the Russian government), written in 1800, is an important document for our
understanding of the development of Karlin hasidism during
the last fifteen years of the eighteenth century, containing
as it does important details about the struggle of those years,
especially in Pinsk itself.[86]

In the passages describing the situation in Pinsk and its
surroundings, including Karlin, we read as follows:

'. . . I am now emboldened to lay my petition in fear and
awe before your Majesty's revered throne. I confess that,
when I was chosen *Av Beth-Din* of Pinsk and of the thirty
small towns belonging to the city [i.e., the district], I did
not wish to have any dealings whatsoever with the sect that
had arisen there, and I was very pleased not to have any.

44

However, I endeavoured, through preaching, to persuade them to return from their errings to the right way, but when I saw that this effort had no effect on them at all, and when there came into my hands their clandestinely printed books in which law and justice were most insolently distorted, I was perplexed in mind, for I did not know how to frustrate their designs. Even though I was the *Av Beth-Din*, I no longer had the power to burn their books publicly, for in all the towns under my jurisdiction the majority already belonged to that sect.

I was accordingly obliged to inform the late *Gaon*, R. Eliyahu of Vilna, of what had happened, since he was the greatest of our Sages, both in revealed teaching [*Talmud*] and in hidden lore [*Kabbalah*]. I told him of the contents of the books of this sect and requested wise counsel from him, for I feared that since their books contain for the most part vain and insolent words, and since they call ourselves our brethren, the matter might come to the notice of the authorities, and therefore [action must be taken] to prevent the innocent from suffering for the crimes of evil-doers. Moreover, I proved to him [sc. the Vilna *Gaon*] that, since their books lead the simple man astray from the straight way, according to the Mosaic Law their books should be publicly burnt in the presence of all the people. And this was indeed done in Vilna, where the order was given to burn the books of this sect in public in front of the synagogue [*Tsavvaath ha-Ribash*]. When this became known to the sect and they discovered that I was opposed to their ideas, they rose up as one man against me, and deprived me of my livelihood, and even eventually incited the others [sc. the mithnagdim] not to give me my due. For who would not lend a willing ear to such advice? And so I was greatly impoverished. In the three towns of Zlobin, Stolin and Dobrovich, which were under my jurisdiction but where the heads of the community were in each case members of this sect, they many times prevailed on the local authorities to forbid me to set foot in them. Afterwards they grew stronger and more numerous in Pinsk and, before the term of my appointment had come to an end and it was time to choose another *Av Beth-Din*, they took the post from me by force and, to my great shame, removed the chair intended for my use from the synagogue, and on the place where it had stood scattered sand and earth. . . . According to the religion of Israel it is a custom among us that who serves as *Av Beth-Din,* even if he has been appointed for a certain period only, cannot be dismissed [from his position as *Rav* before the end of his term of office]. But the sect did not observe this custom, and expelled me with great ignominy two years before the appointed time, and deprived me of all my income. When I saw how they were treating me, without consulting me, unlawfully, I laid a complaint against them, in accordance with your Majesty's decree, before the magistrate, who ordered that it be publicly announced in our synagogue that I was to remain in the rabbinical seat until the court should pronounce its decision. In furtherance of the execution of this order, the magistrate sent his secretary to the synagogue to announce his decision in person. When this became known to the sect, they determined, on solemn oath, to bring about the annulment of the magistrate's decision. They chose one of their persuasion as head of the community and, when the secretary tried to enter the synagogue in order to announce [the magistrate's decision], they took up their stand in front of him and did not let him enter.

According to Your Majesty's exalted decree it is laid down that, in every town where there are people of our religion, the *Rabbanim* shall be the judges in all matters pertaining to our faith. They [sc. the *Rabbanim*] must be men of learning. But the sect dismissed them [sc. the men of learning] and chose in their stead the people they wished, totally lacking in experience. They elected Hershel Kolodner as head of the community, only because he and his family belonged to the sect. He travelled to the governor of the province, Neplyuyev, and in return for libellous tale-bearing against me obtained an injunction not to pay me the remainder of the salary due to me, both for the last six years and for the years before that. Further, he [sc. Hershel Kolodner] ordered, and this, too, in the name of the governor of the province, that it be publicly announced that everyone whom I had either treated dishonestly or from whom I had taken money unlawfully should make a declaration to this effect in the town hall before the governor of the province. Despite the profound humiliation caused me by this order, I was glad of it, for I was sure that even among the sect there would not be a single person capable of saying ill of me. I had never favoured a wealthy man, if he was guilty, and thereby ignored the rights of a poor man. On the contrary, I had always wished, to the utmost of my ability, to help the poor. When a full year had passed after the publication of this same announcement and no complaints against me had been received, the governor of the province issued me a certificate of probity. After the town council had thus been convinced that I was in the right, my enemies drew out the matter for almost six more years. All this time I did not cease to demand the 3,000 *chervontsy*. And although I subsequently went to Minsk more than ten times, and showed the town council [in Pinsk] the order issued by the governor of the province and by the governor-general, Tutelman [Tutolmin], my efforts have still not borne fruit. My case drags on and on, and meanwhile I have been so greatly impoverished that I have been forced to sell all my possessions. I and my family have been left in utter destitution. But I have not lost my faith in Almighty God, as it is written: " If you do afflict them, and they cry out to me, I will surely hear their cry " [Exodus xxii, 22]. I have placed my trust in our exalted laws, that offer refuge to the oppressed. And, indeed, who is better fitted to do this [sc. to offer refuge to the oppressed] than our mighty master, the Tsar Paul I ? . . .

' . . . It is, therefore, with a heart bursting with indignation, that I humbly and respectfully present this petition to Your Majesty. In years past I was rich, whereas now, in my old age, I have been reduced to poverty together with all my family. I therefore wait hopefully for Your Majesty's decision, seeing that it is beyond my power to demonstrate by witnesses the harm done to me by the sect. . . . '

The state of Karlin hasidism, both in the ' principal community ' of Pinsk itself and in the small towns in the surrounding district, is well summed-up in the following

sentences from R. Avigdor's petition: 'Afterwards they
[sc. the hasidim] grew stronger and more numerous in
Pinsk. . . . They chose one of their persuasion as head of
the community. . . . They even eventually incited the others
[sc. the mithnagdim] not to give me my due. . . . The heads
of the community [in the three towns] were in each case
members of this sect.'

The struggle against hasidism was waged by the mithnagdim, from the start, as a 'holy war' fought for the
purpose of rooting-out a dangerous heresy. In this war,
R. Avigdor sought the aid of the *Gaon* of Vilna, since in the
hasidic books, which were 'clandestinely printed,' 'law and
justice were most insolently distorted' and the 'books
contain for the most part vain and insolent words' which
'lead the simple man astray from the straight way.' In the
end, the struggle spread outside the confines of the community in which it had begun. R. Avigdor sought the
protection of the Russian authorities, and the hasidim
retaliated by doing the same. The removal of R. Avigdor
from the position of *Rav* in Pinsk took place, as has already
been shown, in 1793.[87] This year, then, is to be regarded as
the year of the victory of Karlin hasidism over its opponents.

This growth in the influence and power of the Karlin
hasidim in Pinsk and its surroundings must certainly have
been known to the disciples of R. Shelomo of Karlin, with
whom the Karlin hasidim presumably maintained contact.
R. Shelomo's successor in Ludmir was his son, R. Moshe. In
the writings and history of hasidism neither this R. Moshe
nor his descendants—his son, R. Shelomo ; his grandson,
R. Nahum ; and his great-grandson, R. Gedalyah—figure at
all prominently. These descendants became *Tsaddikim* of
the not so large Jewish community in Ludmir and the
surrounding district, but only thanks to the reflected glory
of their ancestor, R. Shelomo of Karlin. Two of R. Shelomo's
disciples, R. Asher and R. Mordekhai, went after their
master's death to R. Barukh of Mezhibozh,[88] the grandson of
the Besht and the father of R. Shelomo's daughter-in-law.
R. Asher was also, for a short time, a disciple of the *Maggid*,
R. Yisrael of Kozhenits.[89] The study of hasidic doctrine as
propounded by these two leading advocates of *tsaddikism*,

R. Barukh of Mezhibozh and R. Yisrael of Kozhenits, must undoubtedly have had an effect on the future leaders of the hasidim of Polesia.

R. Asher apparently at first lacked the courage to return to his native province, Polesia. He lived for a short time in Zhelikhov, which seems to have led to a dispute between him and R. Levi-Yitshak of Berdichev.[90] Amongst the 'holy writings' of the Karlin *Tsaddikim* in the Stolin *genizah*, there was a letter from R. Asher to R. Yisrael of Kozhenits in which mention is made of the Zhelikhov dispute.[91] This letter also informs us that R. Asher was one of the disciples of R. Yisrael of Kozhenits. From Zhelikhov R. Asher returned to his native province, but evidently felt that the time was not yet ripe for him to go to Karlin itself and to try to revive the hasidic centre there. He therefore first made his way to the nearby small town of Stolin where he remained for a while, only later (after 1810) returing to Karlin. The exact date of R. Asher's arrival in Stolin is difficult to determine. In *Sefer ha-Vikkuah*, the work of R. Yisrael-Leibel published in 1798, the author makes no mention at all of R. Asher, though he does mention—and even challenges to a public debate—the two other *Tsaddikim* of the same region of Lithuania: R. Mordekhai of Lakhovich, and R. Shemuel, the son of R. Hayyim-Heikel of Amdur. Nor is there any reference to R. Asher in R. Avigdor's written petition of 1800, in which he recounts how he was not allowed to set foot in Stolin, describes in detail the 'holy war' declared against him by the hasidim, and demands that the 'Karliner leaders' be imprisoned. As against this, the hasidic tradition informs us, in connection with 'the fifth light' of *Hanukkah* (see below), that in 1798 R. Asher was being held in prison together with R. Mordekhai of Lakhovich. In a letter from R. Asher to R. Yisrael of Kozhenits, written (as will be shown below) between 1801-1802 and 1807, the address is explicitly given as Stolin. Stolin, as already stated, was one of the three small towns that closed their gates to R. Avigdor, since the majority of its Jewish community and their leaders were Karlin hasidim.

From the time that R. Asher settled in Stolin he became known throughout the hasidic world as 'R. Asher of Karlin or Stolin '; and the Karlin hasidim were henceforth called, in addition to 'Karliners,' 'Stolin hasidim.'

R. Shelomo of Karlin's second disciple, R. Mordekhai, chose as his place of residence the small town of Lakhovich (also in Polesia) which, according to the administrative division given in the 'Pinkas of the Province of Lithuania,' came under the jurisdiction of the Pinsk community.[92] Stolin and Lakhovich immediately became hasidic centres on the border between Lithuania and White Russia.

R. Shelomo of Karlin's third disciple, R. Uri, was also installed as Rebbe. He settled in the small town of Strelisk in Galicia.[93] From hasidic writings we learn that R. Uri was one of those Tsaddikim that aspired and attained to lofty purity of soul, in the spirit and after the manner of the first teachers of hasidism. His character is still a living influence in hasidic doctrine. On account of his fervently impassioned manner of praying, which he learnt from his master, R. Shelomo of Karlin, he is still known in hasidic circles as 'the Seraph.'[94]

R. Asher in Stolin and R. Mordekhai in Lakhovich soon made a name for themselves throughout Polesia, and even outside its borders. R. Mordekhai of Lakhovich is mentioned in the polemical pamphlets Zimrath Am ha-Arets and Shever Posheim ; and the well-known fanatical mithnaged, R. Yisrael-Leibel, writes in his work Sefer ha-Vikkuah (published in 1798) that R. Mordekhai had a great influence on the hasidim, who believed in his 'wonders.' Thus, for example, they were sure that it was only through the influence of R. Mordekhai that the provincial governor, Radziwil, was dismissed from his post because of his hostility to the hasidim, and another governor appointed in his place. Amongst the Tsaddikim whom R. Yisrael-Leibel challenged to a public debate on 'the perverse ways of hasidism' we find—together with the Tsaddikim of Amdur, Ladi and Chernobil—also R. Mordekhai of Lakhovich, who had gained adherents even in the stronghold of rabbinism —in Vilna.[95]

This was the second period of ascendancy for Karlin hasidism. The first such period, in the time of R. Aharon the Great (1765-1772) had provoked a violent mithnaged reaction which had plunged Karlin hasidism into a crisis lasting twenty long years (1772-1792). This time, the offensive was started by the hasidim and ended in their victory, the first fruits of which were the deposition of R. Avigdor and their own achievement of equal communal rights. By virtue of their determined struggle for equal and independent status in the ' principal communities' of Lithuania, the Karlin hasidim occupy a special place in the history of the mithnaged-hasidic conflict and of the hasidic movement as a whole. It was they that actually transformed the mithnaged attack on the hasidim into a hasidic attack on the mithnagdim. From now onwards it only remained for them to obtain *de jure* recognition of the equality of communal status that they had previously gained *de facto*. However, the mithnagdim also showed that they were determined not to give up the struggle. The Karlin hasidim were therefore obliged, together with other branches of the movement, to fight a further bitter engagement with the *Rabbanim* and the *kahals,* which ended in their final victory only in the year 1801. The Pinsk *Rav,* R. Avigdor, was once again in the forefront of the fray on the mithnaged side, together with the Vilna *kahal.* Although, on the hasidic side, this last engagement was actually fought mainly by the founder of *Habad hasidism,* R. Shneur-Zalman of Ladi, and not by the Karlin hasidim, yet in all the relevant documents R. Shneur-Zalman is referred to as ' the leader of the Karliners.'

D. *Struggle and Victory* (1794-1801)

The spread of hasidism in the province of Polesia in the nineties of the eighteenth century is a clear indication that, by this time, the Jewish masses had already changed their originally extremely unfavourable attitude to the hasidic movement. Through daily contact with the hasidim, the ordinary Jew had grown used to their peculiar customs and characteristics, and had thus ceased to feel ' the danger from hasidism' against which his spiritual leaders, the rabbis, were continually fulminating. The thirty years of the existence of hasidism had provided empirical proof that the religious and social innovations instituted by the new movement had not resulted in a schism in Judaism, or even in any serious divergence from its norms. It is possible that hasidism would have developed differently and would not have contented itself with merely introducing slight changes in the form of the prayers and in the way of life of the individual Jew and the whole community, if it had not met with such violent opposition at the start. Moreover, the changes that hasidism underwent in its own internal development at this same time—the nineties of the eighteenth century—also helped to dispel the fear of the 'hasidic threat.' By then, the doctrines of the first hasidic teachers about the nature of Judaism and the way of life to be followed by the believer had already undergone a contraction, the main emphasis now being laid on tsaddikism —the belief in the *Tsaddik* as 'the true foundation of the world,' and in the material effectiveness of his prayer and blessing and his power thereby to help the individual in time of need. In the psychology of the ordinary, simple Jew this belief now became the principal doctrine of hasidism.

This internal development in hasidism resulted in an increase in the numbers of the movement's adherents. The popular belief in the sanctity and efficacy of the individual *Tsaddik* was such that, as soon as a *Tsaddik* (who was usually the son or disciple of another *Tsaddik*) took up residence in some place, a number of the local inhabitants became hasidim. The main tenet of their hasidism was their belief in the *Tsaddik* (or 'Rebbe'), whom they regarded as a saint and who was for them a greater religious authority than the official spiritual leader of their community, the local *Rav*. These are the factors that explain the extent to which R. Asher of Stolin and R. Mordekhai of Lakhovich succeeded in spreading the hasidic doctrine in the nineties in Polesia. The growing strength of the hasidim went hand in hand with the steady decline of their rivals, the *kahal*. Indeed, even in the stronghold of mithnagdism, in Vilna itself, the number of hasidim apparently increased in the years from 1790 onwards, to judge from the fact that in this period we find hasidim among the members of the *kahal*. In their struggle to free themselves from the jurisdiction of the official *kahal*, the hasidim took full advantage of the latter's moral decline: the essentially religious character of this struggle was thus almost completely overshadowed by secular issues, such as the embezzlements of public funds by the leaders of the *kahal*, and the like. At first, the hasidim had attacked the arrogance of the rabbinical scholars. Now, in the latter part of the struggle, their onslaught was directed against the despotic rule of the *kahal*. Here the hasidim were considerably helped by the restrictions imposed on the independent authority of the *kahal*, partly by the government of Poland during that country's last period of independence, and partly by the Russian government after the last partition of Poland. With their powers thus reduced, the leaders of the *kahal* tried to gain the support of the Russian authorities, and for this purpose employed political arguments in their controversy with the hasidim. In this way, the struggle between the hasidim and the *kahal*, which had originally been essentially religious, now took on an additional political and social character.

A very important part in the last stages of this conflict was played, as already stated, by the leaders of the Vilna *kahal*, the Pinsk *Av Beth-Din*, R. Avigdor, and R. Shneur-Zalman of Ladi. For the first three years—i.e., from 1794 till the death of the Vilna *Gaon* in 1797—the main struggle took place in Lithuania. Then, in 1798, it was transferred to St. Petersburg, where it finally ended in 1801.

In 1794, after the Karlin hasidim in Pinsk had defeated their bitter enemy, R. Avigdor, the Minsk *kahal* decided—as we know from the community records [*pinkas*]—to ban all prayer-meetings of the hasidic *minyan*.[96] A year later, the provincial governor at Minsk, one Tutolmin, who was well versed in the details of this sectarian conflict and supported the hasidim, persuaded the Empress Catherine II to promulgate a decree greatly reducing the powers of the *kahal*.[97] That same year, the communities of Grodno and Vilna, realising the separatist aims of the hasidim, appealed to the Russian government to recognise the elected *kahal* as the sole legally authorised representative of the Jewish population.[98] Meanwhile, the hasidim had managed to circulate large numbers of copies of their writings, in particular *Tsavvaath ha-Ribash*.

They also spread abroad a story to the effect that the Vilna *Gaon* now regretted his hounding of the hasidim; while at the same time a young scholar, who gave himself out to be the *Gaon's* son, travelled from town to town affirming the truth of this story. These acts of the hasidim still further incensed the mithnagdim against them, and at a meeting of the leaders of the Lithuanian communities in Vilna (June, 1796), under the presidency of the Vilna *Gaon*, it was decided to take more stringent measures against the hasidim. A letter was sent out, signed by the *Gaon*, and reaffirming his previous attitude to the hasidim. In this letter the threat to Judaism from hasidism is once again stressed and the Jews are once more called on to root out hasidism from their midst.[99] Two special envoys, R. Hayyim and R. Saadyah, set out with this letter for the communities of Lithuania and White Russia, in order to display it publicly to the Jewish population there. When the letter reached Minsk, the hasidim rumoured it abroad that the *Gaon's* signature was a forgery and that the letter was not his at all. The Minsk community immediately appealed to Vilna for confirmation of the *Gaon's* signature, at the same time complaining that the hasidim had greatly increased in numbers in the provinces of Vilna and Slonim. In response to this request, on the day after *Yom Kippur* 1796, the *Gaon* sent the provincial communities of Lithuania, White Russia, Volhynia and Podolia a letter denouncing the hasidim still more violently. The letter was again carried by envoys. The reason for the specially vigorous anti-hasidic activity of the Minsk community was that the hasidim had become particularly numerous in this province, which included Pinsk, Karlin, Stolin and Lakhovich. Two weeks after the receipt of the *Gaon's* letter, the Minsk community published a proclamation to all the communities in the Minsk province[100]—and no doubt also to the community of Pinsk—demanding that strong action be taken against the hasidim, and that they should not be allowed to travel to their ' Rebbes.'[101] This proclamation was publicly read out in the synagogues and *batei midrash* of Minsk. At the same time, the Lithuanian *Maggid* and mithnaged, R. Yisrael-Leibel, was delivering his anti-hasidic sermons in the synagogues, and his *Sefer ha-Vikkuah* was published with the approval of the Minsk *Av Beth-Din* (1798). As already stated, this book denounces R. Mordekhai of Lakhovich as a demagogic agitator whose aim was to lead good Jews astray. The hasidim resorted to burning the proclamations and driving out the envoys. Thus, sectarian passions were once more roused in Lithuania when, at the height of the tension (1797), the Vilna *Gaon* suddenly died.

From this point onwards the struggle between the two sections of the Jewish population was waged with the participation of the Russian authorities. The *kahal* realised that its weapons—excommunications, proclamations, and the like—made too little impression to be effective. At the same time, the hasidim for their part saw that their chief enemy was now the *kahal*, which derived its powers from the secular authorities. When, after the *Gaon's* death, the third excommunication of the ' Karliners ' [i.e., hasidim] was proclaimed in the Vilna synagogues to the accompaniment of blasts on the *shofar,* an order was immediately published by the governor of the province in Vilna, Friesel, forbidding any proclamation of a *herem.*[102] Obviously this prohibition was issued at the instigation of the hasidim and testifies to the decline in the power of the *kahal* and the extent of the influence of the hasidim at that time. The Vilna community now set up a special committee to continue the struggle. Anti-hasidic feelings rose to a new height of intensity, following a rumour that the hasidim had gone wild with joy after the death of the Vilna *Gaon.*

In 1798, the leader of the ' Karliners ' in White Russia, R. Shneur-Zalman of Ladi—in the Russian documents, ' Zalman Borukhovich ' [i.e., son of Barukh]—and the *Tsaddikim* of the ' Karliner ' sect in Lithuania were indicted before the Supreme Court in St. Petersburg as revolutionaries. On the basis of this indictment, the public prosecutor ordered ' that the whole affair be thoroughly investigated and that Rabbi Borukhovich's leading assistants be brought under heavy guard to St. Petersburg. . . . Immediately after this, twenty-two of the " Karliners " were imprisoned in Vilna and other districts. Seven of them, who were among Rabbi Borukhovich's chief aides, were

left in prison here [sc. in Vilna]. . . . The seven Jews
sent to St. Petersburg . . . were stopped on the way at Riga
and returned [to Vilna]. . . . After an investigation of the
Jewish sect of the Karliners, and after the explanations
provided by R. Zalman Borukhovich, His Royal Highness
the Tsar decreed . . . since he did not find in their acts
[sc. of the " Karliners "] anything harmful to the State, that
they all be set free . . . but that a close watch be kept on
their actions and those of their associates. . . . After this, all
the adherents of the sect still in prison were released.'[103]

According to hasidic tradition, R. Asher of Stolin and
R. Mordekhai of Lakhovich were among those imprisoned.[104]
The day of their release, which happened to be the fifth
day of Hanukkah, became a day of rejoicing for the Karlin
and Lakhovich hasidim and was given the name of ' the
fifth light.'[105] On this day the hasidim used to gather in
their *shtiebel*, eat *latkes* [potato-pancakes], drink and sing,
and recount the miracle of the Rebbe's release. Avraham-
Baer Gottlober records this in his reminiscences, which
contain interesting and typical details. He writes : ' An old
man from Vilna, R. Zalman Miliater, told me that, when the
Vilna *Gaon* departed this life . . . the mithnagdim brought a
false accusation against seven of the leading hasidim, pillars
of this community . . . who were then imprisoned and
condemned to be deported to Siberia. When they were
taken away from Vilna under military guard, the leaders of
the Vilna community added to this another, Jewish guard,
to make sure that the hasidim should not escape by bribing
the soldiers. As they were passing through a small town,
they entered a Jewish house and asked for something to eat.
They were given *terefah* [ritually unclean] food, since the
Jews said to themselves : " They're ' Karliners ' (the name
given by the Lithuanian Jewish masses to the hasidim),
aren't they, so why should they eat ritually slaughtered
[*kasher*] meat ? . . ." This incident shows that the quarrel
between the two groups had become so bitter that they were
almost split into two separate peoples. Thanks to representations made to the authorities, the seven prisoners were
returned [to Vilna] from Riga ; and the fifth light is still a
day of rejoicing for Lithuanian hasidim.'[106] The institution

of a special festive day to mark the occasion testifies to the historical truth of the imprisonment of the Karlin and Lakhovich *Tsaddikim.*

After the release of the 'Karliner' leaders the Russian government decreed (December 15th, 1798) that 'the Karlin sect is not dangerous and may continue to exist as previously.'[107] Encouraged, naturally enough, by this victory, the hasidim proceeded to accuse the heads of the Vilna *kahal* of embezzling public funds.[108] As a result, the heads of the *kahal* were imprisoned in Vilna, the boxes containing the *kahal* documents were sealed, and a date was set for new elections (February, 1799). Under pressure from the Russian authorities, eight hasidim were elected to the new, seventeen-member *kahal.* The hasidim thus achieved equal rights in Vilna, the mithnaged stronghold.

At the same time as in Vilna and Minsk the struggle against the hasidim was being conducted by the *kahal,* in Pinsk R. Avigdor, as we learn from the wording of his request quoted above, was left to fight a lone battle against them. The beginning of this struggle in Pinsk and its environs is described by R. Avigdor in his letter of appeal. He was no doubt helped in carrying on the struggle by the actions of the Vilna and Minsk communities, especially as Pinsk was spiritually close to Vilna and administratively linked to the main provincial community of Minsk. The proclamation of the Vilna *Gaon* (1796) must also have reached Pinsk, as must the *Gaon's* two special envoys, R. Hayyim and R. Saadyah ; and the third *herem* was also proclaimed there. In the *pinkas* of the Minsk community for the year 1798, we find a ban on ritual slaughtering after the manner of the hasidim (with 'sharpened slaughtering knives'). Every animal and bird slaughtered in the hasidic manner was decreed to be *terefah,* and anyone that transgressed this ban was declared to be in *herem.* Similar decrees are found in the *pinkasim* of other towns in Lithuania and White Russia.[109] It may be presumed that Pinsk, too, was similarly torn by sectarian strife in those years.

In the Stolin *genizah* there is a letter from R. Asher of Stolin to a certain R. Yosef of Pinsk which contains an echo of the tense situation prevailing in Pinsk in those years and testifies to R. Avigdor's sectarian fervour against the hasidim. R. Asher writes as follows:

'My dear friend, R. Yosef,

I was enraged to hear that this man had told his followers to bring him a hasid's head. Although this is nothing new to me, still, if I am unable to make peace as we agreed, do you all form a single group and let all the doers of iniquity be dispersed. I warn you to let nothing be changed and not to let him carry out his evil design. Strengthen the weak-kneed and feeble-handed, and may the Lord uphold you with the strength of faith. Truth is strong and everlasting; therefore be not concerned or afraid or cast down, and the Lord will make peace as seems good to Him, for we have fought this battle only for the Lord's sake.

From your affectionate friend who prays
for your welfare,
Asher of Stolin.

Greetings to you all in the name of the Almighty.'

R. Asher does not explicitly name 'this man (who) had told his followers to bring him a hasid's head.' This is in keeping with his regular practice, in his letters dealing with controversial matters, of not mentioning names. In this letter here, the Karlin hasidim in Pinsk are advised to dissociate themselves from the rest of the community and to establish their own separate entity: 'If I am unable to make peace as we agreed, do you all form a single group'—an instruction that was actually carried out, as is evident from R. Avigdor's letter of appeal (the election of Hershel Kolodner, etc.). Although R. Asher's letter bears no date, it was obviously written in the last decade of the eighteenth century.[110]

The subsequent developments in R. Avigdor's fight against the hasidim, in Pinsk and its environs, are described in his detailed letter of appeal which deserves to be treated as a court confession. The Karlin hasidim, like their brethren in Vilna, found a way to the Russian authorities, in this case to the provincial governor in Minsk, and were able to influence him by their representations. In the report of the Pinsk municipal leaders, we read that R. Avigdor was unduly fond of the bottle. That the hasidim were responsible for this statement is clear from the fact that R. Avigdor's intemperance is also mentioned by R. Shneur-Zalman in the reply sent by him to the Tsar Alexander I (May, 1801). We further find references to this weakness of R. Avigdor's in the hasidic writings.[111] However, even when the influence of the Vilna community was greatly weakened after the first release from prison of R. Shneur-Zalman (1798), R. Avigdor still refused to give up the struggle. Seeing that both the local authorities in Pinsk and the provincial governor at Minsk took the side of the hasidim, he appealed over their heads to the highest government institutions in St. Petersburg.

In 1800 after consultation with the Vilna *kahal*,[112] he travelled to St. Petersburg and presented his petition in person. After a long, drawn-out correspondence between the public prosecutor in St. Petersburg and the provincial authorities in Vilna and Minsk, the government decided that the ' Karliner sect ' did not constitute a political danger. With regard to R. Avigdor's demand for the repayment of the debt owing him, the public prosecutor decided, in the Tsar's name, to instruct the provincial governors to investigate the matter. The Minsk governor handed the investigation over to the local authorities. What eventually happened to the financial demands made by R. Avigdor we do not know. All that is certain is that, in his second petition which he presented in April, 1801, after R. Shneur-Zalman's second release from prison, he writes that he has still not received the money.[113]

While R. Avigdor was running from government office to government office in St. Petersburg, mainly in connection with his financial demands, R. Shneur-Zalman was suddenly brought to the same city and imprisoned there. His imprisonment was this time connected with the report on the state of Russian Jewry submitted at that time to the government by the poet and statesman, Dyerzhavin.[114] The order for the imprisonment of R. Shneur-Zalman was received by the provincial governor of White Russia, after Dyerzhavin had visited the governor in connection with investigation of the causes of the famine in the province. Before this, there had been an exchange of letters about the hasidim between the provincial governors in Lithuania and Minsk. During his visit to White Russia, Dyerzhavin had made the acquaintance of R. Shneur-Zalman. Four days after Dyerzhavin submitted his report, R. Shneur-Zalman was thrown into prison. In St. Petersburg, R. Avigdor helped the judges by drawing up in writing questions and charges to be used in the investigation of R. Shneur-Zalman, to which the latter replied also in writing. The whole matter was then handed over by the 'Secret Office' to the third department of the Senate. A fortnight later, R. Shneur-Zalman was released from prison, but ordered to remain in St. Petersburg.

Both parties to the dispute submitted petitions and declarations which contained details about the first imprisonment of R. Shneur-Zalman in 1798. R. Avigdor, in his petitions, demands that all the other 'Karliner' leaders should also be arrested and brought to St. Petersburg,[115] a demand which was not granted. The documents show that the hasidim of Lakhovich, whose influence had meanwhile spread to the 'principal community' of Lithuania, Slutsk, were being violently harried by the mithnagdim, and also that the hasidim as a whole enjoyed the support of the provincial authorities in Minsk. It is characteristic that R. Avigdor quotes the evidence of Jews from Vilna and Slutsk in support of his written charges, but not the evidence of his own fellow-townsmen from Pinsk. As a result of the arguments and other weapons employed by R. Avigdor in this final stage, his struggle against the hasidim lost its originally selfless religious character and degenerated into a private war for the satisfaction of personal demands (such as repayment of debts), carried on by means of denunciations to the Russian authorities, even though R. Avigdor still endeavoured to base his charges on the tenets of Judaism. Before the Senate had had time to study the documents in the dispute, a palace revolution took place in St. Petersburg (the assassination of the Tsar Paul by his ministers, March, 1801). R. Shneur-Zalman was immediately released and permitted to return home ; and thus ended the struggle between him and R. Avigdor.

Amongst all the bitter enemies of hasidism, R. Avigdor

occupies a special place in the hasidic writings and stories. He is referred to simply as 'Avigdor,' with the addition of such appellations as 'the wicked one,' 'the informer,' 'may his name and memory be blotted out,' and the like ; and it is related of him that he was reduced to abject poverty and finally came to beg alms of R. Shneur-Zalman, and also that his sons became hasidim. This tradition about the conversion of R. Avigdor's sons to hasidism is confirmed by one of his own descendants, who writes as follows: 'The Israelit family . . . were . . . on the father's side, descended from R. Avigdor of Pinsk, the well-known adversary of R. Shneur-Zalman of Ladi. . . . From the first beginnings of *Habad* hasidism this family was a stronghold of mithnagdism. However, my grandfather, the grandson of R. Avigdor of Pinsk whose name he actually bore, made a breach, as it were, in this fortress, for he became a fervent hasid. In this he was followed by my father . . . whose house was steeped in *Torah* and hasidism.'[116] What happened to R. Avigdor in the last years of his life is not known. His son was a *dayyan* in Pinsk.[117]

In all the documents, both the official government memoranda and the petitions of R. Avigdor, the hasidim are referred to as 'Karliners'; and the same name is used by the hasidim themselves in their letters. R. Avigdor, in one of his letters, explains the appellation as follows:
Those who flock after him [i.e., R. Shneur-Zalman] are called Karliners because, after the death of the two writers mentioned above [the Besht and the *Maggid* of Mezerich], Aharon and Shelomo [i.e., R. Aharon the Great and R. Shelomo of Karlin] of the community of Karlin in the province of Minsk were the first to follow in their footsteps.'[118] R. Shneur-Zalman, on the other hand, uses the term 'hasidim' and remarks 'that he [i.e., R. Avigdor] calls them Karliners only out of hatred.'[119] The representative of the Vilna community writes, 'because of their wildness the hasidim are called Karliners.'[120] All these statements show that the appellation 'Karliners' was an insulting term of abuse, and it was used in this sense down to the fifties of the nineteenth century.[121]

During the years 1794-1801 the numbers of the hasidim

increased, thanks to the legal status that they enjoyed both in Pinsk itself and also in Polesia. Perhaps their numbers were now swelled by all those who had previously been afraid to proclaim their adherence to the movement openly. Small groups of Karlin hasidim now came into existence not only in central Polesia, but also in other towns of Lithuania. Thus, for example, in Vilna there was a Karlin prayer-house ['shtiebel,' 'shulkhen'], and even a Lakhovich 'shtiebel.' The Lakhovich hasidim, who appear to have been numerous, maintained contact with their Rebbe, R. Mordekhai, through his son-in-law, R. Yitshak the son of R. Wolf, who used to visit them regularly and give them moral support in their struggle to maintain their position.

In the conflict between the mithnagdim and the hasidim, the mass of ordinary Jews came down firmly on the side of the hasidim, and the Tsarist régime gave legal confirmation to the popular verdict: 'If in any town the dispute becomes so bitter that one group refuses to pray with the other in the same synagogue, then either has the right to build a synagogue of its own and to elect its own rabbis. But both groups shall form one community.' ['Polozheniye' 1804].[122]

E.   Rabbi Asher the First (1793-1826)

After their victory in the last decade of the eighteenth century the Karlin hasidim were able to follow their own customs, openly and without fear of molestation. But the bitter animosity between them and the mithnaged majority all around them was not completely extinguished, and from time to time it flared up again into communal and personal strife.

Throughout the nineteenth century Karlin hasidism preserved its character virtually unchanged. The new elements introduced by hasidism into the beliefs and worships of Judaism crystallised, in time, into a fixed pattern of dogma. The leader of the hasidim, in whom they had unbounded faith, was the *Tsaddik* or Rebbe. His opinion and authority were absolutely binding on all members of the sect. These *Tsaddikim* established family dynasties, with the father's power and sanctity passing to the son. The *Tsaddik* knew every single one of his followers personally and was acquainted with their private affairs and worries ; he was always ready with an encouraging word ; he supported them in their griefs and shared in their joys; and at all times he was their guide in piety and worship. The *Tsaddik's* paternal attitude to his hasidim, together with the individual hasid's faith in the sanctity and power of his *Tsaddik*, had a marked effect on the hasid's whole spiritual character, setting him apart from the Lithuanian rabbinical environment in which he lived. The focal point of the Karlin hasid's —as of any other hasid's—life was his Rebbe, because ' the Rebbe, too, is thinking of him all the time.' This intimate relationship with the Rebbe had a similar effect on the relations of the hasidim with each other. The Karlin hasid was like all the other hasidim in that he lived his life within the closed circle of his hasidic environment. But as a result of the special development and stress that it gave to certain basic hasidic tenets, Karlin hasidism took on a form that distinguished it from the rest of the hasidic movement.

During the first quarter of the nineteenth century the Karlin hasidim were led by R. Asher of Stolin, the son of R. Aharon the Great who has already been mentioned. Under R. Asher's leadership, the number of the Karlin hasidim seems to have increased, especially in Polesia and Wolhynia, thanks to the favourable geographical position occupied by Stolin on the borders of the province of Volhynia. R. Asher's father, R. Aharon the Great, had gone to the people ; now the people came to R. Asher, but not always in order to get from R. Asher what R. Aharon the Great had wanted to give them.

Hasidic tradition relates that, during the emergency of the Napoleonic wars, the Karlin hasidim found a safe place of refuge in R. Asher's house. Among the ' holy writings ' discovered in the Stolin *genizah* were two of R. Asher's *pinkasim* [private notes]. In one of these, comprising mainly records of family matters, there is a will drawn up by R. Asher from which it is clear that he possessed considerable wealth in money and landed property. Yet—and this should be stressed—the dynasty of Karlin *Tsaddikim* were not ambitious for material wealth, nor did they aspire to give

F

their 'court' the external magnificence which was so sought after by some of the *Tsaddikim* in Volhynia and the Ukraine. On the contrary, it was the custom of the Karlin *Tsaddikim* to take money from their wealthy hasidim and distribute it amongst their poorer followers.

R. Asher was in the habit, on Sabbaths and Festivals, of expounding a hasidic interpretation of the weekly portion of the Law. A collection of these hasidic sermons, together with 'Rules of Right Conduct,' 'Exhortations,' and several of R. Asher's letters, was published by the Karlin hasidim, and are included in the volume *Beth Aharon*.[123] In the preface to this work, the publishers write as follows: '. . . Excellent sermons . . . delivered . . . by our Teacher and Master, R. Aharon himself [sc. R. Aharon the Second, the son of R. Asher the First] . . . accurately and truly recorded. . . . We have added a separate section for the holy writings . . . of our Teacher R. Asher [the First] . . . and several articles are as written in his holy hand. Also some holy letters, and the daily programme of our holy Rebbes . . . who delivered it from their holy hand to the community of Yeshurun [i.e., the Jews] that thronged the Rebbes' threshold. . . . And the holy writings of our Master and Teacher [R. Aharon the Second] . . . and of his father [R. Asher the First] . . . which were collected together . . . and annotated in the holy hand of our revered Teacher and Master [R. Aharon the Second] of blessed memory, various annotations on various themes. . . . We have thought fit to add other excellent matters, written down by the followers of our Teacher and Master [R. Aharon the Second] as a record of his holy words which they heard from his holy mouth at various times, when they were in the sanctity of his house. Although some of these matters are similar to the sermons already mentioned which were written by our Teacher and Master . . . we have nevertheless, out of reverence for his sanctity, printed every one of them without any alterations. . . .' From these prefatory remarks, and also from the introductions added by the hasidim themselves to every article and their occasional comments inserted in the text, it may be inferred that the hasidim took pains to give the name of the author of every manuscript, although we cannot be sure that they always succeeded. The writings of R. Asher the First—as stated by the hasidim themselves in the 'Preface'—were edited by his son R. Aharon.

About the character and opinions of R. Asher we can learn from the 'Rules of Right Conduct' [*Hanhagoth Yesharoth*] which he gave to his followers and which were printed together with the will of his father, R. Aharon the Great, during the lifetime of his son and successor, R. Aharon the Second (Chernovits 1855). R. Asher charges his hasidim as follows: 'Every one of you must sanctify himself, that the Lord may dwell within him, as it is written: "And you shall make me a shrine that I may dwell there," etc. (Exodus xxv, 8). . . . And every one of you shall divide his days and years between the study of the Bible, the *Mishnah,* and the *Gemara* and *Aggadah,* this being the bounden duty of every Jew. . . . Every one must devote himself to the study of the *Gemara* and *Posekim* and must learn according to his need ; he must not let himself be unoccupied, for in moments of idleness it is better that he should take up the holy Prophets and learn morality and piety from them. . . . Let every one that has the mind and intention to learn and understand the *Gemara* and the *Posekim* be very careful. Let him not be like those that learn—Heaven forbid !— only for their own greater glory, but let him, with his keen mind, fully comprehend all that he learns. Let him not go on from one matter to another until he has fully understood the first, and let him go over it again three or four times until he knows it by heart. . . . A little studying done with his whole heart will be of benefit to him alike in sharpening his wits, improving his memory, and increasing his piety. . . .' 'Let him take care to have a good, faithful and trustworthy friend to whom he can tell all his innermost thoughts for at least half an hour every day. . . .' 'Let every one take care to give a tithe of what he earns, and let him not think this a trivial matter, as expounded in the *Gemara* and *Midrash* and *Posekim.* . . .'

The other writings attributed to R. Asher the First— 'several articles in his own holy hand'—which were printed at a later date (*Beth Aharon,* Brody 1875) also give us an insight into his conception of hasidism. In one of these, which the hasidim attest to have been 'copied from the original manuscript of the same holy Rabbi [R. Asher the First],' we read the following instructions to the hasidim: 'When any one of you has to speak about the affairs of this world, let his thought be that he is going down from a higher sphere, like a man that is going out from his house and intends to return once. Just as such a man, while walking, is thinking when he will return to his house, so let the hasid always think of the higher world, where is his real home, of the Creator Blessed Be He, even when he is talking of the affairs of this world. Let his thoughts return at once to cleave first of all to the Creator Blessed Be He.' 'Let not a man be too strict in examining everything that he does, for this is the intention of the evil impulse [*ha-yetser ha-ra*]—to make him fear that he is not doing this thing as he should, in order to plunge him into melancholy. And melancholy, as we know, is a great hindrance to the proper worship of the Creator. Even if a man has transgressed let him not be so overcome by melancholy as to stop his work. Let him simply regret the transgression, and then once more rejoice in the Creator. Since he is genuinely contrite . . . he should not be melancholy, but should consider that the Creator, who searches the heart and reins, knows that his wish is to do only what is best.' For 'the Holy One Blessed Be He does not upbraid His creatures . . . for everything is judged according to human nature, according to the place and the time, and according to the measure (of each man's) faith and piety and intelligence . . . and purity of heart and strength of mind are enough for you to be able to carry out the commandment: "Know Him in all your ways." How can you "know Him"? In joy . . . and then you will attain true wisdom. . . . Let every one worship the Creator joyfully at all times and rejoice in his lot, the lot given him by God on High.' With regard to the mithnagdim, R. Asher lays down the following 'great principle: When people abuse the hasid for his form of prayer or for other matters, he shall not answer them even in a conciliatory tone, so as not to start a quarrel and give rise to pride, for pride makes man forget the Creator Blessed

Be He. And our Sages have said: "Silence makes a man humble."'

Very typical and instructive—both for R. Asher's estimate of the importance and purpose of the study of the Law and also for his fatherly attitude to his followers—is the letter that he wrote to one of his close associates, which is also included in the volume *Beth Aharon*. In one part of this letter, R. Asher writes:

'. . . Your son-in-law (long may he live!) told me that your honour is neglecting your trade . . . and not doing any business, but wishes just to sit at home. . . . You must know, my dear friend, that this is not the right way. It is plainly written in the *Torah*: "Thou shalt eat the fruit of thy labours," etc. And in the *Gemara*: "He that enjoys the fruit of his labours is greater than the God-fearing man." Believe me, my dear friend, that one loan or one small coin given as charity, or any of the other practical observances, especially entertaining guests . . . is better than several weeks, perhaps even years, of studying the *Torah*. For the end of study is action . . . as you can learn from the questions asked: Did you do business honestly; and did you study the *Torah* regularly? Which shows that whoever does business honestly is not obliged only to study the *Torah* regularly . . . and the way is thus open to businessmen who wish to turn aside from evil and do good: as I wrote, more than by several weeks of study. With God's help it has been granted me to persuade several people, who wished to do as you do, to carry on with their business; and they, thank God, are grateful to me, both in this world and the next. The main thing is that you should not be negligent in any matter of business. For you must know that, when you neglect your business, your study suffers, too. Of this, too, it is written: "Thou shalt not eat the bread of idleness. . . ." God willing, when you follow my advice, I shall write to you at greater length. Your task is to act, and the Lord will bring the work to a good end. . . . I have told my brother-in-law (long may he live!) to look after you and watch over your health; to see to it that you eat properly and sleep properly, and that you get the sleep you require for the health of your body, head and limbs. Please do not treat this matter lightly, especially as you are by nature thin and delicate. Your study of the *Torah* will, God willing, be improved by your care.'

Some time later R. Asher moved to Karlin, the place to which, fifty years before, his father had with such enthusiasm and devotion brought the doctrine of hasidism from Mezerich. The exact year of R. Asher's return to Karlin is not known, but it could not have been before 1810, since in that year he was still living in Stolin, where he was visited by R. Mordekhai of Lakhovich, who also died there.[124] Thus Karlin once more became the centre of the Karlin hasidim.

R. Asher's importance in the hasidic world and his relations with other contemporary *Tsaddikim* are indicated by two documents found in the Stolin *genizah*: a letter from R. Asher to the famed *Tsaddik* of the Polish hasidim, R. Yisrael of Kozhenits ('the *Maggid* of Kozhenits'; both the original and a copy of this letter were found); and a public proclamation written by R. Asher in support of Jews living in Palestine. Although neither of the documents is dated, it is clear that they were both written at the beginning of the nineteenth century.[125] Below are excerpts from the letter sent by R. Asher the First of Stolin to R. Yisrael of Kozhenits:

'With the help of the Holy Name, on the second day of the week . . . here in the community of Stolin.

'Greetings, greetings . . . to his reverence . . . the Rabbi . . . the man of God . . . the renowned hasid . . . Yisrael (long may he live!) together with . . . his wife and children (long may they live!) and all his followers . . . to all of them greetings and peace upon Israel.

'Praise be to God, we are alive and well, I and my pious wife . . . Feige-Bathyah, and my little son, Aharon, and my daughter, Perl, and her husband and his children, and my wife's son . . . Moshe-Baer . . . and his wife and children. . . . The Lord be praised . . . we are all . . . here alive and well, and may we be granted the blessing of prosperity . . . life and peace . . . that it may be vouchsafed me to behold his holy reverence's countenance . . . in life, joy, and peace.

'My dearly beloved friend . . . whom I remember at all

times . . . and whom I entreat . . . to have me engraved on his pure and holy heart . . . and to accept my offering [i.e., gift] which I gladly send to him, that it may please him to recall me, my son, and my wife. Even though I am far away . . . from his reverence, yet is my soul bound to his soul. . . . In almost every prayer, and especially on our holy Sabbaths . . . I am bound to him . . . with bonds of love . . . and in particular . . . his holy words . . . delivered to me by R. Barukh of Zhelikhov who requested me in his holy name . . . to remain silent and calm and not to intervene in the dispute. . . .

'. . . God will remember that, when I was in the community of Zhelikhov, I had several adventures and with the Lord's help I found the middle path. To be sure, here, too, [in Stolin], there were several such incidents . . . but this is not my way. . . . Heaven protect me from matters of this kind and their like [i.e., quarrels], and I shall not go back on what I have said. It may have happened once in a year that I was obliged to speak in public. . . for when . . . a man truly and sincerely desires to receive moral guidance, it is my duty to prevent him from committing a transgression, as my heart and soul prompt me. But apart from this . . . I shall not speak . . . for several private reasons.

'. . . My very dear friend . . . to be sure . . . that my faith is no mere formal observance (Heaven forbid!). . . . My heart cries to the Lord. . . . I have learnt from the holy ones of the Most High, and especially from his reverence's holy lips how to keep our faith. . . . Only he . . . who is in the habit of exaggerating . . . can say, " Accept my opinion and my manner of worship ; this is the way in which they shall all walk.". . . But we have received all the ways of the Lord, loving kindness and truth, from our sovereign David, King of Israel. . . . In short, the wise man in this time will be silent, etc.

'. . . I know that the holy Rabbi (blessed be he and blessed be his name!. . .) weeps out his soul in secret . . . and his heart cries to the Lord for this. . . . Neither do I say, Accept my opinion ; but only . . . that Israel's faith in *Torah,* prayer, and *mitsvoth* should be strengthened, as when they stood at the foot of Mount Sinai and said " We shall do and obey."

'. . . Who is the man that presumes to intervene in the dispute and to delay (Heaven forbid!) the reconciliation? Let my lord believe me that, at the time when I wrote, I could not control myself, so great was my grief. . . . My lord has the wisdom and knowledge . . . to understand . . . the root of the matter. Therefore let him do what seems right to him. I trust in his graciousness and goodness to find me innocent and thereby behold the goodness of my heart. . . . Thus far have I poured out my heart. . . .

'In short, were I to describe to his reverence in detail several matters . . . that I saw with my own eyes and heard with my own ears, and that I can testify to . . . my lord would be astounded by the report and and would certainly, as I think, publicly demand that they abandon this way. I need not mention them by name. . . . There are thousands upon thousands of them, almost a whole State, that speak in the streets only about the mystic secrets of the Law. . . . They have cast truth and faith to the ground and falsely slander the holy ones of the Most High [i.e., the *Tsaddikim*] . . . saying: " Everything with them is as naught . . . they spurn the observance of the *mitsvoth* and despise the plain meaning of the *Torah*.". . . If I were able . . . to describe . . . how the *shiddukh* [marriage agreement] was made with the holy Rabbi and *Gaon* . . . that they might have a specious cause for an otherwise unjustifiable quarrel. . . . They achieved what they desired, but they did not act truthfully. . . .

' May the Lord preserve us from evil and strange thoughts. Far be it from me and from my father's house to intervene in the dispute. I have never presumed . . . to say that I, too, am one of the great ones of our time. I do not stand in the presence of the great ; nay, I pray the Lord . . . at all times and every hour that I may know my place, and that it may be granted me to be the youngest . . . and humblest of the disciples, and to be truly close . . . to the holy ones of our time. . . . I trust in my Lord's graciousness and goodness . . . and in the honesty of my intentions in this, and that all will end well.

' From me who write to his reverence . . . about my heart's friendship . . . and whose soul . . . longs to be . . . in his courts and to behold the delight . . . of his glorious holiness, in life and peace. May he remember me for good . . . at all times and at every hour. . . .

'His friend for ever. . .'

The letter is full of allusions, names being hardly mentioned at all: 'I need not mention them by name.' But it is clear that the main point concerns 'the great controversy.' The key to understanding some of the events hinted at in the letter can be provided by certain details from the contemporary history of hasidism and also from R. Asher's own private life. When R. Asher writes sorrowfully about what he endured in Zhelikhov, he is no doubt referring to the dispute between himself and R. Levi-Yitshak of Berdichev.[126]

'The holy Rabbi, blessed be he and blessed be his name,' mentioned in the letter is presumably the *Tsaddik* R. Barukh of Mezhibozh, whose pupil R. Asher had been for a short time.[127] R. Asher complains of 'thousands upon thousands . . . almost a whole State, that speak in the streets only about the mystic secrets of the Law. . . . They have cast truth and faith to the ground, and falsely slander the holy ones of the Most High,' the reference here, apparently, being to the *Habad* hasidim of R. Shneur-Zalman. It is well known that at this time a violent dispute had broken out between the *Tsaddikim*. R. Avraham of Kalisk (then in Palestine), R. Barukh of Mezhibozh, R. Mordekhai of Lakhovich and R. Asher of Stolin all strongly opposed R. Shneur-Zalman of Ladi, who was supported by R. Levi-Yitshak of Berdichev.[128] The cause of the dispute was, as can be inferred from the letters written by R. Asher[129] and by R. Avraham of Kalisk,[130] not only doctrinal, but also partly personal, especially in the case of R. Barukh of Mezhibozh, on account of R. Shneur-Zalman's great influence. R. Asher, in this letter, after remarking on the spiritual difference between Karlin and *Habad* hasidism, promises not to take any part in the dispute and appeals for moral support to his teacher, R. Yisrael of Kozhenits. The letter is written throughout in a humble and submissive tone, indicating that the writer felt that he was under attack. It is evident from this letter that R. Asher at this period had as yet nothing of the inner confidence and proud status of his father, R. Aharon the

71

Great.[131] The letter was most probably written at some time between 1802, the year of the birth of 'the little son Aharon,' and 1807, the year of the death of Perl's husband, R. Aharon, who is mentioned in the letter with the addition of the words 'may he live!'

The text of R. Asher the First's public appeal on behalf of the Holy Land runs as follows:

'. . . Be silent and hear, O Israel! . . . Blessed be the Lord that has sanctified us with the sanctity of the Land of Israel. . . . For this, sages and prophets have instructed us to set aside a place for our prayer thrice daily for our Land and . . . our holy Temple. . . . Verily, His mercies have not failed us till now. . . . Throughout our borders . . . those that perform His word in the Holy Land . . . are strengthened by great benefactions and fulfil their holy charge . . . interceding for us and for our brethren that dwell outside it. Now I have seen that there is none among you who will rouse you from your deep slumber, that you may defend yourselves . . . and find a place in the Lord's inheritance. . . . Hence I have resolved . . . to make known to you my request and entreaty: My dearly beloved Jewish brethren, awaken your hearts to feel pity and compassion for the poor of our Land, the Land of Life, man and woman, child and suckling. Strengthen and support, I pray you . . . the cities of our God . . . and strengthen your hearts, all you that wait for the Lord. . . . Then they will rejoice in us and in our gift . . . and their good deeds shall never fail us. And you, sons of the Living God . . . do you help each other. Let each one say to his brother, "Be strong and of good courage in the service of the Lord!" Let them strengthen the hands of those engaged in the work . . . by bringing the money to the House of the Lord, that their contribution may last for ever. . . . We are further obliged to make it known to our dearly beloved Jewish brethren . . . since in every town and village there are dissenters . . . who also desire the important office for themselves and their own benefit, who call evil good and . . . wilfully weaken the hands of those that are performing this *mitsvah*. . . . This one comes with a claim of priority: Why was he not given the performance of this *mitsvah*, since he would have carried it out more properly ?. . . Beware of men like these, whose names are already known. . . . Know full well that the Rabbi and *Gaon*, the Righteous Priest, our Teacher and Master from the Land of Israel, has written about these men that they should know they are putting their own lives in danger. . . . Moreover I shall make the facts known to all the honest *Tsaddikim* and hasidim . . . that all should know who they are. . . . Again and again I have uttered the warning of our holy Law and the warning of all the *Tsaddikim* with whom my soul is bound up. . . . Think not that this is a matter of no import, for it has been explicitly stipulated that all the holy money shall be handed over to me. God willing, we shall bring them receipts from the Land of Life [i.e., the Holy Land], them and their wives and children. . . . May He bless you with abundance of strength and peace! Peace upon Israel!. . . From me, who write and sign on behalf of our brethren and on behalf of the Land [of Israel] and of those that dwell therein. . . . May it be vouchsafed them to go up to Zion rejoicing . . . and may the light of our righteous Messiah shine forth. . . .

'Asher, the son of our Master R. Aharon of blessed memory.'

This proclamation undoubtedly contains a reference to the quarrel between R. Avraham of Kalisk, who was at that time living in Palestine, and R. Shneur-Zalman, who was authorised to collect money for the Jewish community in Palestine.[132] A number of other *Tsaddikim*, who had taken part in the fund-raising, were obliged to settle the dispute in favour of one or other of these two *Tsaddikim*. The pressure was particularly strong on the Lithuanian *Tsaddikim*, since they lived in close proximity to R. Shneur-Zalman. R. Asher's proclamation proves that he regarded R. Avraham of Kalisk as the sole authorised collector: 'The Rabbi and *Gaon*, the Righteous Priest, our Teacher and Master from the Land of Israel.' Of R. Avraham's rivals he writes with great bitterness, warning his own followers to 'beware of men like these,' and announcing—doubtless on behalf of R. Avraham of Kalisk—that he, R. Asher, has been appointed to supervise the collection of money for the land of Israel.[133] Found amongst 'the holy writings' in the Stolin

genizah were receipts for various sums of money sent by
R. Asher to Palestine. The proclamation was written between
1801, when the dispute between R. Avraham of Kalisk and
R. Shneur-Zalman was at its height,[134] and 1810, the year
of R. Avraham's death.[135]

In contrast to the humble and submissive tone which
makes itself felt in the letter to R. Yisrael of Kozhenits and
in the proclamation on behalf of the Jewish community in
Palestine, a very different note is heard in the R. Asher the
First's letter to certain Jews who were desecrating the
Sabbath in pursuance of their business. This letter, which is
printed in *Beth Aharon*, was also found in the Stolin *genizah*
bearing the address of certain salt merchants of Kremenets
in Volhynia, some of whom used 'to eat at his table.' Here
R. Asher appears in the role of stern castigator and does not
shrink from upbraiding and rebuking the *Rabbanim*, 'the
religious teachers of Israel,' who ' are paid by the community . . . to teach the Lord's people His ways . . . and should
stand in the breach . . . and warn the children of Israel to
keep well away from what is forbidden. . . . Then why
now . . . do they put . . . their hands to their mouths, and
why are they thus silent ? If they are small in their own
eyes, let them remember that they are the leaders of the
children of Israel.' He goes on to demand of them that
'wherever their authority rules, they should impose . . .
enormous fines on this offence . . . and above all that they
should exhort the mass of the people . . . to act with
reverence for the teachers of the Law.'

This letter supplements what we have learnt about the
personality of R. Asher the First from his 'Rules of Right
Conduct' and 'Exhortations' and from his other letters
quoted above. It shows that, in the course of time R. Asher
gained authority and recognition as a responsible leader
of the Jewish masses, even though he himself admits that
at first he refrained from upbraiding the mithnagdim, for
fear that they would not listen to him. 'When I heard
this . . . I said to myself that I had better be silent and
refrain from words of censure.' It was only, writes R. Asher
further on in his letter, 'when I discovered that the men
who raised their hands were themselves of those . . . that

eat at my table . . . that I thought I might have the power to protest. Perhaps it is my task to warn them that they should hearken to my voice. I have come to perform my duty. For that I will raise my voice.' In contrast to what we know of the early days of hasidism, when the founder of the new movement sought to protect the simple Jew from the harshness of the *Rabbanim*, R. Asher now demands of the *Rabbanim* that they should ' impose enormous fines ' on the desecrators of the Sabbath. A further piece of information provided by this letter is that, in those days, non-Jews were economically dependent on Jewish merchants who used to exploit this fact to compel ' them [the Gentiles] to desecrate their holy day, just as they [the Jews] desecrate their own holy day.' R. Asher protests vehemently against this attitude of the Jews to the Gentiles. The expression ' of those . . . that eat at my table,' used here by R. Asher to denote his own hasidim, is very characteristic, and corroborates the tradition of the Karlin hasidim about the existence of a ' table ' in Stolin and Karlin in the time of R. Asher the First. The letter also provides confirmatory evidence that, already in R. Asher's day, there were Karlin hasidim in the town of Kremenets, which is situated in the southern part of Volhynia. The letter is undated, but must have been written after the struggle with the mithnagdim had ended and R. Asher was firmly established in his ' court '— most probably in the twenties of the nineteenth century.

Among the small number of writings left by R. Asher the First, there is an incomplete collection of dissertations on the Readings of the Law for Sabbaths and Festivals, which were published in *Beth Aharon*. In form and content, R. Asher's dissertations are similar to those of most of the hasidic teachers of that time, being built around words and verses from the biblical text and interspersed with quotations from the *Midrash* and the *Zohar*, interpreted according to hasidic and kabbalistic concepts. R. Asher several times quotes the exegesis of R. Shelomo of Karlin, introducing the quotations with the words: ' And I heard from the lips of my holy Teacher, R. Shelomo, may his soul rest in bliss!' This form of words tends to confirm that the dissertations were actually written by R. Asher himself. On the other hand, in another place we read: 'When R. Asher returned home from visiting the holy and revered Rabbi of Mezhibozh, he related in his name'; or again, 'he gave precise details,' using the third person. Some idea of R. Asher's conception of hasidism, his way of worship, and his humanity can be obtained from several of the sayings attributed to him, like those quoted by R. Aharon the Second: 'I once heard my revered Father, Teacher and Rabbi say, "Know whence [Heb. *me-ayin*] you have come —that means, Know that you have come from nothing" [Heb. *me-ayin*]. And again: "A man must count every day, every moment and all the days of the year"; "Happy the man that fears always—that means, Fears Him Who is always there"; "Knowledge is of Me—that means, what is of Me is knowledge, and what is not of Me is not Knowledge"; "The true mark of hasidism is the love of one's fellow-men"; "Men think that the Holy one Blessed Be He dwells in glory in the heavens above, in the loftiest heights, but no—the Holy One Blessed Be He dwells on the earth below, in the lowest places of the earth, and everyone can reach Him, even the smallest and most insignificant Jew can reach Him"; "For Thou hearest the prayer of every mouth—even if it is only from the mouth."'

The hasidim relate that R. Asher was once asked by a hasid: 'Can I really repent, when I have committed a sin of which it is written in the books that repentance is of no avail to annul it?' R. Asher replied: 'What has this to do with you? Your business is to perform your duty. If you fear that you have forfeited your portion in the world to come, remember what our Sages of blessed memory have said—One hour spent in true contrition and in good works in this world is better than all the life of the world to come.' R. Asher's opinion of the *Tsaddik's* function is indicated by the following story. R. Asher expressed his displeasure with those hasidim that would speak of what was good in their deeds and keep silent about what was bad. To these he used to say: 'Look at the difference between the early hasidim and their latter-day followers! When today's hasidim welcome their Rebbe they show him the good and conceal from him the bad, whereas the early hasidim used to conceal the good and

tell the bad. That is what I used to do when I visited my
teacher R. Shelomo of Karlin. I used to hide the good from
him. Is he in God's place ? Does he dispense reward and
punishment ? But the bad I used to reveal to him. As it is
written: " If any man be afflicted with leprosy, he shall be
brought to the priest and the priest shall see it." '(Lev. xiii, 9.)

Amongst the 'holy writings' found at Stolin were the
following letters from and to R. Asher the First: a letter
of encouragement from R. Asher (quoted above) to a certain
R. Yosef of Pinsk about the persecution of R. Asher's
followers by ' this man ' [R. Avigdor of Pinsk] ; [136] a detailed
letter to one of his own followers, written just before the
'Penitential Days' [ha-Yamim ha-Noraim], explaining the
value and importance of the hasidic-style prayers on Rosh
Hashanah and stressing, not the element of 'judgement' in
these Penitential Days, but rather the joy and confidence
expressed in them ; [137] a letter [dated the day after Sukkoth,
1801] from R. Yisrael of Kozhenits to R. Asher after the
death of the latter's wife, in which the writer expresses a
high regard for the widow of R. Aharon 'the Silent' of
Zhelikhov [or for his daughter ?] ; a letter of New Year
Greetings to R. Asher from the Tsaddik R. Yehoshua-Heshel
of Apta ; various letters from R. Asher to his son, R. Aharon,
about journeys and family affairs ; a list of R. Asher's books,
and of his lucky charms and other proved means of warding
off illnesses. Also found in the Stolin genizah were the
following letters belonging to R. Asher's period: the will of
the Tsaddik R. Mordekhai of Kremenets, the son of R. Yehiel-
Mikhal of Zlochov, whose daughter married R. Asher's son ;
a letter from R. Avraham of Kalisk to R. Nahum of Chernobil
about a contribution of money for Erets Yisrael ; a letter
(dated 1796) from the Tsaddik R. Yehudah-Leib of Sasov
to his followers ; [138] a letter from R. Mordekhai of Chernobil
to R. Shemaryahu of Olevsk about the ritual slaughterer's
licence granted to the shohet Yaakov Koppel and his son,
who were the cause of communal dissension in the town,
and a second letter (1810) from R. Yehoshua-Heshel of Apta,
who was at that time in Mezhibozh, also about the ritual
slaughterers of Olevsk ; a letter from R. Barukh of
Mezhibozh (dated Sunday, Portion of the Week Va-Yakhel,

1810) to a certain R. Yaakov-Shimon about the journey of a family to Rashkov; a letter from the *Tsaddik* R. David Halevi of Stepan to the Jews of the town Rokitno about their behaviour; and a letter from R. Pinhas of Korets and R. Yehiel-Mikhal of Zlochov. The search of the Stolin *genizah* brought to light no letters from R. Shneur-Zalman of Ladi.

One of the 'holy writings' found in the *genizah* was, then, the will of the *Tsaddik* R. Mordekhai of Kremenets, the son of R. Yehiel-Mikhal of Zlochov and, as stated, a relative by marriage of R. Asher. Part of this will is quoted below, to show the spiritual character of this *Tsaddik* who was the father-in-law of R. Aharon the Second of Karlin.

Last Will and Testament, on the fifth day of the week, in the month of Tammuz, [5]580[= 1820].

Now my sons, be strong in the Law of the Lord and in pious awe [*yirah*] of Him, and in prayer.

This shall be the order of your praying: Accustom yourselves to rise early and do not spend time on your ablutions . . . but forthwith say all the blessings and the *hatsoth* prayer [in memory of the destruction of the Temple], followed by passages from the Psalms. Avoid all speaking before prayer, except what is absolutely necessary. Then, stand up to pray in reverence and awe, stressing every single word; and put aside all worldly thoughts while praying, for the time of prayer is when we are most tempted to indulge in vain worldly thoughts, and therefore you must be very strong against this temptation and request the Lord's help to resist it. If you wish to pray before the Ark [i.e., to lead the prayers in the synagogue], so much the better, for most certainly I would have you do this; but let it be only for the Lord alone, and not for the worshipper's own pleasure. . . . Straight after the prayer be sure to study. . . . And above all let it be done with all your heart and soul. . . . If you go in the true way, it will be granted you to understand the profound meaning of prayer.

Order of Study

. . . Study *Mikra* [the Bible], *Mishnah*, *Gemara*, and the *Posekim* and *Musar* [moral] Literature daily. Study a section of the *Aggadah* before sleeping ; and on no account lie down to sleep with your head full of idle matters, but only with thoughts of penitence. . . . Then you will go in the true way and attain to the wisdom of the *Kabbalah*. After midnight is the time for the *Kabbalah,* and you must on no account break off your study in the middle. The essential thing is that it be done with reverence and awe, with humility and self-abasement, and that each one should withdraw completely into himself while studying and confess and entreat the Divine Name to help him in attaining to the innermost meaning of the Law and to devotion [*devekuth*] to the Creator. This I have attempted to do with God's help, and you, too, will surely be aided by Heaven. I admonish you to obey me, as sons are in duty bound to obey their father, for your own good in this world and the next.

Rules for Right Conduct

Keep far away from anger, pride, honour, and dissension. If (Heaven forbid!) there should be any dissension in the town where you dwell, be among the peace-makers and do not take either side in the dispute. All the more so shall you beware of dissension in your own house, and you shall take great care that peace and love prevail between you, as becomes brothers. In every matter of conduct you shall consult each other. Beware of idling and watching the markets and the streets, for the evil impulse blinds man's eyes and says that this is a small matter. But in reality it separates the soul from the true essence of life. Accustom yourselves always to speak gently with everyone and to answer softly, and not coarsely (Heaven forbid!), even with the least of men. By this you will make yourselves beloved of Him Above and popular with those below. And the Divine Name will certainly be with you.

Solemn Injunction to Honour Your Mother

Take very great care indeed to honour your mother, in body and in spirit and in all her needs, and to consult and obey her, in everything speaking to her respectfully and most politely. Let not even a single day pass without your going to her and speaking to her. Only if you are not in your homes are you excused. All this that I enjoin you to do is very little. . . .

Solemn Injunction to My Daughters-in-Law

You, my daughters-in-law, do I solemnly enjoin to treat your husbands with due respect. Do not upset your husbands in any matter, but always speak to them affectionately. I most solemnly enjoin you to refrain from bad language, above all (Heaven forbid!) to your husbands or children. I absolutely forbid this. If you obey me, you will be granted every happiness in this world and in the next. Know that your husbands are men of noble descent in Israel and it is therefore your duty to show them all manner of respect, and by so doing you will be bringing honour to yourselves.

R. Asher the First, 'the old man of Stolin' as the Karlin hasidim affectionately called him, died on the 26th *Tishri*, 1826, at the age of 67.[139] The tomb of R. Asher, with a 'perpetual light' [*ner tamid*] always burning in it, stood in the Karlin cemetery next to the modest stone over the grave of his father, R. Aharon the Great. Into this tomb the caretaker of the last Rebbe, R. Elimelekh, who lived in Karlin, would insert the 'requests' written by the hasidim who used to visit the grave in time of trouble.

F. R. Aharon the Second (1826-1872)

R. Asher's successor was his son, R. Aharon [Perlov] the Second (so called to distinguish him from his grandfather, R. Aharon the Great), who was born, according to a family tradition, on the New Moon of *Sivan*, 1802.[140] R. Aharon was the recognised leader of the Karlin hasidim for nearly fifty years. The information that we possess about his life and time comes partly from hasidic sources and partly from the circles of mithnagdim and *maskilim*. A gifted organiser, R. Aharon applied himself to strengthening the bonds between himself and his followers. To this end, he used to pay them frequent visits in their towns and welcome them most warmly in his 'court' in Karlin. He also had a striking natural simplicity and sense of humour, and regularly made jokes in the Russian vernacular even while teaching his hasidim at his 'table.' He mixed freely with people of all kinds, and his confident and imposing presence was admired even in non-hasidic circles.

R. Aharon the Second's spiritual legacy, which is included in the volume *Beth Aharon*, comprises the following works: 'Daily Conduct and Exhortations'; a large, almost complete, collection of dissertations on the Portions of the Law for Sabbaths and Festivals; 'Selected Sayings' in his name; letters written by R. Aharon to his followers on the eves of Festivals, especially on the eve of Passover; letters to his son, R. Asher; and 'Inspirational Sermons' to his followers in Yiddish.[141]

The 'Daily Conduct and Exhortations' contains rules 'that he wrote . . . in his own holy hand': 'Although it is not my custom to write matters of this kind, since the earliest authorities, the holy ones of the Most High [sc. the *Tsaddikim*], have already written on the ordering of daily conduct. . . . Yet I have done so out of affection for our followers who have come . . . from afar, in the hope that . . . their hearts will draw nigh to listen attentively to their studies.' In the same volume there are also rules 'that he discussed with our followers'; i.e., that were not actually written by R. Aharon, but handed down by the hasidim in his name. R. Aharon testifies: 'They are my true words, as recorded in books and by writers.' A comparison of these pronouncements with those of his father and with the 'Exhortations' of other earlier *Tsaddikim* shows that there is hardly anything new in R. Aharon's words. Nevertheless, together with his biblical interpretations and letters, they enable us to form a picture of Karlin hasidism in his time. R. Aharon stresses the qualities of 'awe and joyfulness,' of truth-seeking and purity of heart, and of 'study that issues in conduct.' 'Let those that are busy fix a regular time for religious study. And of those that have leisure it is said: "The study of the Law is their trade." The main thing is that some good quality should be derived from the studying. . . . Let them learn the *Mishnah,* the *Gemara* with the *Tosafoth,* the works of *Maharsho* [an acronym of the name R. Shemuel Edels] and the *Posekim,* each according to his ability, whether much or little.' 'There is a man that sits down to study on a full stomach without any soul-searching. After his studying, he is very proud of himself . . . and thinks: Who will the King delight in more than in me ?. . . But by what is study measured by God ? The *Torah* is given to study and perform. . . . If anyone prays every day . . . "to study and to teach, to keep and to do and to perform," and then after this prayer does the opposite, this is a complete lie.' A man should endeavour 'to be absolutely honest, inwardly and outwardly,' 'close to the truth,' for 'by the truth we can attain to the highest degree'; 'above all . . . let his thoughts and words be the same . . . and let him not speak much about the vanities of the world and the new discoveries of the time, for this is a great source of idleness. . . . Above all, every prayer and every study should not be just a routine religious act, but should be deliberately undertaken to bring the man closer to the will of God, according to his status and understanding. . . . After the prayer, he should study the Bible, and in busy times at least *Hok le-Yisrael,* and sections of the *Mishnah* every day. The Holy One Blessed Be He counts not pages, but hours.'

In the rules for 'Daily Conduct' which his hasidim handed down in his name, he said: 'A Jew must be very dear to himself and must believe in himself, for all that he does is thereby much improved. We are not speaking of upper worlds, but only of his own world. . . . Just let him not rise above his level nor fall below his level. . . . Let him not look up above himself . . . nor down below himself. . . . Every man must improve . . . his own station. . . . Every Jew can attain to all the hidden treasure and is indeed obliged to attain to it . . . and will be purified and cleansed and whitened till he attains to the goodness and radiance of the Holy One Blessed Be He.' Like his grandfather R. Aharon the Great, R. Aharon the Second used to say: 'The greatest of all the vices is sadness and melancholy.' 'For melancholy is the cause of all the other vices.' 'Sadness results from . . . pride.' 'The sign of a broken heart is gladness.'

These principles and ideas are reiterated by R. Aharon the Second in the 'Holy Letters' that he wrote to his son, R. Asher, and to his followers. Altogether, R. Aharon's writings and homilies had a considerable influence on the character and conduct of the Karlin hasidim. In particular, it was through him that Karlin hasidism came to attach such great importance—perhaps greater than any other section of the hasidic movement—to joyfulness. R. Aharon the Great, according to hasidic tradition, regarded joyfulness as simply the avoidance of sadness. Whereas R. Aharon the Second used to stress the positive aspect of joyfulness as the active and fructifying principle in life. Thus, he would sum up the allegory of R. Elimelekh of Lizhensk in a single sentence: There is light in the world, only it has been hidden away by the Holy One Blessed Be He, so that every Jew is obliged to seek this light, and all Jews, 'even the smallest of the small and the lowest of the low' can find it.

The period of R. Aharon the Second's 'leadership' coincided with the reign of terror under the Tsar Nicolas I, with its persecutions, anti-Jewish decrees, 'kidnappings' and the like. The joyfulness that R. Aharon laboured to implant in the hearts of his followers undoubtedly helped them to bear the trials and tribulations of those difficult days. For a long time afterwards popular stories were told about the courage displayed, both in private and public, by R. Aharon's hasidim in their time of trouble. It was thanks to R. Aharon's encouraging influence that the numbers of the Karlin hasidim increased still further in his time, over and above the increase that had occurred in the days of R. Asher the First. This was the heyday of Karlin hasidism. On Festivals and on Penitential Days the hasidim would leave their wives and families and make the pilgrimage to their Rebbe in Karlin. On *Shavuoth* and *Simhath Torah* as many as three to four thousand—according to an eye-witness report— would come thronging to his residence. 'He who has not seen *Simhath Torah* in the court of R. Aharon'—so used the hasidic elders to say—'has never seen a real celebration of *Simhath Torah.*' Here is the scene as described by an eye-witness: R. Aharon would be sitting clothed all in white, as was his custom on Sabbaths and Festivals, at the head of the long table that stood in the large courtyard next to his prayer-house. Tens of canopies stretched above the court hardly sufficed as shelter for the crowds of hasidim that came to their Rebbe for *Simhath Torah*. When, at the *maariv* [evening] service, R. Aharon himself led the prayers, the worshippers were carried away by spiritual ecstasy, and the 'circuits' of the Scrolls were performed in a frenzy of jubilation that rose ever higher, circuit by circuit, song by song, and dance by dance, as the wine flowed freely. Thus transported, the hasidim would spend the whole night singing and dancing in the courtyard and the nearby streets. Out of this fervent rejoicing were born many of the Karlin melodies that subsequently became famous in hasidic circles and even throughout Jewry. Nor was this the case only at *Simhath Torah*. Every Festival had its own melodies. Outstanding amongst these were the tunes of the Passover *Seder* night of which, according to the hasidim, R. Aharon used to say: 'In my Passover melodies, there is not one crumb of leaven.' In addition to songs and dances, R. Aharon introduced instrumental music and had two orchestras—one of them made up of his followers from Volhynia—which used to play during *melavveh malkah,* on the intermediate days of *Sukkoth,* and similar occasions.

During these visits to the Rebbe's 'court,' the hasid would forget the bitter, dreary, care-ridden reality of his daily life and find a refuge for his tired body and weary spirit. Freed for a while of his cares by the general rejoicing, he would be uplifted into a state of self-forgetfulness. This spiritual exaltation and tense expectancy reached their climax on *Rosh Hashanah* before the blowing of the *Shofar,* when R. Aharon, having 'purified himself' in the *mikveh* and carrying three or four *shofars* thrust into the silver girdle encircling his white *kittel,* would make his way through the throng of worshippers to the pulpit, where, after fervently reciting the forty-seventh Psalm ['To the sons of Korah'], he would perform the commandment of 'hearing the sound of the *shofar*'—'hearing is in the heart,' as he preached in one of his sermons on *Rosh Hashanah*. On one of his *shofars* were engraved the words: 'God has gone up with a trumpet blast.'

This intensely shared life of the Rebbe and his hasidim was something alien in the prevailingly mithnaged environment of Pinsk. The element of a personal cult in hasidism—the hasid's reverence for his *Tsaddik*—was completely foreign to the 'scholars' of this 'principal community.' Moreover, the mithnagdim still at that time held to their view that hasidism discouraged the study of the *Talmud* and thereby had an adverse effect on Lithuanian talmudic scholarship. Thus, for example, the then *Av Beth-Din* of Pinsk, R. Elazar-Moshe Hurwitz, is reported to have adopted a hostile attitude to hasidism and even to R. Aharon himself.[142] And once, on the fourth intermediate day of *Sukkoth*, when R. Aharon and his followers had been rejoicing after their fashion, singing and dancing in the streets of Karlin, one of the leading local mithnaged families—Lourié—who lived in the neighbourhood, enraged by having their peace disturbed for days and nights on end, used their influence to have the Russian authorities order R. Aharon to leave Karlin. He withdrew to his old place of refuge—Stolin. This event shows that sectarian bitterness had not yet completely died away even at this late date, exactly a hundred years after the first *minyan* of the Karlin hasidim was established in this town, in an atmosphere of hostile pressure and actual persecution.

The writer and poet, J. L. Gordon, who, as a young teacher in Pinsk—in the Lourié household—became closely acquainted with the life led by the Karlin hasidim, has given us, in his story *Olam ke-Minhago*, a highly critical and even repellent picture of R. Aharon the Second and his hasidic milieu.[143] Despite the purely fictional and personal elements in this description, it nevertheless contains references to certain historical facts, such as the quarrel between the hasidim and the Lourié family, and the expulsion of R. Aharon from Karlin by order of the Russian police. The fear of the hasidim, which is stressed in the story, induced the author to give his characters fictitious names: R. Aharon appears as R. Leibele, his son R. Asher the Second as

R. Herschele, Hayya Lourié is called Yokheved, and Karlin is changed to Krimvilishek. The whole story is a most important historical document, as showing what the leading poet of the *Haskalah* movement thought of hasidism.

The exact year of R. Aharon's forced move from Karlin to Stolin is not known. J. L. Gordon gives [on pages 107 and 154 of the above-mentioned story] the following as the date of R. Aharon's expulsion: ' October 1st, the 21st of *Tishri*, the day of *Hoshana Rabbah*, the fourth day of the week.' But the year is intentionally omitted: '. . . in the year . . . (the number being deleted).' Now, a glance at the calendar shows that, throughout the relevant period, these dates never all fall on the same day. That means that their choice is either the storyteller's mistake, or a deliberate inaccuracy on his part. Another piece of evidence is a letter written by R. Aharon the Second to his son-in-law R. Avraham-Yaakov, the son of R. Yisrael of Sadagora, ' on the fifth day of the week, on the 17th of the month of *Av,* in the year [5]626 [= 1866], which is extant in the original hand in the family archives. From this letter it transpires that, in the year mentioned, R. Aharon was living in Stolin. In a letter to Aharon, the son of R. Moshe Lourié in Pinsk, dated the 7th of *Av* [5]624[= 1864], J. L. Gordon writes: ' The town where the Rebbe is living is close to you. (But is he still in Stolin ? Or has he chosen another royal city for his residence ? Is R. Aharele [R. Aharon] still reigning, or has his son R. Asherl [R. Asher the Second] already succeeded him on the throne ?).' From this it may be deduced that R. Aharon the Second was already living in Stolin in the year 1864.

That the mutual hatred between the mithnagdim and the hasidim was still very much alive in the nineteenth century is evident from two further facts. One of the finest, most devoted, and most influential of Karlin Jewry's public figures, the above-mentioned R. Shaul Levin (the father of Hayya Lourié), who was known as R. Shaul Karliner, specifically forbade his sons and heirs, in his will (he died in 1834), to have anything to do with the hasidim.

In connection with the bequests to charity made by R. Shaul Karliner in this will, we read as follows: ' A clear

inventory of all my property and effects . . . shall be drawn
up and recorded . . . and signed by the heirs, together with
my wife . . . and the *Rav* who shall be the communal
Av Beth-Din at that time. If the *Rav* at that time is the
Rebbe of the sect of the hasidim, then, with the consent of
my wife and sons, another *Rav* shall be added to the signatories [i.e., instead of the Rebbe], or some upright and
honest person. . . .' In a similar vein, R. Shaul Karliner gives
the following instructions to those of his next of kin to whom
he entrusted the management of the charities to be paid
out from his estate: '. . . Everything shall at all times be
conducted and managed on the principle of relatives first,
provided that they are upright and respectable men, and not
of the sect of the hasidim. . . . Even of the relatives it is
laid down that they shall not be of the above-mentioned
sect, and if they are [members of the sect] they shall be
disqualified. Only those that are truly God-fearing shall be
taken care of, but none of them [sc. the hasidim]. . . . All
the inventory shall be clearly and exactly written [on every
anniversary of the death] in a notebook and shall be signed
also by whoever shall then be the *Rav* or *Moreh-Tsedek*,
but not if he is a member of the sect of the hasidim, so that
the matter may be finally and permanently arranged and
settled.'

These excerpts from the will show the depth of the
hatred and anger felt against the hasidim, even on his
death-bed, by the leader of the Karlin community in the
thirties of the nineteenth century. His opinion of the hasidim
is expressed in his explicit instruction that the money for
charity bequeathed by him shall be devoted 'to some
upright and honest person . . . to those that are truly God-
fearing . . . so that the matter may be finally and permanently arranged and settled.' All these qualities are denied
the hasidim by R. Shaul Karliner. The extent of the influence
of the hasidim in Karlin in those days can be inferred from
R. Shaul's fear that one of them might be chosen as the
Rav of Karlin. Evidently, the conditions in the community
were then such as to make this possible. In fact, however,
no hasid became the *Rav* of the Karlin or Pinsk communities at any time during the nineteenth century.

On the other side, the Karlin hasidim as late as 1870-1871 published a broadsheet headed 'No punishment, but A Warning,' full of abuse and threats against the mithnagdim.

Like his father before him, R. Aharon the Second gave his support to the hasidic settlers in Palestine who were then going through hard times. When an emissary came from Palestine to collect money on their behalf, R. Aharon wrote the following letter (undated in the original) to his hasidim: [144]

'To our beloved followers . . . may they all be rewarded! I write . . . in praise of our Land, the Land of Life, the place to which our prayers are directed . . . the Holy of Holies. . . . Let our brethren the Children of Israel unite . . . with a single heart and with worship that comes from the heart—that is, by prayer. . . . Who am I . . . to go on and on in praise of such exalted matters ? . . . However, my spirit gives me no peace, because of . . . the oppression of the times. For it is now several years that the Lord has called up a famine on the Land, and thousands of precious souls and their children are going hungry with none to offer them bread. Moreover, I have seen that letters written with passionate fervour by all the great ones of Israel to arouse the hearts of our brethren the Children of Israel have borne fruit and succeeded. Therefore am I writing now to my loyal followers [to tell them] that my friend the learned and venerable Rabbi . . . Avraham-Yosef . . . the grandson of the holy Rabbi and *Gaon* of Volochisk . . . the son-in-law of my kinsman, my dear friend the renowned hasid . . . R. Naftali-Tsevi . . . the grandson of the holy *Baal Shem Tov*, has been sent from the Holy Land to collect fresh funds to keep alive our brethren dwelling in the centre of holiness [i.e., in the Holy Land]. I am therefore writing this letter to urge all our followers . . . to welcome its bearer, my friend the Rabbi, warmly and to arouse your hearts to participate . . . generously . . . in the new contribution, everyone according to his means and even more. . . . Pay your contributions promptly and generously . . . to uphold their dwelling in the Holy Land. . . . From me, who love you and send you affectionate greetings and desire your good, and your affection, your unity, and your attachment to the Source of Life. . . .'

In the second, also undated, letter found in the Stolin *genizah* from R. Aharon the Second to his hasidim, we read as follows:

'May the Lord give life and blessing . . . to our brethren the Children of Israel wherever they be . . . long life and peace to them, their housholds and their offspring . . . for ever.

'I have taken up my pen . . . to write words from the heart to the heart . . . that you should freely and generously make your contributions out of love for the Holy Land . . . the Land for which the Lord cares and which is mentioned in all the prayers . . . of the community of Israel. . . . The Divine Name has vouchsafed us the fulfilment of the desire of our holy forefathers, that there should be some of our loyal supporters in the Land of Life [i.e., the Holy Land]. . . . With the Lord's help they have found a resting place for a group of our followers who devote themselves to the study of *Torah* and to prayer, where the feet of the holy *Tsaddikim* trod . . . a permanent place for prayer from the holy . . . *Tsaddik* . . . Menahem . . . whose pious hands established the holy place. With the Lord's help our followers have succeeded in purchasing the holy place that was granted to no other man. Thus far has the Divine Name aided our brethren, the Children of Israel, but they still require further assistance, especially our own followers. . . . You should, therefore, aid and support them generously, so that by their purchase they should have their share in the Holy Land. . . . I am confident that our brethren, the Children of Israel, will pay heed to these my words. . . . May we be granted in abundance . . . all that our hearts desire, for good and for blessing . . . from the Lord of Peace. . . .

'The words of Aharon, the son of R. Asher.'

From a comparison of these two letters it is evident that in the period between the dates when they were written, a group of Karlin hasidim established themselves in the Holy Land and bought the prayer-house in Tiberias which had previously been purchased by R. Mendel of Vitebsk.[145] Also found in the Stolin *genizah* were deeds of sale relating to houses bought by R. Aharon in Tiberias and Jerusalem, as well as a letter from the recipients of the *halukkah* to R. Aharon, appointing him as the 'chief general administrator' of all the funds sent to Palestine, and his son, R. Asher the Second, as his assistant.

Altogether, the Land of Israel [*Erets Yisrael*] occupied an important place in Karlin hasidism; and conversely, Karlin hasidim played a significant role in the history of hasidism in the Land of Israel. The son of R. Aharon the Great, R. Yaakov, settled with his family and his father-in-law, R. Avraham of Karlin, in Palestine and died there.[146] R. Asher the First wrote the public proclamation—quoted above—in support of Jewish settlers in Palestine. And amongst the papers found in the Stolin *genizah* there were, as already stated, receipts for sums of money sent by R. Asher to Palestine. In the credentials carried by an emissary sent by the Jews of Tiberias, in 1846, to collect money for Palestine—R. Moshe Yafe—we find included amongst the signatures of 'the leaders of the holy community of God-fearing Ashkenazi Jews . . . of the community of Volhynia . . .' that of a certain 'Moshe-Dov, the son of the Rabbi and Teacher Aharon of blessed memory from Stolin.' This Moshe-Dov was the step-brother of R. Aharon the Second.[147] Further evidence of the specially close connection between Karlin hasidism and Palestine is provided by the deeds of sale relating to houses in the name of R. Aharon the Second in Jerusalem and Tiberias (which were found, as stated, in the Stolin *genizah*); and also by the letter written by R. Aharon after the purchase of the house and plot of land belonging to R. Mendel of Vitebsk by the Karlin hasidim in Tiberias. It is clear then that, in R. Aharon the Second's time, a group of Karlin hasidim established itself in Tiberias. Detailed information about the exact date when this group established itself and about the early days of its existence is lacking. What is certain is that it was not until the second half of the nineteenth century, with the break-up of the various hasidic communities in Palestine into separate dynasties, that the special Karlin group arose with its own *shtiebelakh* [hasidic prayer-houses] in Tiberias, Safed, and

Jerusalem. It is worth stressing that, as far as is known to us, the fund-raising emissaries from Palestine who came originally from Pinsk and its environs (R. Hayyim the son of the *Gaon* of Karlin, R. Barukh the son of R. Shemuel, R. Avraham *dayyan* Wolfsohn, R. Avraham the son of R. Tsevi Eisenstein of Drohichin, R. Shemuel-Muni Zilberman[148]) were all *Perushim* (i.e., mithnagdim) and disciples of the *Gaon* of Vilna, and not Karlin hasidim. We likewise find men born in Pinsk at the head of the mithnaged community (the Pinsk *Av Beth-Din*, R. Hayyim Cohen, and R. Yeshayah the son of R. Yissakhar-Baer [Bardaki]).[149]

Apart from the letters referred to above, the following documents from the time of R. Aharon the Second were also found in the Stolin *genizah*: (1) a letter from R. Yisrael of Sadagora (dated *Rosh Hodesh Teveth*, 1852 ?) in which the writer complains that he has no money to give the emissaries from *Erets Yisrael* and therefore requests R. Aharon to try to raise the sum required from among his hasidim; (2) a second short, friendly letter from R. Yisrael of Ruzhin (dated the 19th *Elul*, 1848) in which the writer congratulates R. Aharon and promises to pray on his behalf daily; (3) the regulations of a *Mishnah*-reading society in the small town of Yanovo, near Pinsk (dated the 10th *Nisan*, 1830), signed by R. Aharon: the members undertake to study passages from the *Mishnah* in memory of the Jew named Lapidoth, who had donated a Scroll of the Law to this society; (4) the reply of R. Shemuel-Avraham Shapira of Slavuta [the owner of the well-known printing press] to the invitation to R. Aharon's wedding; (5) a short prayer composed by R. Aharon, of which the members of the ' court ' did not permit copies to be made; (6) a letter from R. Aharon to his followers about their regular payments to the ' court ' funds. In one of his letters is an interesting request of his to his family that they should not fast on *Taanith Esther*.[150]

In another letter—undated in the original—now in the possession of his descendants, R. Aharon gives his family his opinion about doctors, as follows:

' My daughter and son (may you be granted long life!),

pray handle medicines with moderation(?) and do not disobey the doctors' orders, for they are expert in the drinking of the waters, and in the amount of walking required after that, and also in eating and drinking and sleeping during the drinking of the waters . . . and carry out their instructions to the letter. May the Holy One Blessed Be He help you and give you complete healing and good health, for His goodness is everlasting!

'From your father . . . who prays for your welfare and eagerly waits to hear from you . . . about the beneficial effect of the treatment. . . .

Aharon of Karlin. . . .'

The close bonds of friendship established between the Karlin and Kozhenits dynasties in the time of R. Asher the First were maintained in R. Aharon the Second's day, too. This is evident from the following letter found in the Stolin *genizah*—undated in the original—from R. Aharon the Second to the Kozhenits hasidim:

'Warm greetings to the beloved of the Lord . . . frequent . . . in the threshold . . . of the Teacher and Master . . . Yisrael of Kozhenits . . . and his descendants. . . .

'Were I to try to relate in detail . . . the love . . . that my Father and Teacher implanted deep in my heart . . . there would not be space enough, for he never ceased praising [R. Yisrael]. Thanks be to God . . . that after him [R. Yisrael of Kozhenits] there came forth a scion of his stock . . . a delightful child, whom . . . I raised and brought up at my table [i.e., in my house] . . . a clever and knowledgeable boy . . . filled with the spirit of wisdom . . . who . . . has now reached the age of marriage. . . . Therefore, let my friends . . . who have followed in their holy path [i.e., that of the Kozhenits *Tsaddikim*] from generation to generation, let them awake and rouse themselves, and let them help one another to contribute gold from their pockets generously, according to their means and beyond their means. . . . For . . . the delightful boy is a fine person . . . and with God's help everyone will find his own satisfaction in him. I trust that the leaders of the generation, too . . . will hasten to fulfil my wishes . . . to awaken the hearts of those that follow them [i.e., their hasidim] and to raise as much money as possible.

May the merits of their holy forefathers aid them and assist them . . . in all their affairs with success and blessing . . . in all that they do and in all that their hearts desire. . . . These are the words of their loved one who prays for their welfare and good. . . .

Aharon the son of R. Asher. . . .'

'. . . A delightful child whom . . . I raised and brought up at my table . . . who . . . has now reached the age of marriage' for whose marriage R. Aharon the Second requests the hasidim of Kozhenits 'to contribute gold from their pockets generously, according to their means and beyond their means,' was one of the descendants of R. Yisrael of Kozhenits, R. Yerahmiel-Moshe. This R. Yerahmiel-Moshe was educated in Stolin, in the house of his step-father, R. Asher the Second, and subsequently became the *Tsaddik* of Kozhenits.

In R. Aharon the Second's days, the influence of the *Haskalah* ('Enlightenment') in Western Europe began to penetrate into Lithuania, bringing with it liberal social ideas. Hasidism now faced a new challenge. It now came under attack from the *maskilim*, just as a hundred years previously it had been attacked by the *Rabbanim*, and it displayed the same stubborn power of resistance in meeting this second onslaught as it had in meeting the first. Eventually, this conflict did great damage to Karlin hasidism and led to its decline, but not until long after the death of R. Aharon the Second.

The teachings of R. Aharon the Second included in *Beth Aharon* are described as follows in the introduction to that volume: 'Excellent sermons . . . what was uttered explicitly . . . by the lips . . . of R. Aharon [the Second] . . . faithfully recorded true words, one out of a thousand of his holy sayings. . . . The writings of our Master and Teacher of blessed memory [R. Aharon the Second] . . . were collected together and annotated in his own hand, various annotations on various subjects. Whenever he referred to these holy writings, he called them *Beth Aharon*. . . . Also, we have seen fit to include other excellent matters which we found written down in the hand of our Teacher's followers, who wrote them down for themselves as a record of his holy words that they heard from his holy mouth at various times when they were in his holy residence.'[151] In the volume *Beth Aharon*, which was published three years after R. Aharon the Second's death, we find many such expressions as the following: 'He began to speak,' 'the Rebbe said,' 'the Rebbe spoke a great deal about this,' 'the Rebbe raised a question,' 'the Rebbe repeated,' 'he reported his Father as saying,' 'he related on the authority of the holy Rebbe, R. Shelomo Karliner,' 'afterwards he spoke a great deal himself and said,' 'he ended with a blessing,' 'he was asked,' 'he said in the name of the holy Rebbe from Mezhibozh [R. Barukh],' 'the holy Rebbe of blessed memory asked a difficult question,' 'in the year 1872, on the holy Sabbath, Portion of the Law *Be-Haalothkha,* before he was laid to rest . . . he said.' These repeatedly stressed expressions confirm that most of the contents of the book were indeed written 'by his followers . . . who wrote them down for themselves . . . that they heard from his mouth.'

On the other hand, we also find such expressions as the following: 'As I heard from my revered Father,' 'in my youth I asked my revered Father,' 'according to the parable related by my revered Grandfather, the holy *Tsaddik* [R. Aharon the Great] of Karlin,' 'as I heard in the name of the *Tsaddik,* our Teacher and Master, R. Sh.[elomo] of Karlin,' 'I have heard it said in the name of our Teacher and Master R. M.[ordekhai] of blessed memory from Neskhizh,' 'we spoke,' 'we said,' and the like. These expressions are evidence that some of 'the holy writings . . . were . . . annotated in his holy hand.' In his sermons, R. Aharon the Second frequently quotes from his father and also from R. Shelomo of Karlin, whom he refers to as 'the holy *Tsaddik* of Karlin.' He also mentions his grandfather, R. Aharon the Great, whom he calls 'R. Aharon Karliner.' He likewise quotes from the homilies and parables of other *Tsaddikim,* such as R. Barukh [of Mezhibozh], R. Elimelekh [of Lizhensk], the *Tsaddik* of Kozhenits [R. Yisrael], the *Tsaddik* of Polonnoye [R. Yaakov-Yosef], R. Yisrael of Ruzhin, R. Nahum of Chernobil, R. Levi-Yitshak of Berdichev, R. Mordekhai of Neskhizh, the Rebbe of Lublin [R. Yaakov-Yitshak], R. Zusya of Anipol, R. Mendel

of Bar, The Rebbe of Apta [the *Tsaddik* R. Avraham-
Yehoshua-Heshel: 'as I heard from the *Tsaddik* of Apta '].
Another source used by R. Aharon is 'the *siddur* [prayer-
book] of R. Yaakov-Koppel.' Sometimes he attributes the
same idea both to his father and to R. Shelomo of Karlin ;
and certain ideas which he attributes to his father are the
same as those attributed by the hasidim, in their 'Collected
Sayings,' to R. Asher the First. In R. Aharon's sermons, there
is not much casuistry. Instead, there are many explanations
and parables, sometimes even in Yiddish, which made the
book more accessible to the simple uneducated hasid. From
references in the text, it is clear that these hasidic homilies
were delivered over a period of many years, from 1841 to
' the holy Sabbath . . . before he was laid to rest ' (1872).

On the way in which a Jew should pray, R. Aharon speaks
as follows: ' In worshipping . . . the Almighty, one should
not keep on repeating the same prayer mechanically, but
should add and add again. Every prayer must have fresh
vitality infused into it.' 'The uniting of the worlds is achieved
primarily by prayer.' ' Even the man of least worth is not
permitted to despair. . . . " For is not my word like fire ? "
Just as fire lights up the darkness, so will the Holy Name
give him light . . . in all his trials.' ' Everyone must take care
to bring himself closer to the Source of Life when he prays,
and, of course, when he studies and when he performs any
of the commandments.' ' Every word that a man utters
should bring him closer to the Source of Life.' One should
stand up to pray only in a joyful frame of mind. ' Whenever
a prayer is uttered something is born. . . . And when is something born ? . . . When the prayer is uttered joyfully. But
prayer uttered (Heaven forbid!) in sadness bears no fruit.
When God has aroused a man's spirit and soul to pray joyfully, then he exalts all the previous prayers.' ' Every word
spoken by man in the presence of the Almighty Blessed Be
He, must be spoken clearly, vigorously, and joyfully. . . .
This is the meaning of " Thou shalt make a window for the
ark " [Heb.: *tevah*]—that you should bring light to the
written letter ' [Heb.: *tevah*]. Not only when praying should
a man be happy, but whatever he does should be done
joyfully, for ' by joyfulness he will be able to remove himself

95

from everything evil and to bring himself closer to the good.' 'One must beware of sadness and melancholy, as of all the other sins and vices.' 'The essential thing is to perform every commandment joyfully, not sadly.' The consonants of the Hebrew word for 'thought' [*mahashavah*] form the word for 'joyfully' [*besimhah*] ; hence 'repentance . . . comes primarily from joyfulness and delight ; and delight and joyfulness come primarily from repentance.'

Apart from prayer, there is still another way that brings the Jew closer to his God—the way of *Torah* (the study of the Law). 'Not only in prayer, but also in our study of the Law, we must continually, every day, find fresh, renewed vitality. "Give us our portion in Thy Law" . . . this means: give every single one of us the share in the Law that is his. . . . One man finds spiritual vigour in the study of a single verse, another in the *Gemara*, a third in the *Zohar*. Each one must seek for and find his own spiritual vigour and sanctity in the *Torah*.' At the same time, R. Aharon stresses the part played by the ordinary Jew in creating this sanctity: 'The People of Israel . . . bring holiness to everything. . . . Here is the proof: a Scroll of the Law written by a heretic is unfit for use . . . even though the letters are exactly the same as those written by a Jew. For the truth is that what matters is the sanctity, drawn from the living power of the Creator, that the Jew infuses into the letters.' R. Aharon is reported to have summed up the relationship between the study of the Law and prayer in the following dictum: The study of the Law is an obligation, prayer a need.

Not only prayer and the study of the Law, but every act that a man performs is a form of Divine worship. 'Not only in the study of the *Torah* and in prayer, but also in things that a man does of his own free will, such as eating, drinking, sleeping, walking, sexual intercourse, and the like, and in all other human activities, everyone must take care not to remove himself (Heaven forbid!) from the Almighty, Blessed Be He, but only to bring himself closer thereby to His Holy Name.

'Whenever a man does good deeds he is sowing a seed in Heaven that will bear fruit. . . . If a man does not sow the seed, he will not reap the harvest. Hence, in spiritual matters a man is obliged to sow *mitsvoth* and good deeds, and thus bring it about that the Holy Name should shower down upon him His great light and every spiritual and physical blessing in this world, and that there should be complete communion. . . . The flesh is purified until it becomes all spirit.'

Prayer, study, and good deeds were given to man for one purpose only—to enable him to attain to the living power of the Creator. 'Everything that is done in the world . . . contains within it the living power of the Creator,' 'and when all creatures are exalted spiritually by us, our righteous Messiah will come.' 'When a Jew is born, he is born with his good portion, with all the faculties required for him to be equipped to receive his good portion. And what is this portion ? "For the Lord's portion is His people "—the living power of the Divinity . . . the vital force which He implanted in His people Israel, was all taken from on high, that is, from His Holiness, Blessed Be His Name! For, as is known, man is a portion of the Most High.' 'Every Jew can attain to the living power of the Holy Name. Even the smallest of all, and the least of all, and the lowest of all.' What, then, prevents them ? 'When a man knows that he is nothing and that there is nothing in him, then, whenever he wishes it, the living force of the Creator can pervade his whole being. . . . But when he thinks himself something, then there is no room for the living power of the Creator to spread in him.'

The purpose for which everything was created is the attainment of perfection, and 'we, the people of Israel, were created for the complete perfection that is to be attained . . . speedily in our days. The world shall be purified and restored to perfection ; all things shall be one, and there shall be peace in the world.' 'Everyone must know that the whole universe and every human being are like a lamp and vessel that receive the living power and light of the Holy One Blessed Be He.' But 'the light of the Holy One Blessed Be He cannot go together with anything physical in this lower world of ours. Hence, His intention . . . in creating this world was to make the two worlds one, that man should be freed from his physical trammels and everything should be raised up to His will . . . but then came the sins of the generation of the Flood and the generation of the Tower of Babel and the men of Sodom. There followed two thousand years of chaos, when the Divine Presence withdrew to the Seventh Heaven and this lower world was separated from the higher world and the Divine Providence almost abandoned man. . . . But afterwards, when the two thousand years of *Torah* commenced and God's light began to shine in this world, when the patriarchs together with all the righteous ones and Moses our Teacher brought back the Divine Glory to earth, and everything was purified and raised up to the Holy One Blessed Be He—then the two worlds were made equal. For this is the essence of His will . . . that every physical thing in this world should be elevated to the spiritual level.' 'For, in truth, the spiritual is far removed from the physical, and the physical is far removed from the spiritual. Only when Israel cleave to the Holy One Blessed Be He by keeping His Law and worshipping Him and obliterating themselves, only then do they bring His Holiness and light down to this world and only then can they ascend to the higher sphere . . . in body.' 'For the worlds were created solely for the purpose that each of them should be filled with the light of the Holy One Blessed Be He and be constantly renewed. Thereby is this world kept in being.'

R. Aharon attributes to the *Tsaddik* the exalted role of radiating some of the 'hidden light' on the world. 'The first light that was hidden away, was sealed up in the *Tsaddikim* . . . not for the world to come, but for the *Tsaddikim* that were to arise in every generation, that they should attain to the light by their good deeds.' 'By their actions, the *Tsaddikim* raise up all things to the heights, where they become a torch . . . a great light for all this world.' 'All the *Tsaddikim* attained to the hidden light by their spiritual self-sacrifice . . . until they became men of great righteousness.' 'It would seem natural to wonder (since the Lord hid the light away), why did He create it at all ? . . . So that afterwards every man should search for the hidden light.' To this end, 'everyone must bind himself in his prayers to the *Tsaddikim*, who are bound to the holy patriarchs.'

Prayer, study, and good deeds hasten the day of redemption. 'Every day, nay every hour, a man must bring the world nearer to the coming of the Messiah : as we have already said on the verse " All the days of your life "—this includes [lit. : brings in] the days of the Messiah, so that everyone must . . . by his deeds bring the world nearer to the days of the Messiah.' Moreover, 'every Jew is also in himself a kind of Messiah,' for ' every Jew is obliged to think and know that he is unique in the world, and that no other person like him has yet existed in the world. For if there had already been anyone like him in this world, there would have been no need for him to exist. . . . Every single person is something new in the world and must in this world perfect his character . . . and his Jewish knowledge which are an integral part of his being, until all the worlds shall be perfected by the whole community of Israel, and . . . the righteous redeemer shall come.'

R. Aharon the Second used to say : Truth, even the slightest trace of truth, is impossible without spiritual devotion. And 'R. Yisrael of Ruzhin once said : "R. Aharon the Great of Karlin was the truth of the world; R. Asher, his son, walked all his life in the footsteps of the truth ; and as for R. Aharon, his grandson, if he knew that a crumb of truth was hidden under the floor, he would pull up the floor with his fingers."'

R. Aharon the Second remained all the rest of his life in Stolin. He died on the 17th *Sivan*, 1872,[152] while passing through the small town of Mlynov, near Dubno, in Volhynia, and was buried there. Thereafter, he was given by his followers the additional names of 'the man of Mlynov' or 'the holy grandfather.' Since the teachings of R. Aharon the Second comprise the major part of the volume *Beth Aharon*, he himself is often referred to by the hasidim by the name of this book, according to the Jewish practice of naming writers after their works.[153]

G. *Ha-Yenuka [The Child]* (1873-1921)

R. Aharon the Second's successor was his son, R. Asher
the Second. The situation then prevailing in the 'court' at
Stolin may be gathered from a letter, signed by R. Asher
the Second and written in the hand of one of his followers,
which was sent by R. Asher to his hasidim after his father's
death.

'With the help of the Blessed Name!

'Life and blessing . . . to my beloved ones . . . our loyal
followers. . . . May they be blessed . . . with every good,
they and their wives and their children and descendants . . .
with a good and long life. . . . Our beloved followers know
the painful burden of debts left . . . by our Master, my
revered Father . . . and they all know how great were [my
father's] sufferings of this account in his lifetime . . . how he
was pained to the very depths of his being . . . and how the
voice of the creditors was heard every day. . . . Now, therefore, I am sending our dearly beloved friend . . . the bearer
of this letter, to all . . . our followers to collect their contributions . . . according to the list that he shows them. Let
them take good note of the greatness of the need. Moreover,
I request that my office in such a great matter as this should
not be changed . . . and everyone that trod the threshold
of the holy residence of . . . my Father . . . should be quick
to carry out these my words, to honour him and to give his
holy spirit rest in Paradise. And also to remove the great
sorrow that is caused by this. Let them all rise up as one
man to pay the sum required . . . generously and gladly. Let
them help . . . and encourage one another to pay their
contribution speedily to our friend, the bearer of this letter
. . . according to the list. Heaven forbid that they should be
late, or should put off . . . their response, but let them bring
it themselves. Let them contribute through the bearer of
this letter, and let them give generously. For he that gives
generously will receive an additional blessing. It is not to be
believed that there will be even one of our followers that
will shut his ears . . . and not feel bound to perform this
great duty, nor remember his reverence for his Teacher. . . .
Even as the love of him was deeply implanted in their hearts

in his lifetime so now it is their bounden duty to be quick in showing respect for his memory. . . . Everything will be . . . under my supervision. . . . I trust . . . that they will hearken to my words for their own good . . . and that the Hidden Light may pour down every blessing upon them . . . to bring blessing upon their houses in peace . . . and in long life . . . and that their names may be constantly mentioned on our lips. . . . Wherever they turn may they prosper . . . that all may be well with them always. . . .

Asher, the son of R. Aharon. . . .'

In his practical interpretation of hasidic doctrine R. Asher the Second occupies a special place among the Karlin *Tsaddikim.* He was very greatly influenced by mystical doctrines and laid greater stress than his predecessors on the importance of immersion in the *mikveh* [the ritual bath] which 'washes away the uncleanness of the body and instead infuses it with holiness.' There are many reports of how he would remain immersed in the *mikveh* for hours on end, to the uncomprehending astonishment of the local mithnaged population. The few passages of biblical exposition attributed to him in *Beth Aharon* all deal with 'purification by immersion in the *mikveh.*' In the 'Rules for Daily Conduct' quoted in his name in the same volume, R. Asher bases the whole order of the day's work on the one principle of joyful 'inner worship,' as against 'sadness and grief (Heaven forbid!),' on religious awe, love, and humility, which 'purifies and perfects all the human qualities.' Again, 'Attachment to the *Tsaddikim* is very efficacious, to prevent any error in soul-searching'; and 'levity is the exact opposite of hasidism.'[154]

R. Asher the Second's period of 'leadership' as the Stolin Rebbe was of short duration. He died only a year after R. Aharon the Second, on the 15th *Av*, 1873, in the small town of Drohobich (Galicia), and was buried there. Hence the additional names given him by the Karlin hasidim: 'the man of Drohobich,' or 'the young Rebbe,' to distinguish him from 'the old man of Stolin,' R. Asher the First, and from 'the holy grandfather,' R. Aharon the Second.[155]

The death of R. Asher the Second caused a crisis in the ranks of Karlin hasidism, since he left no adult successor.

His only son, Yisrael, was then about four years old (hasidic tradition has it that he was born in the month of *Kislev*, 1868), and thus not only the child, but all the Karlin hasidim, too, lost a father. In this critical time, the Karlin hasidim resolved to meet the danger by standing firm in their loyalty to the Karlin dynasty, and therefore proclaimed the *Yenuka* [Child] Yisrael to be their Rebbe. This proclamation of a small child as a Rebbe aroused comment in the Jewish press, particularly in a satirical article entitled *Hithgalluth ha-Yenuka bi-Stolin* [The Revelation of the Child in Stolin].[156] This satire is presented in the form of a long letter, written supposedly by a hasid in the characteristic hasidic style, in which the writer goes into ecstasies about the 'miracles' and 'marvels' of the Karlin *Tsaddikim,* including those performed by the *Yenuka*.

When R. Yisrael grew up, he not only made a name for himself by his intellectual ability and practical vigour, but he also won the deep affection of his followers by the warm paternal interest that he took in every one of them. They loved him for the impartial way in which he used to preach and reprimand as he thought necessary, without making any distinction between rich and poor, between someone from a good family and a simple Jew. His sense of realities and his experience in worldly affairs enabled him to help his followers with good advice in time of trouble. R. Yisrael was also very tolerant and mixed freely with people from all strata of the population, thus winning the respect even of his opponents. With his knowledge of Russian and German he had close connections with the secular authorities, and used to intercede with them on behalf both of the whole community and of its individual members. The hasidim relate that once, when a troop of soldiers descended upon Stolin with the intention of carrying out a pogrom, R. Yisrael invited the commander to a meal ; and when the latter told him that he had not come to Stolin to eat but for 'other matters,' and asked R. Yisrael who his children were since he did not wish to harm them, R. Yisrael replied : 'All the Jews of Stolin are my children.' The story ends with the words : 'So there was no pogrom in Stolin.'[157]

True to the tradition of his father and grandfather before

him, R. Yisrael held open 'court' in Stolin for the Karlin hasidim, especially on Sabbaths and Festivals. R. Yisrael was not in the habit of expounding the *Torah*, and yet on the 'Penitential Days' Stolin—so eye-witnesses relate—was crowded with hasidim who would come from far and near, from Kiev and Warsaw and from as far away as Odessa, and a few even from Palestine. On *Simhath Torah* and on the *Seder* Night of Passover, the tunes of R. Aharon the Second, sung with joyful fervour, would resound through the small town till late into the night. Unlike the other Karlin hasidim, R. Yisrael used himself to pray silently. However, he conducted the *melavveh malkah* to musical accompaniment. He and his three sons together made up a quartet which occasionally performed various pieces of secular music, in addition to liturgical tunes. For R. Yisrael, playing music was one of the forms of Divine worship, which was therefore 'to be preceded by washing the hands.'[158]

The influence of the *Haskalah* movement, which had first begun to be felt in R. Aharon the Second's days, grew stronger in R. Yisrael's time. The nationalist and socialist movements at the turn of the century, together with the secularisation of Jewish education, alienated the younger generation of Jews from hasidism. Indeed, R. Yisrael's own followers used to relate that he himself spoke sadly of Karlin hasidism as a phase that was drawing to a close.

R. Yisrael set down some of the main points of his 'credo' in two testaments, one addressed to his family and the other to his followers.[159]

In the testament to his family R. Yisrael writes as follows: 'When my spirit departs, no time shall be spent on ceremonial tributes of respect. If my end comes while I am travelling, my body shall not be carried to my home, unless the place be only a few hours' distance from Mlynov [the burial place of R. Aharon the Second], Karlin [the burial place of R. Aharon the Great and R. Asher the First], or Drohobich [the burial place of R. Asher the Second]. If it be the local custom to set up an *ohel* [structure over the grave], mine shall not be a large one but only medium-sized. If it be the custom to set up a tombstone, only my name and my father's name shall be inscribed on it, without any titles. . . . [For winding-sheet] they shall take my *kittel* [a white garment worn by Jews on the Penitential Days and on the *Seder* Night], and the other cerements shall be made from the garments of my fathers. . . . In the first year, in all the towns where there are followers of mine, they shall study *Ein Yaakov* [a volume containing the talmudic *Aggadah*], and if there is a *Talmud* study circle, they shall complete one tractate in my memory. And in the circles in which I am registered as a member, care shall be taken to divide up the *Talmud* in such a way that in the course of ten years the whole *Talmud* shall have been studied in my memory.

' I herewith earnestly request my sons to do their utmost to educate their own sons (and to use all their influence with others, too) in traditional Judaism and Hasidism after the old manner without any compromises. The main thing is the study of the *Talmud* . . . which makes all that know it conduct themselves better. When the children grow up, let them be taught writing and language, things that are naturally necessary, and let them not be like the fools of the present day whose whole education is derived from journals and stories. Their parents shall take care that their teacher be an elderly man of known probity. They shall also give good heed to the education of their daughters, for on that depends the corner-stone of Judaism —the family ; and they shall endeavour to find them husbands soon after they reach marriageable age.

' I counsel my sons not to meddle in communal affairs or in any worldly matters, especially not in money cases or matters concerning the secular authorities. For in the course of my long life I have never seen anyone that emerged from all this unscathed and unhumiliated, except in such matters as the study of the *Talmud* and the use of the *mikveh*. The greatest principle of all is not to flatter anyone in the world, for this sometimes leads to the opposite result, as our Sages remarked : " Every flatterer eventually falls into the power of the one whom he flatters." Hence, this shall be the sign to my followers to which of my sons to turn [i.e., which of them to choose as my successor] : the one that shall admit no flatterers, show no special favour to any man, make no special effort to win followers, and not become involved with the secular authorities.'

Then follow the detailed instructions about the division of the property as a whole :

' My Scrolls of the Law shall be divided up between my sons, but the holy Scroll of my grandfather of blessed memory shall remain in Stolin as long as my *beth midrash* stands and those that worship in it pray in the hasidic manner. Afterwards they shall come to some agreement among themselves, according to the decision of pious Jews.'

' This will was written in the hand of our holy Rebbe, in the presence of the undersigned . . . on the second day of the week, the 2nd of *Teveth*, [5]681 [1920], in Stolin.'

Signature of two witnesses.

The following is the text of R. Yisrael's last injunctions to his followers :

' The second day of the week . . . the 12th of *Tammus*, 5681 [1921], Stolin.

' For the sake of my brethren and companions I shall utter . . . words that come from the heart to our loyal followers . . . that these words should be inscribed on the tablets of their heart . . . in the true hasidic manner. . . . Let every single one of them be truthful and sincere ; let him never speak hypocritically, but let his outward manner truly reflect his inner thoughts. Let him obey the injunction of the verse : " Know Him in all thy way " [Prov. 3, 6]. Let every one of them guard his tongue from evil and his lips from uttering deceit, and let him utterly eschew lying and arrogance. As it is written : " The arrogant man is an abomination to the Lord " [Prov. 16, 5]. . . . I pray that the Lord may graciously grant us length of days and years, with all good and pleasant things. True, the net is spread out over all living things ; and since all men are mortal, I exhort our followers (may they live long !) that, in a hundred years from now, there should be no dissension between them arising from the sect of flatterers and hypocrites, for no flatterer shall come into the Lord's presence, but that they should all form one united band. This shall be a true sign for them :

that one of my sons . . . in whom there shall be all these qualities, who shall not be a flatterer or hypocrite, and shall eschew lies, and shall not belong to . . . a company (here, between the lines, the following words have been added in his own holy hand: a company of the Zionists and especially of the *Mizrahi*),[160] but who shall be one of those that fear the Lord, who shall not have his sons and daughters taught in schools, not even in Hebrew schools, nor make any effort to have himself chosen Rebbe—he shall be their [i.e., my followers'] leader and head. (From this point the testament is written in his own holy hand): When I could no longer see clearly enough to write in my own hand, I ordered my family to write at my dictation. In witness whereof I sign my name

Yisrael the son . . . of R. Asher. . . .'
Signature of two witnesses.

R. Yisrael died at the age of 52 on the second day of *Rosh Hashanah*, 1921, far away from his native town, in a convalescent home in Homburg, Germany. He was buried in Frankfurt on Main, and is therefore to this day referred to by the Karlin hasidim as 'the man of Frankfurt.'[161] Amongst the hasidim at large, and even among the mithnagdim, he is known as 'the *Yenuka* of Stolin.'

NOTES TO CHAPTER II

[1] Dubnow, *Toledoth ha-Hasiduth*, p. 463 ff.

[2] R. Rafael Hacohen, later *Rav* in Hamburg, was one of the greatest talmudists of his time and author of numerous rabbinic works ; see : S. M. Rabinowitsch, ' *Al Pinsk, Karlin ve-Yoshveihen*,' *ibid.*, p. 8 ff.

[3] *Salomon Maimons Lebensgeschichte*, pp. 188, 198, 201 ff. The abovementioned book, *Maggid Devarav le-Yaakov* (Lublin 1927 and many other impressions), is the original source for the teaching of the Great *Maggid*.

[4] A. E. Shapiro, *Mishnath Hakhamim*, p. 39, Jerusalem 1934.

[5] Y. M. Kleinbaum, *Shema Shelomo*, Pt. II, p. 25, Petrokov 1928. Karlin, which was later incorporated in Pinsk, gained its communal independence and kept it almost until the Nazi holocaust. Cf., Rabinowitsch, ' *Al Pinsk, Karlin ve-Yoshveihen*,' p. 15 ; R. Mahler, *Toledoth ha-Yehudim be-Polin*, p. 394, Merhavyah 1946 ; *Toyzend Yor Pinsk*, ed. Hofman, p. 56 ff.

Hasidic tradition relates, that R. Aharon the Great had an uncle in Karlin, R. Manele, who also found his way to the Great *Maggid*, and that it was this uncle that influenced R. Aharon to go to Mezerich. M. H. Kleinman, *Zikhron la-Rishonim*, p. 28, Petrokov 1912 ; A. Ayzen, ' R. *Aharon ha-Gadol*,' *Ha-Modya* (daily paper), 6. X. 1954, Jerusalem.

[6] It is possible, that the young hasidic preacher described by Solomon Maimon (*Lebensgeschichte*, p. 205, note) might be R. Aharon, despite the difference between the age of the preacher, as conjectured by Maimon (22), and that R. Aharon who was then about 30. See below the comments added by R. Aharon to the *pinkas* of Maimon's birthplace Nesvizh. R. Aharon continued to be referred to as ' The Admonisher ' for more than a hundred years after his death. See : Had min Havraya, ' *Hithgalluth ha-Yenuka bi-Stolin*,' *Ha-Shahar*, Vol. VI, p. 31, Vienna 1875.

[7] ' *Zemir Aritsim ve-Harvoth Tsurim*,' published by Dubnow, *Chassidiana*, supplement to *He-Avar*, Vol. II, pp. 22, 23, 25.

[8] Solomon Maimon, *op. cit.*, p. 188.

[9] ' Chassidim appelés aussi *Carolins* en Lithuania, du nom d'un village nommé Carolin non loin de Pinsko, ou la secte a pris naissance,' cited by Graetz, *op. cit.*, Vol. XI, p. 557.

In connection with the rise of Karlin hasidism, mention should be made of the words spoken, according to hasidic tradition, by the Karlin Rebbe R. Yisrael of Stolin before his death in 1921 : ' Our hasidism is one hundred and sixty years old.' According to this statement, Karlin hasidism came into being in the early sixties of the eighteenth century. Hausman, *Divrei Aharon* p. 119.

[10] In my search for these writings I was aided by the teacher David-Tsevi Bakhlinski and his assistant Shuchman, both of whom apparently died martyrs' deaths in the Nazi holocaust. The archives of the Karlin *Tsaddikim* were housed in the cellar of the old Rebbe's residence (the ' court ') in Stolin—this is the Stolin *genizah*. They comprised correspondence of the Karlin *Tsaddikim* and of the *Tsaddikim* of other dynasties, public appeals, *pinkasim*, a pledge of loyalty [*shtar hithkashruth*] signed in 1575 in Safed by disciples of R. Yitshak Luria and R. Hayyim Vital ; a manuscript of *Sefer ha-Tsoref*, written by the Shabbatean, R. Yehoshua-Heshel Tsoref, and other writings. Cf., W. Z. Rabinowitsch, ' *Min ha-Genizah ha-Stolinaith*,' *Zion*, 5th year, pp. 125-132, 244-247, Jerusalem 1940 ; Idem, ' Al " *Sefer ha-Tsoref*," ' *Zion*, 6th year, pp. 80-84, Jerusalem 1941 and below, the last paragraph of this book.

[11] R. Aharon's postscripts are published in part by Dubnow, *Toledoth*

ha-Hasiduth, p. 478. Cf., also: Benzion Dinur, *Be-Mifneh ha-Doroth,* pp. 144-146, Jerusalem 1955 ; I. Halpern, '*Yahaso shel R. Aharon ha-Gadol mi-Karlin klappei Mishtar ha-Kehilloth,*' *Zion,* 22nd year, p. 86 ff., Jerusalem 1957.

¹² *Siah ha-Sadeh,* Shklov 1787 ; *Reiah ha-Sadeh,* Shklov 1795. R. Eliezer, son of R. Meir Halevi was formerly *Av Beth-Din* in Homsk (a small town near Pinsk) and afterwards ' *Rav* of the synagogue and *Moreh-Tsedek* of the holy community of Pinsk.' See: A. Yaari, '*Ha-Defus ha-Ivri bi-Shklov, Kiryath Sefer,* Vol. XXII, p. 63, Jerusalem 1945.

¹³ The letter is published by Dubnow, *Toledoth ha-Hasiduth,* p. 477 and by Kleinbaum, *Shema Shelomo,* Pt. II, p. 21.

¹⁴ M. Teitelbaum, *Ha-Rav mi-Ladi u-Miflegeth Habad,* Pt.I, p. 23, n. 2, Warsaw 1910 ; H. M. Heilman, *Beth Rabbi,* Pt. I, p. 8, n. 4 and p. 125, Berdichev 1903.

¹⁵ H. Lieberman, '*Hearoth Bibliografiyoth,*' *Sefer ha-Yovel le-Alexander Marx,* p. 15 ff., New York 1943.

¹⁶ Infr., p. 37. Similarly we find no historical data in hasidic literature on the relations between R. Aharon and R. Tsevi, son of the Besht, who lived in Pinsk and, at stated above (p. 6), died and was buried there.

¹⁷ See above the letter of the Great *Maggid* of Mezerich to the Pinsk *Moreh-Tsedek* R. Eliezer Halevi.

Nadav, in his study *Toledoth Kehillath Pinsk* (in ms.), holds R. Eliezer, the son of R. Meir Halevi—whom the Great *Maggid* of Mezerich, R. Baer, request in his letter ' to live together in peace and to work in partnership and harmony with our distinguished and renowned friend, R. Aharon. . . . Why, then, should you turn away [from him] ? . . . Set aside evil thoughts, that there be no schism between you '—was, at the time when this letter was written (probably between 1769 and 1772), not one of the mithnagdim but, on the contrary, closely connected with hasidism in Pinsk and with the Great *Maggid* of Mezerich and a friend of R. Aharon and R. Shelomo of Karlin. Nadav is also of the opinion that hasidism had at that time a great influence in Pinsk, even amongst the towns talmudic scholars.

With regard to the problem of the date of the penetration of hasidism into Lithuania, v. Tishbi's view, *op. cit.,* p. 23 and cf., *ibid.* (pp. 16-24) on R. Shemuel the son of R. Eliezer of Kalvariya and his book *Darkhei Noam.*

¹⁸ '*Zemir Aritsim ve-Harvoth Tsurim,*' published by Dubnow, *op. cit.,* pp. 24, 25, ; Heilman, *op. cit.,* p. 85.

¹⁹ Heilman, *op. cit.,* p. 85.

²⁰ There is the legend among hasidim that in the Shklov debate the hasidim were represented by R. Aharon the Great, but there is no historical substantiation for this. On the name ' *Talk hasidim* ' see: D. T. Hilman, *Iggeroth Baal ha-Tanya,* p. 156 ff., Jerusalem 1953 ; Heilman, *op. cit.,* Pt. I, p. 8, n. 1.

²¹ '*Zemir Aritsim ve-Harvoth Tsurim,*' in Dubnow, *op. cit.,* p. 25.

²² *Ibid.*

²³ *Ibid.,* p. 21, 22.

²⁴ *Ibid.,* p. 11 ff. and p. 26.

²⁵ *Ibid.,* p. 14 ; *Maimons Lebensgeschichte,* p. 203. The *Tsaddik* R. Aharon the Second of Karlin (the grandson of R. Aharon the Great) used to relate the following hasidic tradition: ' My revered Grandfather . . . used to set on the table in front of his holy teacher [sc. R. Baer] twelve haloth [round loaves] at every meal of the holy Sabbath ' (*Beth Aharon,*

by R. Aharon of Karlin, p. 289, Brody 1875).

26 'Zemir Aritsim ve-Harvoth Tsurim,' pp. 10, 24, 25 ff.; Dubnow, Toledoth ha-Hasiduth, p. 113, n. 4.

27 See above the account by Maimon of pilgrimages to the Tsaddik.

28 Cf., infr., Chap. 3: Amdur Hasidism.

29 'Zemir Aritsim ve-Harvoth Tsurim,' p. 11 ff.

30 Ibid., p. 12 ff., 21 ff.

31 Dubnow, Toledoth ha-Hasiduth, p. 114.

32 M. H. Kleinman, Mazkereth Shem ha-Gedolim, p. 7, Petrokov 1908 ; Kehal Hasidim, pp. 53, 54 (no place and date of publication).

33 Tsavvaah mi-Kethoveth Yad Kodesh. . . . R. Aharon . . . mi-Karlin . . . ve-Hanhagoth . . . mi-Beno . . . R. Asher . . . mi-Karlin, Chernovits 1855 ; Beth Aharon, pp. 1, 11, 15-16, 293.

34 On the legends regarding R. Aharon's religious feeling see: Heilman, op. cit., p. 127 ; M. H. Kleinman, Zikhron la-Rishonim, pp. 22-45, Petrokov 1912 ; Idem, Mazkereth Shem ha-Gedolim, pp. 6-13 ; Kehal Hasidim he-Hadash, passim. Lemberg 1904 ; [M. Bodek], Seder ha-Doroth mi-Talmidei ha-Besht p. 35 (no place and date of publication).

35 Beth Aharon, p. 1.

36 Op. cit., p. 293.

37 Ibid.

38 Op. cit., p. 1.

39 Ibid.

40 Op. cit., p. 11. The 'Zemer' was subsequently included among the Sabbath songs in several siddurim [prayer-books], such as the following: Beth Yaakov, compiled by R. Yaakov Emden, p. 318, Warsaw 1881 ; the collection of Sabbath songs, Sheloshah Sefarim Niftahim . . . ed. . . . by Y. A. L. Oppenheim . . . p. 60, Petrokov 1910 ; the Koidanov siddur, Or ha-Yashar (v. infr. Chap, 4, n. 32) ; the siddur, Zemiroth le-Shabbathoth ve-Yamim Tovim, published by A. B., Jerusalem 1947.

41 Entsiklopediyah Yisraelith (Eshkol) ,Vol. I, s.v. Aharon Ben Yaakov mi-Karlin, Berlin 1929 ; A. Ben-Ezra, Ha-'Yenuka' mi-Stolin, New York 1951 ; Horodets, edited by A. Ben-Ezra and Y. Zusman, p. 52, New York 1949 ; M. S. Geshuri, 'Niggunei Karlin u-Stolin,' Stolin, Sefer Zikkaron, edited by A. Avatihi and Y. Zakai, p. 167, Tel Aviv 1952.

42 Kleinman, Zikhron la-Rishonim, p. 28.

43 Shivhei ha-Besht, edited by Horodetzki, p. 38.

44 Besides the works listed in n. 34, hasidic literature contains many other stories about R. Aharon the Great. There is reason to suspect that the hasidim were not particularly careful in their handing down of the details and mixed up words spoken by R. Aharon the Great with those spoken by one of his descendants, especially by his grandson, R. Aharon the Second.

As regards the vidduy [confession] printed in Beth Aharon (pp. 12-15) as the personal confession of R. Aharon the Great, it has already been proved by Y. Tishbi that this is merely a copy of an original composed by the author of the book Hemdath Yamim. Tishbi rightly maintains that R. Aharon the Great copied the confession out into his own siddur, and that the hasidim mistakenly thought that he was the author of it (Tarbits, Year 15, p. 175, note, Jerusalem 1944). This mistaken assumption is implied in the introductory remarks to the confession in Beth Aharon: 'Copied letter for letter from the wording of the confession in his holy siddur' (Beth Aharon, p. 12).

[45] These sayings about melancholy and joyfulness are of Yiddish origin. Kleinman, *Zikhron la-Rishonim*, p. 13.

[46] These sayings about melancholy, bitterness, and joyfulness are also attributed, *verbatim*, to the *Tsaddik* R. Hanokh of Alexander. A. Z. Eshkoli, ' *Ha-Hasiduth be-Polin*,' in the book *Beth Yisrael be-Polin*, Pt. II, p. 129, ed. I. Halpern, Jerusalem 1953.

[47] This idea is also attributed to the *Tsaddik* R. Mordekhai of Lakhovich. M. H. Kleinman, *Or Yesharim*, p. 30, Petrokov 1924.

[48] This may be an allusion to the persecutions R. Aharon experienced at the hands of the mithnagdim. The fact that he had prepared his will at the age of 36 perhaps indicates that his death was not a sudden one. Or perhaps it is to be explained by the belief that a man should face every day as his last.

[49] *Beth Aharon*, p. 15. Up to destruction of the Pinsk community (1941-1942) these words could be read on the gravestone of R. Aharon in the Karlin cemetery.

[50] '*Zemir Aritsim ve-Harvoth Tsurim*,' *op. cit.*, p. 21 ff.

[51] *Op. cit.*, pp. 12, 23.

[52] Graetz, *op. cit.*, Vol. XI, p. 557.

[53] J. Hessen, *Istoriya Yevreyskogo Naroda v Rossii*, Vol. I, p. 54, Leningrad 1925.

[54] Hessen, *op. cit.*, p. 49 ff.

[55] '*Zemir Aritsim ve-Harvoth Tsurim*,' *op. cit.*, p. 23.

[56] Cf., the Pinsk and Slutsk *herem*, published by E. T. Zweifel, *Shalom al Yisrael*, Pt. II, pp. 41, 42, Zhitomir 1869.

[57] '*Zemir Aritsim ve-Harvoth Tsurim*,' *op. cit.*, pp. 21, 22.

[58] Kleinman, *Mazkereth Shem ha-Gedolim*, p. 63 ; W. Z. Rabinowitsch, ' *Min ha-Genizah ha-Stolinaith*,' *Zion*, 5th year, p. 244 ; Kleinbaum, *Shema Shelomo*, Pt. II, p. 1, note and p. 58.

[59] Kleinbaum, *op. cit.*, Pt. II, passim.

[60] Bodek, *Seder ha-Doroth mi-Talmidei ha-Besht*, p. 37 ; Valden, *Shem ha-Gedolim he-Hadash*, *Maarekheth Sefarim*, p. 69, s.v.: *Reiah ha-Sadeh*, Warsaw 1874. Cf., supr., p. 15.

[61] There is a hasidic story that before R. Shelomo became a disciple of the Great *Maggid*, R. Aharon said to the *Maggid*: ' I have a young man in Karlin, named Shelomo, who, when he recites the Psalms on *Yom Kippur* after the *Kol Nidrei* leaves no holy spark in Poland, Lithuania and White Russia which he does not bring before the throne of glory ' (Kleinbaum, *op. cit.*, Pt. II, p. 3).

[62] V. infr., Chap. 3: Amdur Hasidism.

[63] Maimon, *op. cit.*, p. 210.

[64] '*Zemir Aritsim* '. . . etc., *op. cit.*, pp. 12, 26 ; *Shever Posheim* and *Zimrath Am ha-Arets*, cited by Dubnow, *Toledoth ha-Hasiduth*, pp. 369, 447.

Dubnow discussed the authorship of these collections of polemical writings: Dubnow, *Toledoth ha-Hasiduth*, pp. 412-417 ; *Sefer Shimon Dubnow*, ' *Mikhtevei Dubnow el Pinhas Torberg*,' ed. S. Rawidowicz, pp. 353-361, London 1954. An attempt to decide this question is made by A. Rubinstein, ' *Shever Posheim le-R. David mi-Makov—Zoth Torath ha-Kanauth le-R. Yehezkel mi-Radzimin*,' *Kiryath Sefer*, Vol. XXXV, pp. 240-249, Jerusalem 1960 ; Idem, ' *Ha-Kuntres " Zimrath Am ha-Arets " bi-Kthav-Yad*,' *Aresheth*, ed. N. Ben-Menahem and Y. Rafael, Vol. III,

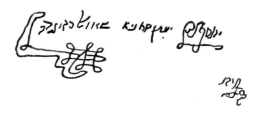

Signatures of the disciples of R. Yitshak Luria ("Ha-Ari") and R. Hayyim Vital (1575) [from the Stolin *genizah*]

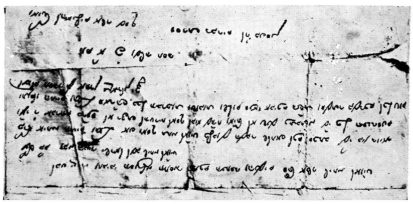

Letter from R. Aharon the Second of Karlin to his son, R. Asher

The grave of R. Aharon the Great in Karlin [photographed in 1932]

p. 193 ff., Jerusalem 1961.

[65] Dubnow, *Toledoth ha-Hasiduth*, p. 133 ff. ; Hilman, *Iggeroth Baal ha-Tanya*, p. 95.

[66] *Peri ha-Arets*, by R. Mendel of Vitebsk, at the end of the volume, Kopys 1814.

[67] Heilman, *Beth Rabbi*, Pt. I, p. 128.

[68] Idem, *ibid*.

[69] W. Z. Rabinowitsch, ' *Min ha-Genizah ha-Stolinaith*,' *Zion*, 5th year, p. 244 ; Hilman, *op. cit.*, pp. 32, 107, 177. Cf., the comment of this letter, infr., p. 37.

[70] Zweifel, *op. cit.*, Pt. II, pp. 37, 38 : The wording of the Grodno *herem*.

[71] Bodek, *op. cit.*, p. 66-68.

[72] Dubnow, *Toledoth ha-Hasiduth*, p. 193 ff. ; Horodezki, *Ha-Hasiduth ve-ha-Hasidim*, Vol. II, p. 71 and others.

[73] Regarding the time when R. Levi-Yitshak was driven out of Pinsk we have the following reports :
From the approval given by R. Levi-Yitshak to the book *Erkhei ha-Kinnuyyim* on *Lag ba-Omer* 1775—which he signed ' here in the holy community of Zhelikhov '—and from his approval to the book *Meir Nathiv*, dated the 4th *Elul*, 1776—which he signed ' *Rav* of the holy community of Pinsk '—it may be deduced that R. Levi-Yitshak came to Pinsk between the above two dates (H. Lieberman, *Hearoth Bibliografioth, Alexander Marx Jubilee Volume*, p. 15, New York 1943).
Among my late father's papers there is a letter from S. Dubnow, in which it is mentioned that my father saw in Pinsk a *pinkas* containing the signature of R. Levi-Yitshak in his capacity as the *Av Beth-Din* of Pinsk and dated the 8th *Heshvan* [= 6th November], 1780. But in the writings of the mithnagdim, R. Levi-Yitshak is referred to, even in later years—the end of 1781 and in 1784—as ' the man of Zhelikhov,' especially by the *Rav* of Brest-Litovsk, R. Avraham Katzenellenbogen (Dubnow, ' *Kithvei Hithnagduth*,' *Devir*, Vol. I, p. 304-305, No. 6, Berlin 1923 ; Dubnow, *Toledoth ha-Hasiduth*, p. 152, n. 3).
In the Stolin *genizah* there was a legal decision signed by R. Levi-Yitshak of Berdichev from the year 1780, in the matter of a dispute between two Jews of Petrikov (a small town not far from Pinsk). Although we do not know in what capacity R. Levi-Yitshak signed this judgement, it may be presumed that he gave his verdict as the *Av Beth-Din* of Pinsk and its district, which is the title that appears at the head of his approval of R. Meir Margalioth's books, *Meir Nethivim* (Polonnoye 1791) and *Sod Yakhin u-Boaz* (Ostrog 1794).
The evidence of the approvals and other documents quoted here, to the effect that R. Levi-Yitshak held the office of *Rav* in Zhelikhov before he became *Rav* of Pinsk, is confirmed by the order of the titles given him in hasidic literature. Thus, for example, the *Tsaddik* R. Yaakov-Yitshak of Lantsut writes : ' I heard from the *Rav* of Pinsk (long may he live!), who was formerly *Rav* in the holy community of Zhelikhov ' (quoted by Dubnow, *Toledoth ha-Hasiduth*, p. 216, n. 1).
R. Yosef Levinstein, in his letter to Dubnow dated the 1st *Av*, 1895, mentions the rabbinical offices held by R. Levi-Yitshak of Berdichev in the same order, Zhelikhov-Pinsk-Berdichev (Wilensky, ' *Hearoth la-Pulmusim bein ha-Hasidim ve-ha-Mithnagdim*,' *Tarbits*, Vol. XXX, p. 402, Jerusalem 1961 ; cf., Chap. 3, n. 11).

I

74 Dubnow, *Toledoth ha-Hasiduth*, pp. 141 ff., 146; Idem, '*Kithvei Hithnagduth al Kath ha-Hasidim*,' *Devir*, Vol. I, p. 297 ff., Berlin 1923.

75 Zweifel, *op. cit.*, Pt. II, p. 37; Dubnow, *Toledoth ha-Hasiduth*, pp. 147, 148.

76 Dubnow, '*Kithvei Hithnagduth*,' *op. cit.*, pp. 304, 305; Zweifel, *op. cit.*, p. 41. There are differences in the wording and the signatures between the version given by Dubnow—which is cited here—and that given by Zweifel. But in both these versions the signature of the Pinsk *Av Beth-Din* is missing.

77 Zweifel, *op. cit.*, p. 41.

78 '*Zemir Aritsim ve-Harvoth Tsurim*,' *op. cit.*, p. 25; 'And they decided to disperse the *minyan* of the Karlin hasidim [in Vilna, Passover 1772].' V. Supr., p. 16.

79 In the Russian government archives and in R. Avigdor of Pinsk's denunciation of the hasidim. V. infr., p. 62.

80 Heilman, *Beth Rabbi*, Pt. II, p. 128, n. 2. This account is attributed to a descendant of R. Shneur Zalman. S. Y. Zevin, *Sippurei Hasidim*, *Kerekh Moadim*, p. 156, Tel Aviv 1957.

81 Cited by Dubnow, *Toledoth ha-Hasiduth*, p. 157, n. 1.

82 Dubnow, *op. cit.*, p. 479. The chronology of his career as *Rav* and the various places in which he held his office are listed by H. Lieberman. '*Hearoth Bibliografioth*,' *Sefer ha-Yovel le-Alexander Marx*, p. 15 ff.

83 Dubnow, *Kithvei Hithnagduth*, *op. cit.*, p. 293.

84 Teachings attributed to R. Shelomo of Karlin and legends about him were collected and published by Y. M. Kleinbaum in his book *Shema Shelomo* (two parts), Petrokov 1928. However, this apocryphal work cannot be regarded as original source-material. The first part contains *hanhagoth* [rules for good conduct] and hasidic teachings attributed to R. Shelomo of Karlin, most of them from the volume *Beth Aharon* by R. Aharon of Karlin. The second part contains hasidic writings and traditional lore. Here and there in these legendary tales an echo of certain historical events can be heard. The sayings and stories about R. Shelomo quoted in this chapter have been taken from the books *Beth Aharon* by R. Aharon of Karlin, and *Imrei Kadosh ha-Shalem*, attributed to R. Uri of Strelisk, and also from the book *Shema Shelomo*.

85 Heilman, *Beth Rabbi*, Pt. I, pp. 8, 9; and other writers.

86 Dubnow, *Yevreyskaya Starina*, Vol. III, p. 84 ff., St. Petersburg 1910. On 'the lease of the Rabbinate of Pinsk in Lithuania . . . for ten years and also [the giving of] a loan to the community of 400 *chervontsy* without interest for the duration of that period,' see Dubnow, *Toledoth ha-Hasiduth*, p. 276.

87 Hessen is of the opinion that the deposition of R. Avigdor from the office of *Rav* occurred in 1794-1795; Hessen, *Yevreyi v Rossiyi*, p. 151, n., St. Petersburg 1906.

In Dobrovich—i.e., Dombrovitsi—which is mentioned by R. Avigdor in his appeal to the Russian government as having refused him entry, there was a *shulkhen* [prayer-house] of Karlin hasidim, built in the first quarter of the nineteenth century.

88 *Beth Aharon* by R. Aharon of Karlin, p. 27; Kleinbaum, *Shema Shelomo*, Pt. II, p. 42. On descendants of R. Shelomo of Karlin, see: Valden, *Shen ha-Gedolim he-Hadash*, p. 104, s.v.: Moshe . . . of . . . Lodmir; L. Grossman, *Shem u-Sheerith*, p. 69, 90, Tel Aviv 1943; S. N. Gottlieb, *Oholei Shem*, p. 264, Pinsk 1912; A. Hausman, *Divrei Aharon*,

p. 252, Jerusalem 1962; *Toledoth Anshei Shem*, Pt. I, ed. A. Z. Rand, p. 18, s.v. Uri-Aharon Gottlieb and Moshe Gottlieb, New York 1950.

[89] Kleinbaum, *op. cit.*, Pt. II, pp. 26, 30. V. infr., p. 48.

[90] Kleinbaum, *op. cit.*, Pt. II, pp. 26, 42.

[91] V. infr., p. 69.

[92] *Pinkas Medinath Lita*, ed. Dubnow, p. 18, Berlin 1925.

[93] [Bodek], *Seder ha-Doroth mi-Talmidei ha-Besht*, pp. 66-68.

[94] Kleinman, *Mazkereth Shem ha-Gedolim*, pp. 134-142; [Y. Berger], *Eser Tsahtsahoth*, pp. 76-83, Petrokov 1910; *Imrei Kadosh ha-Shalem* . . . *Uri ha-Saraf mi-Strelisk*, collected by . . . B. Z. Shenblum, Lvov (no date of publication).

[95] Dubnow, *Toledoth ha-Hasiduth*, pp. 223, 224, n. 457; Zweifel, *op. cit.*, Pt. II, p. 48. V. infr.: Lakhovich Hasidism, p. 151.

[96] For details of the part played by the communities of White Russia, in co-operation with those of Lithuania, in the struggle against hasidism in the nineties of the eighteenth century, see Dubnow, *Toledoth ha-Hasiduth*, p. 220.

[97] Hessen, *Yevreyi v Rossiyi*, p. 157 ff.

[98] *Akty Izdavayemyye Vilenskoy Kommissiyeyu dla Razbora Drevnikh Aktov*, Vol. XXIX, no. 244, Vilna 1902.

[99] Dubnow, ' *Kithvei Hithnagduth*,' *op. cit.*, p. 302, Letter No. 4, of the Vilna community.

[100] On 'the provincial *kahal*,' see Dubnow, ' *Kithvei Hithnagduth*,' *op. cit.*, p. 301; Idem, *Toledoth ha-Hasiduth*, p. 161.

[101] Dubnow, ' *Kithvei Hithnagduth*,' *op. cit.*, pp. 299-302, Letter No. 3.

[102] Hessen, *Istoriya Yevreyskogo Naroda v Rossiyi*, Vol. I, p. 106, Leningrad 1925.

[103] For the report ' on the sect of the Karliners ' sent by the Governor of the Lithuanian province to the Attorney-General, see Dubnow, *Yevreyskaya Starina*, Vol. III, p. 257 ff.

[104] Heilman, *Beth Rabbi*, Pt. II, p. 54, n. 1, and the sources quoted in the following note.

[105] *Yevreyskaya Entsiklopediya*, Vol. XIV, p. 570, s.v.: *Stolinskiye Tsaddiki*; W. Z. Rabinowitsch, ' *19 Kislev ve-Hey Hanukkah*,' *Haolam*, 26th year, No. 13, Jerusalem 1937.

[106] A. Friedkin, *A. B. Gottlober un Sayn Epokhe*, p. 75. See also: *Yizkor-Bukh fun Rakishok un Umgegend*, p. 59, Johannesburg 1952; Y. Lifschits, *Zikhron Yaakov*, Pt. I, p. 15, Kovno-Slobodka 1924.

In the course of time the reason for the festival was forgotten. Thus, for example, in the year 1932 the last Rebbe of Karlin, R. Elimelekh, in my presence asked his aged caretaker, who knew every detail of the customs followed by the Karlin *Tsaddikim*, to explain the rejoicing of ' the fifth light,' and though the caretaker had witnessed this celebration for the past seventy years, he was unable to give an answer. Moreover, the *Tsaddik* R. Yohanan of Karlin denied the historicity of the connection, though he had heard about it: Hausman, *Divrei Aharon*, p. 207.

[107] Dubnow, *Yevreyskaya Starina*, Vol. III, p. 273, document 21.

[108] Hessen, *Istoriya Yevreyskogo Naroda v Rossiyi*, Vol. I, p. 109; cf, M. Teitelbaum, *Ha-Rav mi-Ladi*, p. 87. The struggle in the Vilna community has been critically investigated by Yisrael Klausner, *Vilna bi-Thkufath ha-Gaon*, pp. 20-45, Jerusalem 1942. In May, 1798, the hasidim

in the small town of Vidz, to the north of Vilna, led by their *shohet* [ritual slaughterer], submitted to the authorities a writen denunciation against the Vilna *kahal* (Klausner, *op. cit.*, p. 31). This incident shows that in north-western Lithuania there were small towns in which hasidism had established itself. This denunciation greatly enraged R. Shneur-Zalman. In one of his letters he writes: 'The Vidz denunciation literally made me shudder' (Hilman, *Iggeroth Baal ha-Tanya*, p. 207), because its authors were almost certainly *Habad* hasidim.

109 Y. Brafman, *Kniga Kahala*, quoted by Dubnow in the monthly *Voskhod*, 1892, No. 11, p. 7.

A note that I found in the *pinkas* of the Pinsk *Hevra Kaddisha* [burial society] states that the society's previous *pinkas* was burnt in the great fire of 1799. Apparently the town *pinkas* was also burnt in the same time, and thus was lost material of the first importance for our knowledge of the sectarian struggle of those days. See: S. M. Rabinowitsch, '*Al Pinsk, Karlin ve-Yoshveihen,*' *op. cit.*, p. 13.

110 At the time, the bitterness of the dispute led to the use of physical violence by both sides. R. Yisrael-Leibel writes in his *Sefer ha-Vikkuah*: 'As they did . . . to the great *Rav* of the holy community of Volpe—they stripped off his clothes and forced him to enter the town stark naked.' (Dubnow, *Toledoth ha-Hasiduth*, p. 258.) It should be noted that in Karlin there was a synagogue called 'The Volpe synagogue.' 'The *Rav* of Volpe' is also mentioned by S. M. Rabinowitsch (*op. cit.*, p. 15). Moreover, people in Karlin used to relate that the hasidim there hounded the '*Rav* from Volpe.' It may be that Karlin was also the scene of the attacks on the *Rav* of Volpe mentioned by R. Yisrael-Leibel in his *Sefer ha-Vikkuah*.

111 Dubnow, *Yevreyskaya Starina*, Vol. III, p. 278; *Shivhei ha-Rav R. Shneur-Zalman*, published by Druker, p. 13, Lemberg (no year of publication).

112 Hessen, *Yevreyi v Rossiyi*, p. 170 ff.

113 Dubnow, *Yevreyskaya Starina*, Vol. III, pp. 253-261; and Documents 9, 10, 11-13, 24.

114 Hessen, *Yevreyi v Rossiyi*, pp. 176-180.

115 Dubnow, *Yevreyskaya Starina*, Vol. III, p. 271, Document 20.

116 Heilman, *Beth Rabbi*, Pt. I, p. 34, n. 2 and p. 68; Teitelbaum, *Ha-Rav mi-Ladi*, p. 23, n. 3; *Shivhei ha-Rav*, pp. 3, 12 et al.; N. Israelit, '*Mishpahath Israelit,*' *Pinkas Kletsk*, p. 51, Tel Aviv 1959.

117 *Entsiklopediyah Yisraelith*, Vol. I, s.v.: *Avigdor ben Yosef-Hayyim*, Berlin 1929. From a letter written by one of the hasidim to the son of R. Shneur-Zalman in 1806, in which the writer violently abuses R. Avigdor, we may conclude that R. Avigdor was still alive in that year. The source of this letter—H. A. Bikhovski, *Ginzei Nistaroth, Or Rav*, p. 7, Jerusalem 1924—is known not to be entirely reliable.

The writer Zalman Shneur has included an imaginative literary reconstruction of the personalities of the Vilna *Gaon* and R. Shneur-Zalman, and of R. Avigdor's denunciation, in his story *Ha-Gaon ve-ha-Rav*, Tel Aviv 1958.

118 Dubnow, *Yevreyskaya Starina*, Vol. III, p. 266, Document 15.

119 Dubnow, *op. cit.*, p. 273, Document 21.

120 Hessen, *Istoriya Yevreyskogo Naroda v Rossiyi*, Pt. I, p. 111, n. 19.

121 Friedkin, *Gottlober un Sayn Epokhe*, p. 75. V. supr. p. 57.

122 P. S. Marek, '*Vnutrenyaya Borba v Yevreystve v XVIII Veke,*'

114

Yevreyskaya Starina, Vol. XII, p. 163, Leningrad 1928. On the existence of a Karlin and Lakhovich *minyan* at that time in Vilna, see Dubnow, *Toledoth ha-Hasiduth*, p. 223 ; Klausner, *op. cit.*, p. 24 ff. On the hasidim in Vidz see above, n. 108. Even after the Russian government in St. Petersburg had released R. Shneur-Zalman from prison, the mithnagdim in Vilna still continued their fight against the hasidim and went on applying the name 'Karliner' to any and every hasid. Thus, in the regulation of 'the *beth midrash* of the pious *Gaon, Rabbenu Eliyahu*,' of the 24th *Adar*, 1801, we find it explicitly stated that 'great care shall be taken to ensure that, among the above-mentioned students in the *beth midrash*, there shall not be a single one of the new sect of the so-called Karliners' (quoted by S. Y. Fuen, *Kiryah Neemanah*, p. 275, Vilna 1860). The same attitude to the hasidim as prevailed in 'the *beth midrash* of the *Gaon*' in Vilna was also found at this time in the talmudic study groups in the small towns, which were controlled by the mithnagdim. In the *pinkas* of 'the holy circle for the study of *Talmud* and *Mishnah*' in the small town of Radoshkovich (close to Minsk), the original manuscript of which is in the National Library in Jerusalem (4° 636), there is a resolution of the 26th *Tishri*, 1800, prohibiting the admission of hasidim to this group. (I. Halpern, '*Havuroth la-Torah ve-la-Mitsvoth ve-ha-Tenuah ha-Hasidith be-Hithpashtuthah*,' *Zion*, 22nd year, pp. 194-213, Jerusalem 1957.) Instructively characteristic is the gradual change for the better reflected by the *pinkas* of this group in the attitude to the hasidim in the first years of the nineteenth century. Up to 1804 we still find the resolution of 1800 in full force. But already in 1805 the resolution is no longer quoted in full, but is simply included in 'the minutes made in the above *pinkas* of decisions taken up to this day.' The same formula appears in the regulations for 1806 and 1807. However, in 1808 this resolution was completely annulled, since 'at this time the majority of the community is unable to conform to this resolution and it may lead to unseemly conduct and violent quarrels.' The majority of the community evidently by now contained so many hasidim that it was no longer possible to keep them out of the study circle.

123 *Tsavvaah mi-Kethoveth Yad Morenu . . . R. Aharon [ha-Gadol] mi-Karlin . . . ve-Hanhagoth Yesharoth . . . mi-Beno R. Asher*, Chernovits 1855 ; *Beth Aharon . . . R. Aharon . . . mi-Karlin u-Miltha . . . Morenu Asher u-mi-Pi . . . R. Aharon ha-Gadol . . . mi-Karlin. Gam . . . meeth Beno . . . R. Asher . . . mi-Stolin*, Brody 1875. Here the *Hanhagoth Yesharoth* [Guides to God Conduct] (pp. 2, 3) of R. Asher the First are printed with slight textual alterations, as also his *Azharoth* [Exhortations] (pp. 3-5), *Derashoth* [Sermons] (pp. 17-41). Letters (pp. 293, 297, 315) and *Dibburim Nehmadim* [Delightful Sayings] reported in his name (pp. 285-287). Since *Beth Aharon* also contains the Sermons and Letters of R. Aharon the Second, as well as the Daily Conduct of his son, R. Asher the Second, the book actually comprises the whole spiritual legacy of the Karlin dynasty. A. Hausman, in his book *Divrei Aharon*, pp. 5-20 (Jerusalem 1962), cites 'Sayings' which the Karlin hasidim attribute to R. Asher the First and used to relate in his name. Cf., n. 161.

124 Kleinman, *Mazkereth Shem ha-Gedolim*, p. 108. The grave of R. Mordekhai of Lakhovich is in Stolin. *Divrei Shalom* by R. Shalom of Koidanov, p. 14, Vilna 1882.

125 Parts of the two documents are quoted in the orginal in Dubnow, *Toledoth ha-Hasiduth*, pp. 481-483. *Beth Aharon* (p. 297) contains a small

excerpt from the letter to R. Yisrael of Kozhenits, and also the Proclamation (p. 315), printed with slight textual alterations and mistakenly attributed to R. Aharon the Second.

[126] V. supr., p. 50. R. Barukh of Zhelikhov, who is mentioned in this letter, is elsewhere described as a disciple of R. Asher: Hausman, *op. cit.*, p. 17 ; on pp. 6, and 17 R. Shalom of Horodok is named as a disciple of R. Asher.

[127] V. supr., p. 49.

[128] Heilman, *Beth Rabbi*, Pt. I, p. 83 ff. Compare this letter of R. Asher's with the letter from R. Avraham of Kalisk to R. Shneur-Zalman. A. Y. Braver, ' *Al ha-Mahloketh bein R. Shneur-Zalman mi-Ladi ve-R. Avraham Hacohen mi-Kalisk,*' *Kiryath Sefer*, Vol. I, p. 144 ff., Jerusalem 1924. The bitterness between the Lithuania *Tsaddikim* and R. Shneur-Zalman goes back to the time of R. Shelomo of Karlin. It continued right down to the first quarter of the nineteenth century, as can be seen from the fact that, in his Proclamation On Behalf of *Eretz Yisrael*, dated 1821, R. Noah, the son of R. Mordekhai of Lakhovich, specifically mentions R. Shelomo of Karlin, R. Barukh of Mezhibozh, and his father R. Mordekhai, ' who were in the habit of supporting the poor of *Eretz Yisrael*,' while ignoring the activities of R. Shneur-Zalman in the same cause. V. supr., p. 37 and infr., p. 157.

[129] Cf., infr., The Proclamation of R. Asher On Behalf of *Eretz Yisrael*.

[130] Braver, *op. cit., ibid.*

[131] Cf., supr., p. 12 : the postscripts made by R. Aharon the Great in the Nesvizh *pinkas*.

[132] Dubnow, *Toledoth ha-Hasiduth*, pp. 335-338.

[133] In other sources, however, it is stated that R. Avraham of Kalisk's emissary, R. Meir of Bykhov, appointed R. Mordekhai of Lakhovich as head of the fund-collectors on behalf of *Erets Yisrael*. A. Yaari, *Sheluhei Eretz Yisrael*, p. 625, Jerusalem 1951 ; Hilman, *Iggeroth Baal ha-Tanya*, pp. 177, 182.

[134] Yaari, *op. cit.*, p. 624.

[135] Dubnow, *Toledoth ha-Hasiduth*, p. 337.

[136] W. Z. Rabinowitsch, ' *Min ha-Genizah ha-Stolinaith,*' *Zion*, 5th year, p. 244 ; V. supr., 58.

[137] *Beth Aharon*, by R. Aharon of Karlin, p. 294.

[138] V. infr., p. 156.

[139] *Beth Aharon*, p. 2 ; Shapira, *Mishnath Hakhamim*, p. 39.

[140] Shapira, *op. cit.*, p. 39. The family name of the Karlin dynasty— Perlov—is derived from ' Perl,' the name of R. Aharon the Great's mother.

[141] *Beth Aharon*, Brody 1875. The volume contains the following works by R. Aharon the Second: ' Daily Conduct and Exhortations ' (pp. 6-10), Sermons for the Weekly Portion of the Law and for Festivals (pp. 42-285), ' Collected Sayings ' (pp. 287-290), Words of Inspiration and Encouragement ' written down as uttered by his holy mouth,' in Yiddish (pp. 290-291), Letters to his son and his followers (pp. 297-312, 316). ' Words of Our Teachers,' in Yiddish (p. 313).

In *Divrei Aharon* (pp. 21-80), Hausman published twenty-four letters from R. Aharon the Second to his followers. Written chiefly for the various Festivals, these letters reflect R. Aharon's opinions on such questions as change of dress, and the like. Hausman's book contains various ' Sayings ' attributed by the hasidim to R. Aharon the Second, and also corrections and additions to the volume *Beth Aharon* 'from old manuscripts which were written before the holy book *Beth Aharon* was published in the year 1875' (p. 60). Cf., n. 161.

142 *Toyzend Yor Pinsk*, ed. Hofman, p. 267 ff. ; Had min Havraya, '*Hithgalluth ha-Yenuka bi-Stolin*,' *Hashahar*, Vol. VI, p. 33 ff., Vienna 1875 ; the Rabbi from P. [i.e., Pinsk] referred to by the author of this article was, at that time, R. Elazar-Moshe Hurwitz, of whom Perets Smolenskin writes in such glowing terms: Mossessohn, '*Masa be-Russia*,' *Hashahar*, Vol. VI, p. 357.

143 Y. L. Gordon, *Olam ke-Minhago*, the second story—*Aharith Simhah Tugah*, Vilna 1873. In contrast to Gordon's description of the lack of respect shown to R. Aharon by the Russian authorities, there is the evidence of one of the Karlin elders, R. Mordekhai Kerman, himself a mithnaged and maskil, who was an eye-witness of R. Aharon's expulsion. In describing this event, he related that, when the Pinsk Minister of Police summoned R. Aharon to his office, he sent a special coach to fetch him, but R. Aharon refused to travel in it, for fear that there might be *shaatnez* [a forbidden mixture of wool and linen] in the upholstery. R. Mordekhai Kerman further relates that, when R. Aharon refused to desecrate the Festival—it was the day of *Hoshana Rabbah*—by writing, he was not compelled to sign an undertaking to leave the town. Y. L. Gordon's story is quoted by the writer H. Chemerinski in his memoirs *Ayarathi Motele*, p. 176, Tel Aviv 1951.

The expulsion of R. Aharon the Second from Karlin is also mentioned in hasidic literature: *Meoroth ha-Gedolim*, ed. by R. Aharon Zeilingeld, Pt. III, p. 39, Bilgoray (no date of publication).

About his story *Aharith Simhah Tugah*, Gordon writes as follows in one of his letters to his pupil Aharon Lourié of Pinsk (Y. L. Gordon, *Iggeroth*, Vol. I, pp. 121, 185, Warsaw 1895): 'Let me know . . . how your revered grandmother, Hayyah, is. . . . I have several stories ready for publication . . . among them one called *Aharith Simhah Tugah*. The heroes of this story, which is based on actual events in the life of the hasidim . . . are your revered grandmother . . . and father. I have, of course, been careful not to mention their names, but all those who know them will recognise them, for they are " a seed blessed of the Lord." When you read my story, you will easily recognise the identity of the nasty people referred to.' See also Gordon, *Iggeroth*, Vol. I, p. 95, Letter of 1864.

In an article: '*Gad-Asher Levin*' (no author's name), in the *Pinsker Stot Luah*, 1904, p. 41, note, Vilna 1903-1904, we find the following: 'Hayyah Lourié was, in her day, a well-known character. . . . All her life, she actively opposed the hasidim and carried on a personal feud with the *Tsaddik*, R. Aharon of Karlin.' On R. Shaul Karliner see: A. Lourié, '*Di Tsavoe fun a Pinsker Baal-Bayith fun Onheyb 19ten Yorhundert*,' *YIVO Bleter*, Vol. XIII, pp. 390-428, New York 1938 and *Toyzend Yor Pinsk*, p. 87, note, where the broadsheet, '*Ein Onshin Ela Mazhirin*' ['No Punishment, but a Warning']—v. infr.—is also quoted. This broadsheet was originally published by Y. Gottlieb, *Pinsker Wort*, No. 75. Excerpts from reminiscences about R. Aharon the Second and his time can be found in Mordekhai Kerman's memoirs *Meine Zikhreines* (*Hundert Yor Pinsk*), published as Stencil, without place or year of duplication.

144 *Beth Aharon*, p. 316.

145 R. Aharon's letter, which was written after the purchase of the prayer-house belonging to R. Mendel of Vitebsk (according to a hasidic

source, after the Passover Festival of 1872), was published, with slight alterations, by Shapira in *Mishnath Hakhamim*, p. 40 ; Cf., Hausman, *Divrei Aharon*, p. 74.

146 Grossman, *Shem u-Sheerith*, p. 89 ; Kleinbaum, *Shema Shelomo*, Pt. II, p. 26. The immigration of R. Avraham of Karlin and his companions to Palestine was evidently regarded as an event of considerable moment: it was mentioned—as Hilman points out—(*Iggeroth Baal ha-Tanya*, p. 145, n. 9)—thirty years later by R. Avigdor of Pinsk, in one of the documents submitted by him to the Russian government in St. Petersburg.

147 Yaari, *Sheluhei Eretz Yisrael*, p. 788. Cf., the letter, quoted above, from R. Asher to R. Yisrael of Kozhenits, in which the name of R. Moshe-Dov is mentioned. This R. Moshe-Dov was the son of R. Aharon 'the silent' of Zhelikhov (Grossman, *Sheerith li-Sheerith*, pp. 13, 20, supplement to *Shem u-Sheerith*, no place or year of publication). According to hasidic tradition, it was R. Moshe-Dov that originally instituted the Karlin *minyanim* in the Holy Land. Together with the signature of R. Moshe-Dov on the letter from the Jews of Tiberias, we also find the signature of the ' Naftali Tsevi of the holy city of Tiberias ' who is mentioned by R. Aharon the Second in the letter quoted above, p. 89, on behalf of the emissary from Palestine.

148 Yaari, *Sheluhei Erets Yisrael*, pp. 779, 780, 786, 798 ; see Ben-Ezra, ' *Rabbi Avraham Eisenstein*,' Drohichin, ed. D. B. Warshawski, p. 118 ff., Chicago 1958.

149 Yaari, *op. cit.*, p. 769.

150 R. Yisrael's letter from Sadagora is dated—another piece of information that I owe to the late David-Tsevi Bakhlinski—*Rosh Hodesh Teveth*, 1852. However, this is evidently an error, since R. Yisrael of Ruzhin died on the 3rd *Heshvan*, 1850.

151 From the 'talk' of the Karlin hasidim: Once, after a session at the 'table,' R. Aharon the Second saw one of his followers pick up a page of notes that he had dropped. On being informed, in answer to his question, that this particular hasid was in the habit of writing down his ' words on the *Torah*,' so that they could be published in a book, R. Aharon asked him: ' Are you making sure that my hasidim have a good soporific ? ' Similar stories are told of R. Mendel of Kotsk.

152 *Beth Aharon*, p. 6.

153 As has already been remarked, the exact authorship of each of the sections of *Beth Aharon* is uncertain. In *Mishnath Hakhamim* by R. Avraham-Elimelekh Shapira (Jerusalem 1934), there is a collection of ' Words of our Rabbis ' from the ms. of the Karlin *Tsaddikim*. In the introduction to this volume we read: ' I received the ms. as a gift . . . from my revered father-in-law . . . our Teacher and Rabbi, R. Yerahmiel-Moshe . . . of Kozhenits, who grew up and was educated in Stolin in the household . . . of R. Aharon . . . the author of *Beth Aharon*. . . . In the ms. it is written that most of the articles are . . . by our Teacher, R. Asher [the First] of Stolin . . . and that some are by . . . our Teacher, R. Aharon the Great . . . and also some by . . . our Teacher, R. Aharon [the Second] . . . the author of *Beth Aharon*. . . . But there is no indication which these " some " are.' R. Shapira's book comprises explanatory comments on Biblical verses and rabbinical sayings, together with hasidic material similar in content and spirit to that found in *Beth Aharon*. At the end of the book, the author prints a story about R. Aharon the Great

from the time when he was living in the house of his Teacher in Mezerich, together with two letters from R. Aharon the Second to his followers in Palestine, and chronological details with an important bearing on the history of the Karlin *Tsaddikim*.

154 *Beth Aharon*, Brody 1875. R. Asher the Second is the author of the following material printed in this volume: 'Daily Conduct' (p. 10), and 'Sayings' quoted in his name (pp. 161, 198, 289, 314).

In *Divrei Aharon* (pp. 81-88), Hausman published several letters from and to R. Asher the Second in which there are some historical details.

155 In order to perpetuate the names of their *Tsaddikim*, the Karlin hasidim used to call their children 'Aharon' or 'Asher.'

156 Had min Havraya, '*Hithgalluth ha-Yenuka bi-Stolin*,' *Ha-Shahar*, Vol. VI, pp. 25-44. The author of this satire was the writer and *maskil* Yahalal [Yehudah-Leib Levin], as he himself states in his book *Zikkaron ba-Sefer*, p. 45, Zhitomir, 1910.

157 A. Ben-Ezra, *Ha-'Yenuka' mi-Stolin*, p. 16, New York 1951.

158 Ben-Ezra, *op. cit.*, p. 11. R. Yisrael kept composers of songs in his 'court.' The best known of these was R. Yaakov of Telekhan (a small town close to Pinsk), whose melodies attained such popularity in hasidic circles that they were sung for two generations by the hasidim of Karlin, Lakhovich, and Koidanov. The next best-known composer of Karlin melodies was R. Yossele Talner. A second edition of *Beth Aharon* was published in R. Yisrael's time (Petrokov 1914). It is identical with the first edition (Brody 1875).

159 The text printed here is that of a copy of the two testaments which belonged to a Stolin hasid in Pinsk closely associated with R. Yisrael of Stolin. Both the testaments were published by Ben-Ezra, *op. cit.*, pp. 19-24. There are slight differences between these versions. The testament to his followers is included in the third edition of *Beth Aharon*, p. 314 (Brooklyn 1952), and also in the fourth edition, p. 315 (Jerusalem 1965).

160 R. Yisrael's cool attitude to the Zionist movement is illustrated by the following story, which was told me by Dr. Moshe Lutski the curator of Hebrew mss. in the library of Columbia University, New York, originally from the small town of Kozhan-Horodok (not far from Pinsk). As a young man, Dr. Lutski asked R. Yisrael's advice about where he should go to study *Torah*. R. Yisrael replied: 'If you want to study hasidism, go to one of the Lubavich *yeshivoth*; and if you want to go to a mithnaged *yeshivah*, go to the *yeshivah* of Hafets Hayyim in Radin. But, if you go to Radin, don't stop in Lida' (a hint that he should not enter the well-known *yeshivah* of Rabbi Reines, the founder of the 'Mizrahi' party). As against this, amongst the 'holy writings' found in the Stolin *genizah* there were deeds of sale relating to houses bought by R. Yisrael in the Holy Land; and he also used to send a special emissary to collect funds for the 'Karlin *kolel*' in Palestine (Ben-Ezra, *op. cit.*, p. 24, n. 20).

161 The collection of letters of the Karlin *Tsaddikim* published by Hausman in his work *Divrei Aharon* (Jerusalem 1964), constitute a valuable supplement to the book of Karlin hasidism, *Beth Aharon* (v. supr., nn. 123, 141, 154, and infr., Chap. 6, n. 11). Hausman's volume contains (pp. 89-124) thirty-six letters from the *Tsaddik* R. Yisrael and sayings attributed to him. This material reflects the close personal relations existing between R. Yisrael and his followers, as well as his concern for the welfare of the Karlin hasidim in Palestine—in Jerusalem, Safed, Haifa, and above all in Tiberias —and for the prayer-house of R. Mendel of Vitebsk which the Karlin hasidim had purchased in the time of R. Aharon the Second (supr., Chap. 2, p. 90). R. Yisrael's letters are thoroughly hasidic in spirit, with special stress being laid on the importance of the study of the *Talmud*. He opposed the establishment of a Jewish school of a different type from the traditional *heder*; and he writes with pride of the values of Judaism. He is also reported to have expressed his opposition to the Zionist movement.

To this large collection of letters Hausman has appended a painstakingly complete and almost legalistically precise list of Karlin hasidic customs (pp. 210-240), and also a genealogical table of the Karlin *Tsaddikim* and the ramifications of their families (pp. 242-253), based on a critical study of the sources.

For details of the life of R. Yisrael of Stolin and a description of how he lives on in the memory and imagination of his followers and their descendants, see: Stolin, *Sefer Zikkaron*, ed. A. Avatihi and Y. Ben-Zakai, the section Hasidism, Tel Aviv 1952, and the pamphlet *Or Zarua*, by the same editors, Tel Aviv 1952.

Chapter III

Amdur Hasidism

WE HAVE SEEN that Lithuanian hasidism originated in Karlin, a suburb of the 'principal community' of Pinsk. From there, as will be shown below, its influence, and that of its offshoots, spread over an area covering the towns of Pinsk, Koidanov, Slonim and Kobrin.[1] The hasidim also penetrated in small numbers into the other 'principal communities of Lithuania.' For example, the Lakhovich hasidim gained a foothold in Slutsk;[2] and even in Vilna, 'the Jerusalem of Lithuania,' there were *minyanim* of Karlin, and particularly Lakhovich,[3] hasidim, as well as the *minyanim* of hasidim belonging to the *Habad* movement. All of these hasidim were, in the main, from 'the Karlin domain.' However, an attempt was also made to establish a second centre of hasidism in Lithuania, parallel to Karlin, in the small town of Amdur or Hamdura (Indura), which was close to the 'principal community' of Horodno (Grodno).[4] The author of this attempt was R. Hayyim-Heikel of Amdur who, like R. Aharon the Great of Karlin, was also one of the Great *Maggid* of Mezerich's disciples. But whereas the hasidism of Karlin overcame its mithnaged opponents and enjoyed a long history, the Amdur branch of the movement withered after only two generations. Here Lithuanian rabbinism defeated hasidism in a struggle which gave rise to a prolific polemical literature on the part of the mithnagdim.[5]

The founder of Amdur hasidism, R. Hayyim-Heikel (or Heike), the son of R. Shemuel,[6] was a children's teacher (*melammed*) in the small town of Amdur. In 1768, about two years after the influence of hasidism had begun to make itself felt in Lithuania,[7] his name appears in the Amdur communal register as an ordinary member of the *Hevra Kaddisha* (burial society).[8] According to one of his contemporaries, the fanatical mithnaged R. David of Makov,

121

R. Hayyim-Heikel first learnt the hasidic doctrine in Karlin.
'Heike of Amdur used to teach small children, by which
he earned a bare living. What did this needy man do ? He
went to the holy community of Karlin and there learnt the
hasidic form of worship.'[9] This piece of information is borne
out by what we are told of the state of hasidism in
Lithuania by Solomon Maimon. In his description, which is
to be dated to the latter sixties of the eighteenth century,
Maimon depicts K. [Karlin] as a kind of pilgrimage-centre
for the hasidim.[10] One of these pilgrims was R. Hayyim-
Heikel. From Karlin he found his way to Mezerich. The
statement quoted above, to the effect that R. Hayyim-Heikel
first learnt the doctrine of hasidism in Karlin, probably
from R. Aharon the Great, is not supported by any reference
in hasidic literature. However, the remarks of a contemporary of R. Hayyim-Heikel's even though he was a
mithnaged, are more trustworthy than later hasidic sources,
especially as these particular remarks contain no tenden-
tious note of censure.[11] On R. Hayyim-Heikel's stay in
Mezerich we find the following statement in one of the
hasidic sources: 'As we have heard from the late lamented
Tsaddik, our Teacher and Master, Heike Hamdura of
blessed memory, who used to fast and mortify his body
several times from Sabbath to Sabbath, and used to stay up
a thousand nights to study the *Torah.* Yet, despite all this,
he did not feel that he had attained to spiritual perfection
until he came to the holy Rabbi, the *Maggid* R. Dov-Baer
of Mezerich, of blessed memory. Then he achieved full
perfection forthwith.'[12] However, whereas R. Aharon the
Great established a centre of hasidism in Lithuania in the
lifetime of his Teacher, the Great *Maggid* R. Dov-Baer, it is
almost certain that R. Hayyim-Heikel set up a *Tsaddik's*
court only after the death of the Great *Maggid,* like most
of the latter's disciples. In the pamphlet *Zemir Artisim
ve-Harvoth Tsurim* (a collection of mithnaged broadsheets,
letters, and descriptions of the spread of hasidism in
Lithuania up to the year 1772), there is no mention at all
of Amdur, or even of Grodno, the 'principal community'
of Amdur, which lay between Vilna and Brest-Litovsk, even
though the names of these last two communities are men-

tioned together with those of Shklov and Minsk. Moreover, in the same work the name ' Karliner ' occurs as a general designation for all the hasidim.[13] On a deposition against the hasidim made by a certain mithnaged, which is quoted in ' A copy of the letter sent by the *Gaon*, the *Av Beth-Din* of the holy community of Tiktin,' the date given is ' Wednesday, 26th *Nisan*, [5]532 [= 1772].' Appended to this is another deposition by the same man, in which it is stated that ' R. Hirsch the son of R. Iser of Horodno [Grodno],' wrote down the names of all those who wanted to travel to the holy community of Minsk (to R. Menaham-Mendel of Vitebsk), and who were harassed on their journey by the mithnagdim.[14] But there is no mention in this connection of Amdur as a pilgrimage-centre for hasidim, as it is described in later documents.

After the death of the Great *Maggid* of Mezerich, R. Hayyim-Heikel set to work in Amdur. In ' A letter sent from Vilna to the holy community of the city of Brody ' the following passage occurs: 'The men of Horodno [Grodno] have strayed from the true path and wicked men in their midst have laid destructive hands on the main tenets of our faith, burning our writings openly and in public and thus stirring up contempt and wrath in plenty, on account of their desecration of the Great and Terrible Name. It were fitting to requite them according to their deeds. . . . But, since they walk in devious ways and know how to speak smoothly to the minister and ruler of the Gentiles in presenting their complaint to him, and lest all our community (Heaven forbid!) should suffer in consequence, we have resolved . . . to blot out their memory for fear of punishment and to set a ban to our lips. . . . Now we are sending the revered Teachers of the Law copies of the text of various depositions and also a copy of the letter from the holy community of Horodno, all signed by the learned servants of the community. But, for fear of informers, we have not copied the names of the signatories. It is well known to you exactly who they are that have transgressed the solemn bans of excommunication in the matter of the pamphlets that are being printed, and they should be requited accordingly. . . . Therefore, we entreat the revered Teachers of the

Law to inspire greater fear and awe, and to pour out their wrath on these sects . . . to publicly reprimand those that support them, so that they should return from their evil way and all declare their loyalty to the Lord.' This letter is undated. However, since it contains mention of the printing and burning of certain mithnaged writings—probably the pamphlet *Zemir Aritsim ve-Harvoth Tsurim*—and also of depositions made against hasidic practices, it may be assumed to have been written between the summer of 1772 and the intermediate days of Passover, 1773, or the month of *Tishri*, 1773. This date is established by the fact that almost all the depositions that have come down to us are from *Tishri*, 1773.[15] The letter provides reliable evidence for the state of hasidism in Grodno in those years. It shows that there arose in the town a group of hasidim who 'laid destructive hands on the main tenets of our faith, burning our writings openly and in public,' and that amongst these hasidim were men 'who know how to speak smoothly to the minister and ruler of the Gentiles'— so much so, that the Vilna community, when it forwarded the letter from the Grodno community to Brody, dared not copy the names of the signatories 'for fear of informers,' i.e., for fear of being arrested and exiled by the Russian authorities. These hasidim in Grodno must have been the followers of R. Hayyim-Heikel of Amdur: Amdur was close to Grodno, and R. Hayyim-Heikel was at that time the only *Tsaddik* in the northern part of Lithuania.

The following eye-witness description of the way in which R. Hayyim-Heikel propagated hasidism is given by an active opponent of the movement, the above-mentioned R. David of Makov: 'Heike of Amdur . . . started to ensnare souls with his smooth tongue. He gathered round him worthless and reckless fellows and began to teach them his doctrine, and he also sent agitators to other communities.'[16] Further, 'he sent emissaries to all the cities of Israel to lead them astray by telling them: "This is a new way. . . . When you go with me to the Rebbe of the community of Amdur, you will hear from his mouth more and more about this way." '[17] From this it may be deduced that R. Hayyim-Heikel was an inspired propagandist, who preached hasidism fearlessly in the region around his place of residence.[18] He and his group of followers must undoubtedly have been one of the causes of the renewed attack of the mithnagdim on the hasidim in 1781.

The *kahal* of Grodno was the first of the Lithuanian communities that took part in ' the day of the great market ' in the town of Zelva (itself in the province of Grodno and not far from Amdur), at which a ban (*herem*) was proclaimed against the hasidim. This ban was signed by the *Rav* of Grodno, who was also the *Rav* of the whole region. Below is the text of the ban, in one version of which the hasidism of Amdur is merely hinted at, while in the other it is mentioned by name:[19]

' Today we have had before us a noble letter, written in the language of the righteous, from the heads of the holy community of Vilna, together with the two *Geonim*—the Light of the Exile, the true *Gaon*, the Divinely pious man, the Rabbi Eliyahu, may his light shine forth! and the *Rav* and *Av Beth-Din* of the aforementioned holy community— concerning the sect of the hasidim (may their name be blotted out!) who have once again formed themselves into organised groups calling themselves by the name of *hasidim*. Their leaders are worthless men, for most of their deeds are confusion ; the Sages reject them, because they alter our prayers into the Sephardi version. They gather around them all manner of dissidents, destroyers of the world, at whose loud cries the earth gapes . . . . They are not what they seem. Now, in the aforementioned holy community there is a flourishing root of the above sect, spreading gall and worm-wood ; (they are increasing from day to day, while the *Torah* and the true faith are growing ever weaker. Therefore) [the Rabbis] have girded up their loins to stand in the breach . . . to remove the stumbling block, that the plague should not spread in the midst of Israel . . . (and all the concern of our community [sc. Grodno] is directed to checking this growth and withdrawing support from the aforementioned sect) of hypocrites. Moreover, they have proclaimed the great *herem* of Joshua the son of Nun [Josh. vi] and the *herem* prescribed in the volume *Kol Bo*, and all the bans and excommunications, curses and execrations written in the Book of Deuteronomy. (These will fall upon [the hasidim] and upon whosoever does not hearken to our solemn injunction which we have proclaimed against every man) not to join them and not to support them ; and that no one of our community [Grodno] should travel to the place of the aforementioned sect of the hasidim to keep their company (or should stand in their presence, still less look upon the face of the wicked man, the godless priest of their community,[20] who calls out to idols of gold, "These are your gods, O Israel!"). . . . Assuredly, the aforementioned leaders and *Geonim* were right to proclaim what they proclaimed, for all their words were carefully weighed in the scales of justice, according to the prescriptions of our *Torah*. . . . Wherefore we have acceded to their request on both counts: to make the preventive vows and restraints that the above Sages have proclaimed binding also on the other cities of our provinces (both near and far, to enforce upon them and their offspring the injunction publicly issued here in the presence of the whole community, all of them holy and famous men ; and their leader, the *Rav* of the province, who rules over all the cities of Israel, has commanded to sound a loud blast of the *shofar*, that it may be known far and wide that his decree is binding on all the cities of those of the children of Israel in his province that recognise his authority. That no one at all shall travel from our community to the place where is the sect of the accursed and abominable hasidim (may their name be blotted out!) in order to come into the company of the unclean ; and in particular, no one shall visit the holy community of Amdur).

It is hereby proclaimed . . . for all to know, that our solemn injunction in the above decree is also binding upon the cities of our province that recognise our authority, that no one shall change any part of the form of public prayer from the Ashkenazi to the Sephardi practice. . . . Whosoever shall transgress this injunction shall incur all the bans, excommunications and curses, and shall be banned and excommuicate in both this world and the next. Further details of the aforementioned letter are written and explained on the attached sheet[21] (in the communal register, the large *pinkas*). Such are the words of the leaders and governors, those who are the heads of our holy community of Grodno (together with the distinguished *Rav*, the Light of the Exile, the famed *Gaon*, *Av Beth-Din*, and head of the *yeshivah* of the above holy community and of the province,[22] the *Rav* and *Gaon* of the holy community of Grodno and the *Beth-Din*, assembled here on the day of the Great Market in Zelva.

' [Given under our hand] this day, *Rosh Hodesh Elul*, [5]541 [= 1781], here in Zelva.

'Eliezer, *Rav* of the holy community of Grodno and the provinces.'

In addition to this ban from the year 1781, we also find, in ' the text of the regulations of the town of Shklov ' (dated 11th *Teveth*—31st December, 1786), an order which was sent from Shklov to all the other communities as a broadsheet against the hasidim, to the effect that ' all restrictions imposed by the holy community of Grodno are to be rigorously observed.' The original document does not specify what these ' restrictions ' are. This detail can be inferred, however, from a comparison of ' the text of the regulations ' with the second letter that was despatched one day earlier by the same Shklov community. On the 10th *Teveth*, 1786, this community sent out an anti-hasidic letter, the contents of which are almost identical with ' the text of the regulations ' of the 11th *Teveth*, 1786, the only difference being that ' the holy community of Grodno ' is replaced by the holy communities of Brody and Vilna. In this letter it is explicitly stated that all journeys to the leaders of the [hasidic] sect are forbidden.[23] There is thus no doubt that, in these years, the heads of the Grodno community were very strict about not permitting the hasidim to travel to Amdur. The mithnaged source stresses that these measures so frightened the Lithuanian hasidim that many of them repented of their error and returned to the fold. This, however, is hardly in accord with the evidence of R. David of Makov, who states that R. Hayyim-Heikel lived as he pleased in the ' court ' that he had built for himself in Amdur and, so far from being on the defensive, used actually to attack the mithnagdim.[24] Indeed, R. Hayyim-Heikel proved himself stronger than his opponents. Whereas R. Shelomo was forced to leave Karlin and move to Ludmir before the

K

year 1784, and R. Levi-Yitshak was driven out of Pinsk in 1785,[25] R. Hayyim-Heikel remained firmly entrenched in Amdur. From 1785 to his death in 1787, he was the one and only *Tsaddik* in Lithuania; and he was succeeded in this position in Amdur by his son, R. Shemuel.

R. David of Makov has left us a detailed eye-witness account of the life led by R. Hayyim-Heikel in his 'court' at Amdur in the years 1773-1787.[26] For all the abusive tendentiousness of this description, it does contain a germ of historical truth which is confirmed by later sources and by historical facts of the nineteenth century. R. David's account indicates that many of the customs followed in the 'courts' of the *Tsaddikim* which are known to us only from later periods actually date back to the time of the disciple of the Great *Maggid* of Mezerich. From the same account we also learn, as already stated, that R. Hayyim-Heikel was an active propagandist ('a stirrer-up of discontent and leader astray,' as R. David calls him) on behalf of hasidism: 'He sent agitators to the other communities, as he did just now when he sent his servant to stir up discontent and lead men astray.' R. David mentions two of these agitators by name: Isaac Reubens from the town of Zabludovo and Yisrael of Vilna. The former used 'to travel from town to town and incite the masses to believe in their [the hasidim's] Rebbe.' The 'agitator' used to describe R. Hayyim-Heikel's form of worship as follows: 'You have never in your life enjoyed praying because you have always prayed silently, without any tune and without drawing the prayer out. With our Rebbe it is quite different. The worshippers raise their voices in song, and our Rebbe in particular has a most tuneful voice and knows how to sing. So it is with all the worshippers there: some sing songs and others hum tunes, while our Rebbe Heike beats time with both his hands, clapping them together. There you will at last know what it is to pray properly, on all the three levels of cries, utterance, and thought' and R. David is sadly forced to admit: 'When this simple Jew comes there and hears their tuneful singing, he becomes passionately attached to them and follows them like an ox to the slaughter.' He then goes on to relate how this 'attachment' to the Rebbe has led to bitter dissension between son and parents, or between a husband and his wife and her father, ending in the destruction of the family or dissolution of the marriage, with the hasid leaving his home and finding shelter in the 'house of the hasidim.'[27] 'When he [the young man] has no money, he steals from his wife or father and departs secretly with the agitator, without telling his father, his mother or his wife. When this becomes known to his wife and children, they begin to scream bitterly and she weeps and sobs over the husband of her youth, for she is now like a widow, while his children lament, "We are become orphans, we have no father."'

'For such is their practice : wherever there is a group of their followers, they appoint as their head one who has greater knowledge of their ways and customs. They instal him in a special room on a chair covered with gilt paper called "Goldpapier," and proclaim him their Rebbe, and are blessed by him after every prayer on the Sabbath, even though he is a stupid am-ha-arets [ignoramus]. Just as that rabid Heike, who is their Rebbe in Amdur . . . used to sit on a chair covered with "Goldpapier" in their special room, with his disciples standing all around him, on his left and on his right.' R. Hayyim-Heikel had 'a deputy, the second in rank to him—Isaac Manshes, who lived at the edge of the town in the hotel next to the cloister [i.e., church]. . . . He did to one particular guest that stayed at his house in 1781 . . . as they did to the husband of the daughter of that rabid Heike . . . from the community of Tiktin, whom they forced against his will to say: "I want to divorce my wife."' R. David writes with his usual indignation about two practices in the Amdur 'court' which were particularly offensive to him: the confession to the Rebbe, and the granting of 'redemption' [pidyon]. He puts the following words into the mouth of the 'agitator' who is inciting simple Jews to make the 'pilgrimage' to the Rebbe: '"Go to our Rebbe Heike in his inner chamber and confess to him all the sins that you have committed from the day you were born till this day. He will make you whole and give you redemption, so that your iniquity will depart from you and your sin be atoned for. If you do not tell him but try to hide your sins from him, *he* will tell *you,* for he can read men's thoughts.". . .

When the "agitator" comes to him [i.e., to a young man] and tries to lead him astray, he says to him: "take some gold coins, and carry the money tied up in a bundle, and go to a country that I shall show you. There you shall spend the money on whatever you desire, and you shall eat there, for fasting and mortification of the flesh may not be mentioned there [i.e., in Amdur], and you shall rejoice and be happy all the time; and you shall also have money to requite the Rebbe for your redemption. . . ." It is true that some of the money which he takes for redemptions from those that have means he also gives for maintenance to the sons of poor families who live with him. For such is their practice, when anyone comes to stay with them for a year, or half a year, or at least a quarter of a year. The longer a man stays, the more highly he is regarded. . . . The sons of poor families amongst them receive their needs according to their status: this one gets a half gold piece or 20 large Polish groschen, and the most important gets a gold piece. All of them pay all that they can to R. Heike's father-in-law, who is known everywhere as a great *am-ha-arets,* and in return for their coins he cooks them a large pot of what they call "krupnik," which they all eat together. Thus his father-in-law, too, earns a very respectable living from the work that he puts into preparing the meal. At night they all sleep together in a single upper room.' R. Hayyim-Heikel ate together with his followers only on the Sabbath. On all the other days of the week he took his food in his room, while the hasidim ate at the table of his deputy, Isaac. 'In any case, the people in Amdur earn a comfortable living, because the place has many inhabitants. People are continually coming and going.'

The forms of prayer practised in Amdur, as described by R. David of Makov, are very similar to what we find in Solomon Maimon's account of the prayers in the house of the Great *Maggid* at Mezerich and of the behaviour of R. Avraham at Kalisk ('the hasidim of *Talk* ')from the very early days of the growth of hasidism. In all these cases, the aim was to stimulate the sense of joyfulness in prayer by artificial means that were hardly in keeping with the solemn dignity of a place of worship.[28] R. David quotes the following report by someone who on one occasion took part in Sabbath prayers at Amdur: 'I, too, was amongst those that came to the *beth ha-midrash* of R. Heike at Amdur on a Sabbath morning to pray there, and I stood facing the wall on the east side. When the prayer-leader came to "Moses will rejoice" in the repetition of the prayer, I heard a great commotion behind me in the entrance doorway, which was open because it was summer-time. Feeling impelled to look behind me, I turned and saw some wicked men and young wastrels standing in the outer hall, near the doorway. When I came near to them, I saw a group of them all piled up on top of one of their number. One of them fell, his eyes wide open and his face pressed into the ground, while the others formed a wall around him and many of them attacked him, bending down together and each one raising his hand and striking him. . . . To find out the reason for this evil deed, I asked the wicked one, "Why do you smite your fellow?" I was answered by the victim himself, who called to me from where he lay on the ground, "Who set you over us? I myself will hide my face and you shall see my behind. I offered my back to the smiters, I did it, and I am ready to suffer." I asked them: "Why do you act so in the middle of prayers?" They answered that, during the prayers, they felt that they were not praying with the joy which should accompany the performance of a *mitsvah* and that a little sadness was stirring inside them. So they took note of this and did what they did; and as a result grief and sighing fled, and in their place came gladness and joy.' 'At the third meal on the Sabbath,' writes R. David of Makov, 'the hasidim say that the profoundest mysteries issue from his [R. Hayyim-Heikel's] mouth, and moreover that every mystic saying splits into a number of facets to suit the interests of every single one of his hearers.'

R. David's own detestation of R. Hayyim-Heikel is forcefully expressed in the following words: 'Everyone that knows R. Heike, their Rebbe in Amdur, and that is not of their sect, will testify that he is a fool, an evil-doer, and a coarse ignoramus.'[29] Of R. Hayyim-Heikel's attitude to the revealed and hidden teachings, to the *Baal Shem Tov* and his opponents, the fanatical mithnaged writes: '. . . It has already been made known by sworn depositions that the rabid fellow Heike of Amdur stood up in his house of prayer before a large crowd on the 26th *Iyyar* in the year [5]546 [= 1786] and declared: " May my tongue cleave to my palate." Fools [here he used a coarse swear-word in Yiddish] and unbelievers are those that study *Gemara* and not the writings of the *Ari* [R. Yitshak Luria]. ". . . With my own ears I have heard that the rabid Heike said to his disciples: 'If there were no more praises of the *Ari* of blessed memory that what is written in *Shivhei ha-Ari*, then our Teacher Israel *Baal Shem* was greater than him. . . .' R. Hayyim-Heikel's servant said: " If he [the servant] finds the *Gaon* and famous pious man, our Master and Teacher Eliyahu of the holy community of Vilna, he will stick a knife into his stomach." '

The particular bitterness of the war that the mithnagdim waged against the Amdur hasidic ' court' no doubt evoked in R. Hayyim-Heikel and his hasidim a similar intensity of hatred for their adversaries. A fanatical contemporary opponent of hasidism, R. Yisrael-Leibel, asserts that ' they [sc. the hasidim] are now permitted to kill their opponents, to beat them and to hand over their money . . . as they did to the *Rav* and *Maggid* of the holy community of Horodno [Grodno].'[30]

A different picture of R. Hayyim-Heikel emerges from the collection of writings that he left to posterity, comprising a signed letter to his followers (with no indication of the year),[31] instructions to his son and successor, R. Shemuel,[32] and ' Rules of Conduct' that he prescribed for his followers.[33] Apart from his views on the meaning of the *mitsvoth,* and on the proper forms of worship and religious study—i.e., Bible and *Mishnah,* no mention at all being made of the *Talmud* and its commentaries—these writings also contain echoes of contemporary events: instructions on the prevention of schism ; reprimands for the distortion of the true character of hasidism by excessive transports of joy bordering on riotous abandon ; replies to the mithnagdim, and also to critics of the *mitsvoth* whose opinions R. Hayyim-Heikel considered to be heretical.

On the proper way for a Jew to be faithful to his Maker, R. Hayyim-Heikel writes: 'When a man rises up in the morning . . . he shall sanctify every organ—his sight, his hearing, and his speech. He shall not direct his eye to any object until he has drawn the Creator Blessed Be He to his sight, and so with his hearing, comprehension, and speech. Then of a surety all his deeds throughout that day will be holy. . . . He shall always take care to observe the nature of his thought. If it is a thought that speaks of love, then he shall immediately bestir himself to love the Creator, Blessed Be He. If it is a thought of hatred and anger, he shall at once rouse himself to fear the Holy Name. And if it is a thought of self-admiration, he shall at once sit down to study *Torah* . . . to do some work that is eternal or perform some act of human kindness, whether in word, or in deed, or in thought. . . . In short, let him not do anything small or great, until he has considered from what human quality this thing springs and how he shall please the Holy Name thereby. Also in matters concerning the body let him act as described above, that he may not fail to rejoice and to cleave to the Creator, Blessed Be He, who is exalted above all intelligence. . . . The most important thing is that he should always unceasingly drive out untruth from his heart . . . for the essence of perfection is to worship the Creator truthfully. . . . Let him see to it that he commune privately in thought with the Creator every day, filling himself with awe of His greatness, and let him practise this until he becomes accustomed not to forget the Creator even when he is speaking with others. . . . When any strange thought comes to him, he shall at once pluck it out by the roots and not wait to let it spread to the organs of his body. . . Let a man realise that he is standing in the presence of His Providence and that the Holy One Blessed Be He has all created things under His Providence at all times. . . . Books of moral instruction have likened the world to a sea, and man to a vessel that always requires a helmsman to steer it ; and this is the fear of God which guides man. When the helmsman takes his hand off the wheel, the ship is in danger of sinking. Who is there that will not save his soul from sinking in worldly vanities which have been likened to the raging ocean ? '

On the value of prayer : 'Let him take care to pray every day with true devotion ; and if he has not enough time for every prayer, let him at least be sure to utter one blessing, or read one chapter with true religious feeling in the Lord's presence. . . . Let him take care, when praying, to make his prayer part of the prayers of all Israel and to forget all his own personal needs. . . . We must . . . remove our own needs from our heart, and each one of us must forget himself in his devotion to the Blessed Above All Beings.' On the subject of study, R. Hayyim-Heikel takes issue with those scholars 'who think themselves wise and learned in the *Torah*, but whose knowledge shows only one thing : that faulty learning leads to wantonness. In truth, our Creator gave us the *Torah* only that we should know His ways . . . and cleave to Him. Is it really possible to cleave to Him ? Yes, if we cleave to His attributes. . . . And how do we know His attributes ? Because the *Torah* reveals the attributes of the Creator to us. . . . Let each one fix a time every day for studying the Bible and *Mishnah,* and in the rest of his free time let him be busy with his own inner qualities.' On the proper attitude to the *Tsaddikim,* he writes : 'Let him be sure to bind himself to the *Tsaddikim,* who diminish themselves for the glory of their Creator. . . . The *Tsaddik* is above the nature of the world. . . .'

In the matter of the ills that flesh is heir to, R. Hayyim-Heikel has this to say : 'Man ! Every day will bring you a fresh trial, whether verbal insults and abuse or financial loss. See to it that you are prepared for this in advance, and then you will be able to accept it joyfully ; you will not spurn your tribulations, but will patiently endure all your sufferings and losses.'

An echo of the war waged by the mithnagdim against the hasidim can be heard in the following passage : 'A very important principle [for the hasid] : when other men abuse him for his form of prayer or any other of his practices, he shall not answer them back, not even civilly, in

order to avoid getting involved in a dispute.'³⁴ R. Hayyim-
Heikel spoke up in defence of the *Tsaddikim* against the
aspersions cast upon them by the mithnagdim: 'Just I
have seen many of our people who have thrown off
restraints . . . and with the sharp sword of their tongue
they presume to speak against the worshippers of the Divine
Name . . . against the *Tsaddikim* who have never committed
the slightest sin nor ever indulged in the slightest worldly
pleasure, but only perform the Lord's will and devote their
souls, bodies and possessions to the sanctification of His
Name. . . . They [the mithnagdim] assert that they never
heard of their fathers or forefathers worshipping in this
pure way, and they say that it is a disgusting act. But they
should hide their faces in shame and ignominy . . . for they
turn light into darkness and darkness into light, and say
that they know where the light is to be found, and how
man should behave with the Creator, Blessed Be He.'

In his letter to his followers, and particularly in his letter
to his son R. Shemuel, R. Hayyim-Heikel raises his voice in
protest against the distortion of the true character of
hasidism by unbridled rejoicing. 'My beloved brethren,' he
writes to his followers, 'I shall give you counsel, and may
God be with you. Do not be of those men that stupidly
imagine themselves to be like a son in the presence of the
Lord. This is the parable that they have made: When a
son comes into his father's presence and wants to help him
and relieve him of heavy work, the father replies that he
does not want the son to do heavy work of this kind, but
only to pour him out a glass, that is what he wants. By this
parable alone they have permitted themselves to indulge
in eating and drinking, for this, too, is the way a father
behaves with his son. When the son does not want to eat,
if the father could put himself into his stomach and throat
so as to be able to eat, he would do so out of his love for his
son. But I am amazed . . . that they should imagine that
they are like a son in the presence of his father. May it be
granted us . . . to be the least of His servants. . . . Therefore,
my dearly beloved ones, do not go in their way and do not
listen to their counsel . . . who make all their days like
Festivals and Feasts, killing cattle and slaughtering

sheep. . . . Let us gird up our loins manfully . . . and when we humble ourselves and bow our backs—that is, our bodies —before our Creator. . . . . His love will light upon us and we shall love Him with a great and strong love, until of our own accord we weary of worldly vanities. . . . For in truth, this world is only a passage . . . and the aim of the Creation was that we should clothe the Divine Presence with our deeds, our words, and our thoughts.' He ends his letter with the these words: ' I earnestly beg you to be sure to read this letter every day. In it you will find wherewith to satisfy your thirst and to restore your flagging spirits, and you will be of the company of those that serve the Lord in purity of heart and with great fervour, for of a surety our King does not take heed of our outward conduct but of the hidden thoughts in our conscience, which is the heart.'

To his son, R. Shemuel, R. Hayyim-Heikel writes as follows: ' My dearly beloved son! How my spirit longs to speak to your heart, that you should take care to strengthen yourself and make your mind control every deed that you perform. Do not act like the well-known fools who have chosen a new way for themselves, giving themselves up to riotous rejoicing and saying that they are sages and pious men [hasidim]. . . . Only take care that, in everything that you do, your intention is to come nearer to Him Above . . . for our Creator asks nothing of us but that we should fear Him. Certainly, if several other things had been intended, they would have been written in His Law, which is the true Law. . . . Everyone must take care to come nearer to Him with every mitsvah, that means coming near in heart and putting aside all material desires. . . . But let me advise you my son to see to it . . . that all that you do should first be done, then spoken about, and then thought about ; and your thought should be directed to your Creator alone. . . . And I request you to study my few words. For though small in quantity, they are great in quality. . . . For our coming to this world is solely for us to choose good from evil.'

Apart from R. Hayyim-Heikel's letter and rules of right conduct to his followers, and his letter to his son R. Shemuel, there are also passages of teaching attributed to him in the book ' Hayyim va-Hesed.'[35] On the title page of this volume we read: 'This holy manuscript was written in the year [5]550 [= 1790] and stored away by the holy *Tsaddik*, our Teacher and Master of blessed memory, Aharon of Karlin, amongst his treasured archives.' And, in the approval of the book by the *Tsaddik* R. Yisrael of Stolin, we find: 'The learned young scholar, the Teacher and Master Bezalel (long may he live!), descended from the holy stock of the Divine *Tsaddik* R. Hayyim-Heikel of blessed memory of Amdur, came into the presence of his reverence our Master and Teacher [R. Israel of Stolin] (long may he live!) with holy manuscripts written by his grandfather, the above-named *Tsaddik*. He wishes to have these manuscripts printed, and has therefore requested his reverence's approval. . . . Since similar writings are found among the pages studied by his holy ancestors (may their souls rest in peace!) in a manuscript of venerable antiquity from the year [5]550 [= 1790], and since it is there . . . explicitly written that the words were uttered in holiness and purity by the Great Man [i.e., R. Hayyim-Heikel] . . . in view of this, his reverence [R. Israel of Stolin] has acceded to his request and it has been permitted to give him the manuscript from his reverence's archives. The two manuscripts are better than one, in order to avoid errors and corruptions.'

On the strength of this detailed examination and approval by the *Tsaddik*, R. Yisrael of Stolin, it may be assumed that the manuscript in question was indeed written by R. Hayyim-Heikel. When his dynasty came to an end and his 'court' at Amdur ceased to exist, the manuscript was presumably brought to the archives of the 'court' of the Lithuanian *Tsaddik* nearest to Amdur (i.e., to Stolin), where it was kept among the 'holy writings' for a hundred years, until at last it found a publisher. From the actual words of the approval we learn that the manuscript was written in the year 1790 ; in other words, it was written—or the writing of it was completed—three years after the death of R. Hayyim-Heikel in 1787. It follows, then, that some at least, if not all, of R. Hayyim-Heikel's sermons in this book were not written by him, but by one of his followers. Many other volumes containing the words of hasidic teachers were similarly compiled by their disciples and published after their death.

It is true that, in the volume *Hayyim va-Hesed* we do not find the expressions customarily used in works of this kind, such as: 'The Rebbe of blessed memory started by saying,' 'he began to speak,' 'he continued speaking,' 'the Rebbe spoke at length to them,' and the like. Nor does the volume contain the words of other *Tsaddikim*, for example those of the Great *Maggid* of Mezerich. *Hayyim va-Hesed* is a collection of exegetic sermons on verses from the Bible, on sayings of the *Talmud*, and on statements from the *Zohar*. The ideas expressed in the work are hasidic and based on kabbalistic concepts and assumptions. There is no such orderly arrangement of thoughts as in *Yesod ha-Avodah* by R. Avraham of Slonim. Our volume belongs to the type of hasidic literature that is full of esoteric allusions, like *Maggid Devarav le-Yaakov*, the book which contains the teaching of the Great *Maggid* of Mezerich, R. Hayyim-Heikel's teacher. Indeed, we find the same principles and ideas in both these works.

In his sermons, too, R. Hayyim-Heikel places the main emphasis on utter devotion to God, even in physical matters, and on praying with one's whole being [*be-kavvanah*]; and he speaks in glowing terms of the virtues of the *Tsaddik*. 'Man is a part of the *Shekhinah* [the Divine Presence]. When man acts righteously, the *Shekhinah*, too, is perfect.' On the verse, 'Great is the Lord and greatly to be praised in the city of our God, His holy mountain!' (Ps. xlviii, 2), R. Hayyim-Heikel comments: 'When will the Lord be praised in the city of our God? When we arouse ourselves spiritually . . . and attach ourselves . . . to His holy mountain —that is, to Wisdom.' And on the verse, 'Let us lift up our hearts on our hands to God in heaven' (Lam. iii, 41), he remarks: 'The heart and hands, which are the physical parts of us, must be raised to God in heaven.' On the verse, 'The first of the first fruits of your ground you shall bring into the house of the Lord your God' (Ex. xxiii, 19): 'The primary thought . . . which comes from examination of the body's needs [this is the physical meaning of "your ground"], this same thought you shall bring into the house of the Lord your God . . . which means pious awe [*yirah*].' Speaking of the offering of the *omer* [sheaf of corn],

R. Hayyim-Heikel says: ' The significance of the *omer* is that when a man deprives his physical body of its spiritual qualities, he is not possessed by the true spirit of life and the holiness of the Divine Presence, for then these two cannot exist, and the people are divided against themselves. Thus, when the Israelites in Egypt followed their material desires, they were divided against themselves. But when Moses came to the Israelites and told them the name of the Holy One Blessed Be He, His name entered into every single one of them and in consequence they became united. This is the significance of the *omer*, which is a close binding in unity. For the Holy One Blessed Be He created Israel in order to bind everything to Himself, and therefore He commanded to offer first fruits to Him and all the other sacrifices.

But we have offended in this and taken for ourselves, and therefore we must repent of our ways and return to binding everything to the Holy One Blessed Be He. This is the meaning of " You shall bring the *omer* " (Lev. xxiii, 10) —you shall take care to restore the bond with the Holy One Blessed Be He. " The first fruits of your harvest to the priest " (*ibid.*)—the first reaping shall be for the Lord. This is the sign : if anything else seems important to you besides the Holy One Blessed Be He, then you are not utterly devoted to the Divine Name, for the bond is not perfect.' Again, ' The *Tsaddik* is the intermediary between the Holy One Blessed Be He and the act . . . to bind ourselves to the Holy One Blessed Be He. . . . When you dissociate yourself completely from worldliness, then you will understand the fear of the Lord, and then the mind and all that overcomes worldliness will begin to grow stronger. . . . Thus will the love of the Creator be implanted in you ; and when you free yourself completely from physical desires, then you will understand and know there is a God in the world and your heart will be filled with the fervent . . . joy of worshipping Him and studying His Law. . . .Then you will understand that this world is very contemptible, and you will greatly rejoice to leave it and will praise the Creator for this, and will marvel how you could ever have been bound to worldly desires . . . which are nothing.' ' " They band

together upon the soul of the righteous " (Ps. xciv, 21). . . .
When can a man join himself to the Holy One Blessed Be
He ? When he is upon the soul of the righteous [*Tsaddik*]—
that is, when he joins himself to the soul of the *Tsaddik*.'

The legends about R. Hayyim-Heikel in hasidic literature
and oral tradition are few in number.[36] There was almost
certainly an oral tradition about R. Hayyim-Heikel, but it
ceased with the end of Amdur hasidism's brief existence,
before its hasidim were able to commit it to writing, and
was then forgotten for want of anyone to preserve it. A
further factor was the isolated position of Amdur, surrounded
on all sides by mithnaged communities and cut off from the
main centres of hasidism. Nevertheless, the reverence in
which R. Hayyim-Heikel was still held in the middle of the
nineteenth century, even by those of the hasidim who were
talmudic scholars, can be seen from the following words
of R. Yitshak-Isaac of Komarno, one of the great learned
Tsaddikim in Galicia : ' " If a man's hair has fallen from his
head " (Lev. xiii, 40)—that is, if all his hair has fallen out
from dread and fear of the Divine Name, then he is certainly
pure. For this is a high degree vouchsafed only to an out-
standingly holy and pure man, such as was R. Heike of
Amdur.' [37]

R. Hayyim-Heikel died in Amdur on the 23rd *Adar*,
1787.[38] ' I saw the Rebbe's grave,' writes one of the leading
hasidic bibliographers, ' and I wept over it. It was also
granted me to see his *beth midrash* and place of prayer.'[39]

R. Hayyim-Heikel had two sons. One of them, R. Dov,
went to live in Poland (in the town of Siedlce),[40] the other,
R. Shemuel, succeeded his father in Amdur. R. Shemuel was
an influential figure—witness the fact that his name appears
amongst the *Tsaddikim* who were challenged by the violent
anti-hasid, R. Yisrael-Leibel, to a public debate on the
nature of hasidism : ' I therefore issue a challenge to all the
rabbis of the above-mentioned sect to a public debate with
me and my noble supporters who are zealous for the Lord
of Hosts : to R. Shemuel of Amdur, to R. Mordekhai of
Lakhowich, and to R. Motel of Chernobil.'[41] We also find
R. Shemuel's name in the list of the *Tsaddikim* in the *Sefer-
ha-Vikkuah* written by R. Yisrael-Leibel (published in 1798)

and in the manuscript *Shever Posheim*, which was completed between the years 1798-1800.[42] This shows that R. Shemuel was still in Amdur in the year 1798. But in the hard time of the third *herem* against the hasidim—from 1796 onwards—his activity was limited to preserving what his father created. The hasidim in the district of Grodno are mentioned in a letter sent by the heads of the Minsk community to the *Gaon* R. Eliyahu of Vilna in 1796. ' We are able,' they write, ' to do with them [i.e., the hasidim] as we wish and to subdue them wherever our power reaches in our district and, in our view, once they begin to fall before us, they will not rise again, not in the districts of Vilna and Slonim either.'[43] We have no information about what actually happened in Grodno, or what action was in fact taken against the Amdur hasidim in those days.

None of R. Shemuel's teachings were committed to writing. The one letter of his that has come down to us was written to his brother, R. Dov, and hints at difference of opinion—probably on personal grounds—between the two brothers.[44] ' My beloved brother, since I am not a man of words, and particularly since a high wall has come between us, I am therefore writing . . . to remove every obstacle between us . . . and also forgivingness is greater than wisdom. Of this it is said: " For it is a stiff-necked people, but pardon " (Ex. xxxiv, 9). I need say no more. . . . Let the yoke of His Kingdom be upon us and His awe upon our countenances, that we should not pursue the transient vanities of passing time . . . and not be like this vain life, which is as insubstantial as the fleeting shadow of a bird.'

R. Shemuel died in Amdur[45] after the year 1798. His last years saw the decline of Amdur hasidism—partly as a result of the organised attacks upon it, partly because R. Shemuel himself was apparently not endowed with the qualities required for waging a spiritual struggle against the mithnagdim. He left two sons: R. Moshe-Aharon, the son-in-law of R. Mordekhai of Lakhovich, and R. Hayyim-Heikel (the Second), the son-in-law of the *Tsaddik* R. Moshe of Shershov, the disciple of R. Hayyim-Heikel. Neither of these two sons seems to have held the status of *Tsaddik*. R. Hayyim-Heikel the Second also died in Amdur.

On the state of hasidism in Amdur during the last two generations before the Second World War, we have the following eye-witness account: '. . . In Amdur there was a large synagogue, three *batei midrash*, and also a prayer-house of the hasidim. . . . The Amdur prayer-house of the hasidim served as a centre for several score hasidim who lived in the town under the spiritual guidance of various Rebbes. These were the hasidim of Slonim, Stolin, Kobrin, Karlin, Kotsk, and in recent years also the hasidim of Novominsk. . . . Since, in the past fifty years, the difference between the mithnagdim and the hasidim has become less pronounced, there were hasidim that prayed and studied in mithnaged synagogues and *batei midrash*. Hence, there was not always a *minyan* in the hasidic prayer-house, especially in winter when there was a shortage of wood for heating. Tradition has it that, on the very same spot where the hasidic "shtiebel" now stands, there formerly stood the prayer-house of R. Hayyim-Heikel of Amdur . . . one of the greatest of the hasidim, at whose grave even mithnaged Rabbis used to prostrate themselves in prayer. I was myself present when the *Tsaddik* of Novominsk visited the cemetery at Amdur and prayed with hasidic fervour at the grave of R. Hayyim-Heikel, may he rest in peace! A visit to R. Hayyim-Heikel's grave was widely considered to be a specific against ills.'[46]

One of R. Hayyim-Heikel's disciples was R. Moshe,[47] who settled in the small town of Shershov, also in the district of Grodno, between Amdur and Kobrin. According to hasidic tradition, the *Tsaddik* R. Moshe of Kobrin, as a young man travelled regularly, for two years, to R. Moshe of Shershov, in order to be taught hasidic doctrine by him.[48] ' He [R. Moshe of Kobrin] heard that in Shershov there was a great and holy *Tsaddik, the* Teacher and Master of Shershov of blessed memory, the disciple of the holy Rebbe, the Teacher and Master Heike of Amdur, of blessed memory, and that he spent all his time in studying, fasting, and mortifying the flesh . . . and he felt that this place was not suited to his spirit.'[49] This was at the end of the eighteenth or the beginning of the nineteenth century.[50] Apart from this echo of R. Moshe of Shershov's hasidic practices, we have no other information about him. He died at Shershov.[51]

142

The *ohel* over the graves of R. Aharon and R. Noah the
Second in Lakhovich [photographed before the holocaust]

The grave of
R. Yisrael
(the "Child")
of Stolin in
Frankfurt-
am-Main

שׁי
אזכרה מנמאזלך
וזרב ר׳ ישראל
בהרהג ר׳ אשר זלל
עטר בים גב לדה
תרמב לפק
תזבה

Title-page of the "Testament" of R. Aharon the Great of Karlin (Chernovits 1855)

The prayer-house of the Karlin hasidim in Tiberias, erected in Tiberias by R. Menahem Mendel of Vitebsk in the last quarter of the 18th century

A second pupil of R. Hayyim-Heikel's, R. Shemuel, settled in the small town of Rosh (Rosi, in the region of Volkovisk, between Grodno and Slonim). He is mentioned in the memoirs of a former inhabitant of Amdur: 'Moshe Burak (the caretaker of a prayer-house in Amdur) used to relate that he was for some time caretaker to R. Shemuelke of Rosh, a *Tsaddik* whose authority extended over the small town of Rosh, in the district of Volkovisk.'[52] Both these attempts, the one in Shershov and the other in Rosh, to establish a *Tsaddik's* 'court' in Lithuania were unsuccessful.

However, it was probably in one of these centres that the well-known *Rav* of the Kovno community, one of the great figures of Judaism in the nineteenth century, R. Yitshak-Elhanan Spector, made his youthful acquaintance with the doctrines of hasidism. He was a native of the small town of Rosh, where his father, R. Yisrael-Iser, officiated as *Rav* and was a follower of the Amdur *Tsaddikim* and also of the *Tsaddik* R. Shemuel of Rosh.[53]

The beginnings of Amdur hasidism go back to the period of the first generation of the disciples of the Great *Maggid* of Mezerich, to the very days of the first *herem* against the hasidim, when one of these disciples—R. Hayyim-Heikel—established a *Tsaddik's* 'court' in the north-western part of Lithuania and endeavoured to create a centre of hasidism there, corresponding to the Karlin centre in the south-eastern part of the province. The establishment of this 'court' was one of the most important causes of the great increase in the polemical activity of the mithnagdim to which we owe a valuable literary output, directed in the main against the hasidism of Amdur. But this 'court' did not hold out for long against its enemies. Even the recorded homilies of its founder were fated to be put away and forgotten for a hundred years. Amdur hasidism was the only branch of the movement in Lithuania to fall before the onslaught of the mithnagdim. The fact that it was doomed gives it a deeper historical significance.

1 V. infr., Chap. Four.

2 V. supr., p. 61 and infr., p. 152.

3 V. supr., pp. 51, 63 and infr., p. 153 ff.; Dubnow, *Toledoth ha-Hasiduth*, p. 223.

4 V. supr., p. 25.

5 R. David of Makov, *Shever Posheim*, sects. 35-41; *Zimrath Am ha-Arets*, sects. 42-48. Quoted by Dubnow, *op. cit.*, pp. 158, 364, 367-370, Appendix III, p. 442, and Appendix XI, p. 475.

6 *Hayyim ve-Hesed* by R. Hayyim-Heikel of Amdur, with an introduction by the author's great-grandson, Jerusalem (no date of publication); first edition, Warsaw 1891.

7 V. supr., p. 10.

8 Dubnow, *op. cit.*, p. 159, n. 2.

9 *Shever Posheim* and *Zimrath Am ha-Arets*, quoted by Dubnow, *op. cit.*, p. 158.

10 V. supr., p. 11.

11 The closeness of the relations between Karlin and Amdur is indicated by the fact that the ms. of the book *Hayyim ve-Hesed*, which is attributed to R. Hayyim-Heikel, was preserved, till its publication in 1891, in the archives of R. Aharon the Second in Stolin (see the introduction to the volume). Hasidic legends relates how R. Aharon the Great found R. Hayyim-Heikel in Amdur, in the course of his search for young men fitted to be disciples of the Great *Maggid* and propagators of hasidism throughout the world (*Divrei Shalom* by R. Shalom of Koidanov, p. 80; Buber, *Tales of the Hasidim, Early Masters*, p. 196; M. Wilensky, ' *Teudah " Mithnagdith " bi-Devar Serefath " Zemir Aritsim ve-Harvoth Tsurim,"* ' *Tarbits*, Vol. XXVII, p. 552. Jerusalem 1958). The details contained in the letter from R. Yosef Levinstein (the author of *Dor ve-Dor ve-Dorshav*) to Dubnow, which is now in the ' Hasidic Archives ' of the YIVO *Institute* in New York and which is quoted by Wilensky, are merely traditional legends of uncertain historical value. It is even related there that R. Hayyim-Heikel was, under pressure of the anti-hasidic attacks, forced to leave Amdur and move for some time to other places—to Makov, Lomzha province, where his son-in-law, R. Nathan of Makov, lived, and to the village Bartnik, close to Prasnysh, Plotsk province: Wilensky, *op. cit.*, p. 551; Idem, ' *Hearoth la-Pulmusim bein ha-Hasidim ve-ha-Mithnagdim,*' *Tarbits*, Vol. XXX, p. 399 ff. Cf., infr., Chap. Two, n. 73.

12 *Tifereth Shelomo* by R. Shelomo of Radomsk, Portion *Tsav*, p. 153, Petrokov 1889; [Bodek], *op. cit.*, pp. 29, 31; Valden, *op. cit.*, p. 47; *Hayyim ve-Hesed* by R. Hayyim-Heikel of Amdur, in the introduction.

13 V. supr., p. 16. Kleinman, *Mazkereth Shem ha-Gedolim*, p. 55, also states that R. Hayyim-Heikel's ' rule lasted 14 years,' viz.: from 1772-1773 to his death in 1787.

14 Dubnow, *Toledoth ha-Hasiduth*, Appendix VI, p. 447. The appellation of Grodno ' added to the man's name indicates his place of origin, but does not necessarily mean that the event mentioned in this deposition actually occurred in Grodno.

15 Quoted by Dubnow, *op. cit.*, p. 129, from the ms. of *Shever Posheim*, sect. 9, and *Zimrath Am ha-Arets*, sect. 19. Cf., Wilensky, ' *Teudah Mithnagdith,*' *Tarbits*, Vol. XXVII, p. 552.

144

[16] Quoted by Dubnow, *op. cit.*, p. 158, from *Shever Posheim*, sects. 35-41, *Zimrath Am ha-Arets*, sect. 42, etc.

[17] Idem, *op. cit.*, p. 367 ff.

[18] The scanty hasidic traditions about R. Hayyim-Heikel hint at a closeness of outlook between him and the well-known propagandist for hasidism, R. Yisrael of Polotsk. [Bodek], *op. cit.*, p. 31.

[19] The text of this Grodno *herem* has come down to us in two different versions. One of these was published by Dubnow, '*Kithvei Hithnagduth*,' *Devir*, Vol. I, p. 303, No. 5, from the manuscript *Mahshavoth Kesilim*; and the other by Zweifel, *Shalom al Yisrael*, Pt. II, p. 37. The main difference between the two versions is in the special stress laid on the prohibition of the pilgrimage to Amdur, which is explicitly mentioned only in the Zweifel version. The additions in the Zweifel version have been incorporated by me, in part, into the text in the booklet *Mahshavoth Kesilim*, where they are indicated by round brackets.

[20] The reference is to R. Hayyim Heikel.

[21] May it be that 'the appended paper' contained the additions found in the version of the Grodno *herem* published by Zweifel. In the Zweifel version, in place of the words 'in the appended paper,' we find 'in the book of records, the large *pinkas*.'

[22] '*Av Beth-Din*, the Rabbi and Teacher of the above-mentioned holy community and of the whole district' is the Vilna *Av Beth-Din*: cf., the Pinsk *herem*, Zweifel version, *Shalom al Yisrael*, Pt. II, p. 41. The Zweifel version contains twelve signatures, in addition to that of the Grodno *Av Beth-Din*.

[23] Dubnow, *Toledoth ha-Hasiduth*, pp. 228, 448.

[24] *Shever Posheim*, sect. 32 ; *Zimrath Am ha-Arets ha-Shalem*, sect. 38, at the end. Quoted by Dubnow, *op. cit.*, pp. 150, 158, 367-370, 475.

[25] V. supr., p. 36 ff., and p. 38.

[26] *Shever Posheim*, sects. 35-41, *Zimrath Am ha-Arets*, sects. 42-48. Although the writing of these works was completed at a later date, viz., near to the year 1800 (Dubnow, *op. cit.*, pp. 289, 423), the compiler, in his descriptions of the life of the *Tsaddik* and his 'court,' mentions the name of R. Hayyim-Heikel who died in 1787. In the body of the ms., the years 1781 (Dubnow, *op. cit.*, p. 368) and 1786 (*op. cit.*, p. 475 ; according to another source, 26th *Iyyar*, 1781: M. L. Wilensky, 'The Polemic of Rabbi David of Makov against Hasidism,' *op. cit.*, p. 151) are mentioned. All this is evidence that these parts of the above compilations were written during the lifetime of R. Hayyim-Heikel. The name of R. Shemuel, the son of R. Hayyim-Heikel, is mentioned only in the list of the great *Tsaddikim* (Dubnow, *op. cit.*, p. 458) which was apparently drawn up after the compilations had been completed. These two mss. have not been published in their entirety to this day: A. R. Malakhi, '*Sefer she-lo Zakhah li-Roth Or*,' *Sefer ha-Yovel shel ha-Doar*, pp. 286-300, New York 1952. I have drawn on the quotations from these mss. given by Dubnow in various parts of his *Toledoth ha-Hasiduth*. A detailed analysis of the description of 'the court' in Amdur found in the anti-hasidic pamphlet *Zimrath Am ha-Arets* is given by A. Rubinstein, '*Ha-Kuntres "Zimrath Am ha-Arets" bi-Kthav Yad*,' *Aresheth*, Vol. III, ed. by N. Ben-Menahem and Y. Rafael, p. 193-230, Jerusalem 1961, and v. supr., Chap. Two, n. 64.

[27] R. David of Makov mentions 'the house of the hasidim' in Minsk. These hasidim were probably the followers of R. Mendel of Vitebsk, who

settled in that town in the lifetime of the Great *Maggid* (v. supr., p. 26 ff).

28 V. supr., p. 16, and also the depositions about the acts of the hasidim in the years 1772-1774: Dubnow, *op. cit.*, Appendix VI, p. 446 ff.

29 Dubnow, *Toledoth ha-Hasiduth*, p. 158, 475. The extent to which the writer was simply giving vent to his hatred is evident from his statements about R. Shneur-Zalman of Ladi and the latter's book *Tanya*: 'The work *Tanya* is *lahma anya* [i.e., bread of affliction]. The fools say that it is full of brilliant new ideas, all most holy, which only those endowed with wisdom by the Lord can understand, and that the author was inspired by the *shekhinah* and the book reveals the most mystic secrets. But I say: there is neither prophecy nor vision here, and their opinion is the opinion of fools' (quoted by Dubnow, *op. cit.*, p. 289). The hasidim apparently did not forget R. David of Makov's attitude to them, even after his death. Amongst the writings in Dubnow's 'Hasidic Archives,' in the *YIVO Institute* in New York, there is a single page containing anonymous details about R. David of Makov and his descendants. On this page it is related of R. David that, 'after his death, his disciples desired to set up an *ohel* over his grave, but it was knocked down every night by the hasidim. Until the *Tsaddik* our Teacher Nathan (the son-in-law of the *Tsaddik* our Teacher Heikel of Hamdur) died in Makov, and the hasidim wanted to erect a monument over his grave and were therefore compelled to let the mithnagdim put up an *ohel* over the *Maggid's* [R. David's] grave, too.' The page containing the details about R. David of Makov was written by Rabbi Yosef Levinstein of Serotsk (*Sefer Simon Dubnow*, ed. S. Rawidowicz, p. 360, Jerusalem 1954), although the handwriting of this page is different from that in the body of the letter written by Rabbi Levinstein, which is also in the 'Hasidic Archives.'

30 *Sefer ha-Vikkuah* by R. Yisrael-Leibel, quoted by Zweifel, *op. cit.*, Pt. II, p. 48.

31 *Hayyim ve-Hesed* by R. Hayyim-Heikel of Amdur, pp. 10-17, Jerusalem (no date of publication). *Iggeretn ha-Kodesh . . . me- . . . Morenu . . . Menahem-Mendel . . . mi-Vitebsk ve-Avraham mi-Kalisk . . . ve- . . . Ish Elokim Morenu Hayyim-Heikel mi-Hamdura u-mi-Elimelekh . . . u-mi-Sefer Rav Yeyvo. . . . Nosaf la-Ze Sefer ha-Zekhirah . . . mi-Morenu Levi-Yitshak . . . mi-Berdichev . . .* (no place and date of publication). There is a difference of wording between the text of R. Hayyim-Heikel's letter as printed in the *Iggereth ha-Kodesh* and that in *Hayyim ve-Hesed*. In the former we read: 'The words of the *Rav* . . . R. Heikel'; and in the latter: 'A copy of the letter of R. Hayyim-Heikel.'

32 *Hayyim ve-Hesed*, p. 17.

33 *Op. cit.*, pp. 8-10. These two letters and the *Hanhagoth* ['Rules of Conduct'] were printed in the first edition of *Hayyim ve-Hesed*, pp. 148-155, Warsaw 1891. A. Y. Heshel writes that when he was in Europe, he came into possession of a ms. by R. Hayyim-Heikel of Amdur, which he left in Warsaw: A. Y. Heshel, '*Unbakante Dokumentn zu der Geschichte fun Hasiduth,*' *YIVO Bleter*, Vol. XXXVI, p. 114, New York 1952.

34 The same injunction was also written by R. Asher the First of Stolin (v. supr., p. 69 ff., the letter to R. Yisrael of Kozhenits). The *Tsaddikim* in Lithuania chose to remain silent in the face of insults, in order to avoid public conflict as much as possible.

35 '*Sefer Hayyim ve-Hesed, Imaroth Tehoroth* [pure sayings] by . . . our Teacher, Rebbe Hayyim-Heikel (of blessed memory) from Amdur.

This book was stored in manuscript in the literary archives of the *Tsaddik* . . . our Teacher R. Aharon . . . in Stolin, whose grandson the *Rav* and *Tsaddik* (long may he live!) of Stolin [R. Yisrael] . . . gave this holy ms. into my keeping for it to be printed and published. . . . The famed *Rav* and *Tsaddik* in Koidanov [R. Aharon] called this holy book *Hayyim ve-Hesed* . . . I have printed it following the order of the ms., without any changes, in accord with the wishes of the great ones and *Tsaddikim* of our times ' (from the introduction to the first edition of the book ' the author's grandson . . . who is having it published . . . Betsalel Levin . . . in the community of Lakhovich,' Warsaw 1891). I have used the second edition, Jerusalem, with no date of printing [1953 ?], in which the homilies are arranged according to the order of the Weekly Portions of the Law, then Prophets and Writings, Rabbinical Sayings, For Festivals, etc. In this edition, the ' Rules of Conduct ' and the letters of R. Hayyim-Heikel are printed at the beginning of the book and not at the end, but otherwise both the wording and contents are the same as in the first edition.

36 Kleinman, *Mazkereth Shem ha-Gedolim*, p. 49 ff. ; Idem, *La-Yesharim Tehillah*, p. 109 ff., Jerusalem 1960 ; *Tifereth Shelomo* by R. Shelomo of Radomsk, p. 153, Petrokov 1889 ; S. Y. Zevin, *Sippurei Hasidim, Vol. Moadim*, p. 155, Tel Aviv 1957.

The National Library in Jerusalem has recently acquired a ms. (No. 3282 — 8°) which contains two pages attributed to R. Hayyim-Heikel of Amdur. On the first of them the following is written: ' This book belongs to the Rabbi who is distinguished for his learning and piety, the sage . . . whose praise is beyond words, our honoured Teacher and Master R. Shemuel, the son of our Teacher R. Hayyim-Heikel of blessed memory.' At the bottom of the same page is written: ' This book belongs . . . to the distinguished *Rav*, the hasid and recluse, the great and renowned *Gaon* . . . Hayyim-Heikel (of blessed memory) of Amdur.' Only pages 103a, b and 104a, b are attributed to R. Hayyim-Heikel and they are bound together with other mss. The content of the hasidic writings that we find here is similar to that in the work *Hayyim ve-Hesed*, e.g.: ' the evil impulse was also created in the *Torah*, for everything was created in the *Torah* ' ; ' " And because the midwives feared God, He gave them families " (Ex. i, 21)— this shows that man has an aspect described as a " midwife " and this is his thought. . . .'

37 *Sefer Shemoth min Hamishah Humshei Torah* . . . *Heikhal ha-Berakhah* [a commentary on Exodus] . . . prepared and edited by . . . our Teacher and Master, Yitshak Yehudah Yehiel Sifron . . . the son of . . . R. Alexander Sender . . . of the holy community of Komarno, Portion of the Law *Tisa*, leaf 262, p. 2, Lemberg 1867.

38 *Hayyim ve-Hesed*, in the introduction.

39 Valden, *Shem ha-Gedolim he-Hadash*, p. 47, s.v.: *Hayyim Heike me-Hamdura*.

40 *Hayyim ve-Hesed*, in the introduction.

41 *Sefer ha-Vikkuah* by R. Yisrael-Leibel, quoted by Dubnow, *Toledoth ha-Hasiduth*, p. 259. A different version of the text, including R. Shneur-Zalman of Ladi amongst those challenged to the debate, is printed by Zweifel, *Shalom al-Yisrael*, Pt. II, p. 48, and Dubnow, op. cit., p. 224, n. 2.

In 1798 R. Hirsch ben David of Vilna is supposed to have handed a written denunciation of the hasidim to the secular authorities, depicting R. Levi-Yitshak of Berdichev, R. Hayyim-Heikel of Amdur, R. Asher of

Stolin and R. Shelomo of Karlin as revolutionaries. As the actual text of this denunciation has not come down to us, we cannot form any opinion about its genuineness. However, we do know that, in the year in question, both R. Shelomo of Karlin and R. Hayyim-Heikel of Amdur were no longer living (Dubnow, *op. cit.*, p. 259; Teitelbaum, *Ha-Rav mi-Ladi*, p. 72). Moreover, R. Asher of Stolin had no influence in the lifetime of R. Shelomo his teacher; indeed he only acquired the appellation 'of Stolin' after R. Shelomo's death.

During these years (1790-1794), the saintly R. Alexander Suesskind was living and teaching in Grodno. His book *Yesod ve-Shoresh ha-Avodah* (Warsaw 1875) and· his *Tsavvaah* (Lemberg 1870) contain certain ideas which were stressed and developed by hasidism (the need to love one's fellow-Jews, the importance of finding joy in the performance of a *mitsvah*), as well as others that are at variance with hasidic practice. But the author makes no mention at all either of the hasidic movement, or of the war then being waged against it in Lithuania (Joseph Klausner, ' *R. Alexander Suesskind-mi-Horodno—he-Hasid bein ha-Mithnagdim,*' *Sefer Asaf*, pp. 427-432, Jerusalem 1953.

[42] Dubnow, *op. cit.*, pp. 457 ff., 289, 423.

[43] Subsequently, the province of Grodno: Dubnow, *op. cit.*, p. 246.

[44] *Hayyim ve-Hesed* by R. Hayyim-Heikel of Amdur, p. 18.

[45] *Op. cit.*, in the introduction.

[46] Y. Efron, ' *Mein Geburt-Stetele Amdur,*' *Grodner Opklangen*, Vols. V-VI, Buenos Aires 1951. In the article ' *Amdur* ' by M. Friedman (*Grodner Opklangen*, Vol. II, p. 60, no date or place of publication), we read: ' In the *pinkas* of the burial society [in Amdur] it was recorded that once, on a Sabbath eve [R. Hayyim-Heikel] was condemned to be beaten in the corridor of the prayer-house, as a result of a false charge brought against him by the mithnagdim. Over his grave, which lay in a structure, stood an old headstone bearing a very badly blurred inscription. In the month of *Elul* the hasidim from other towns would visit his grave to pray there.'

Y. Rivkind, himself a native of Amdur, writes in his reminiscences (*Grodner Opklangen*, November, 1955) that the mithnagdim were traditionally believed to go into mourning and sit *shivah* when a member of the family became a hasid.

[47] *Hayyim ve-Hesed*, in the introduction; Kleinman, *Mazkereth Shem ha-Gedolim*, p. 50.

[48] V. infr., p. 171.

[49] Kleinman, *Or Yesharim*, p. 136.

[50] R. Moshe of Krobin was born in 1784. After leaving R. Moshe of Shershov, he was the disciple of R. Mordekhai of Lakhovich who died in 1810. It follows, then, that in the period mentioned hasidim used to go to R. Moshe of Shershov to learn hasidic doctrine.

[51] *Hayyim ve-Hesed*, in the introduction. R. Moshe of Shershov died on 30th *Tishri*, 1826 (Levinstein, *Dor va-Dor ve-Dorshav*, p. 96) or on 24th *Elul*, 1828 (Grossman, *Sheerith li-Sheerith*, supplement to *Shem u-Sheerith*, p. 23).

[52] Y. Efron, ' *Amdurer Kelei Kodesh,*' *Grodner Opklangen*, Buenos Aires, 1955 ; R. Shalom of Koidanov mentions him in his book *Divrei Shalom*, p. 52: ' The hasid, our Teacher the *Rav* Shemuel of blessed memory, one of the leading disciples of the holy Rebbe of Amdur.'

R. Avraham Abele (Roisen) of Makov, the author of *Birkath Avraham* (Warsaw 1895) is described on the title-page of that work and in the imprimaturs as 'an old disciple of the *Rav* . . . R. Heike of Amdur.' And, in the introduction, his grandson writes about him as follows (*op. cit.*, p. 4): '. . . I have heard from reliable sources from the elders of the hasidim, who were with him [i.e., the author] and heard him speak, that he was an old disciple of . . . R. Heike of Amdur . . . not a one-day pupil, but a regular student that studied with him for a whole year. . . . When he set out to return home, R. Heike placed his two hands upon him and authorised him to be a Rebbe and leader in Little Poland.' R. Hayyim-Heikel of Amdur is not mentioned at all in the author's introduction to his book, nor is the author himself known to have taken any part in the hasidic movement.

53 Y. L. Maimon, *Sarei ha-Meah*, Vol. VI, p. 68, Jerusalem 1956; *Yevreyskaya Entsiklopediya*, Vol. XIV, p. 522, s.v.: Spektor, Isaak Elhanan.

Chapter IV

The Karlin 'Heder'

IN THE EARLY DAYS of hasidism it was customary for the teachers and leaders of the movement to show a special personal interest in certain of their disciples and sometimes even to educate them in their own homes. After the Rebbe's death, some of his followers would choose as his successor the one of these favourite disciples with whom they felt most spiritual affinity. The deceased teacher's disciples would usually continue to propagate their master's doctrine, founding an independent 'dynasty' of their own, side by side with that of their master. This was the way in which the movement spread and branched out. Of the Karlin *Tsaddikim* only R. Aharon the Great and R. Shelomo trained up disciples of this kind. R. Shelomo of Karlin was, as already noted, the disciple of R. Aharon the Great (though he was also one of the disciples of the *Maggid* of Mezerich) ; and R. Shelomo's disciples were R. Asher of Stolin, R. Mordekhai of Lakhovich, and R. Uri of Strelisk. Karlin hasidism thus had four offshoots—in Lakhovich, Koidanov, Kobrin, and Slonim—whose influence was confined, in the main, to the territory of Lithuania.

A. *Lakhovich Hasidism*

R. Mordekhai, the founder of the Lakhovich dynasty, who has already been mentioned in the chapter on Karlin hasidism, was born, according to hasidic tradition, in 1742.[1] His father was R. Noah of Nesvizh.[2] R. Mordekhai was one of the outstanding disciples of R. Shelomo of Karlin ; and when R. Shelomo was forced to take refuge in Ludmir, R. Mordekhai accompanied his master. After R. Shelomo's martyrdom in 1792, R. Mordekhai went, together with his friend, R. Asher of Stolin, to learn hasidic doctrine from the *Tsaddik* R. Barukh at Mezhibozh. But he remained there

150

only a short time and in 1793 returned to Lithuania, settling in the small town of Lakhovich (close to Slutsk) in which the rabbinical authority was, still in the lifetime of the Great *Maggid* of Mezerich, vested in the person of one of his most gifted disciples, the *Tsaddik* R. Pinhas Horowitz, the author of the book *Haflaah*. From the polemical writings of the mithnagdim, no less than from hasidic sources themselves, it is evident that R. Mordekhai was a well-known and influential personality throughout the whole region. The fanatical anti-hasid, R. Yisrael-Leibel, challenged R. Mordekhai to a public debate;[3] and R. Mordekhai's name is included in the list of *Tsaddikim* appearing in the anti-hasidic pamphlets, *Shever Posheim* and *Zimrath Am ha-Arets*.[4] In 1798 R. Mordekhai was arrested together with R. Asher of Stolin.[5] In the dispute between R. Shneur-Zalman and R. Avraham of Kalisk, R. Mordekhai actively supported the latter.[6] While the mithnagdim sarcastically describe him as a 'wonder-worker,'[7] the hasidim write about him with the most enthusiastic admiration.[8] Various documents testify that R. Mordekhai gained a following even in the two 'principal communities of Lithuania '—in Slutsk and Vilna.

In reply to the indictments laid before the court in St. Petersburg by R. Avigdor of Pinsk, R. Shneur-Zalman of Ladi writes (at the end of 1800) as follows: 'The members of the holy community of Slutsk also hate us and have bitterly harassed the hasidim of Lakhovich, as is well known, with the result that a decree was issued by the secular authorities of Minsk, according to the findings of the investigation.' R. Yisrael-Leibel, the fanatical fighter against hasidism, who was a preacher in Slutsk, is especially vehement against R. Mordekhai in his *Sefer ha-Vikkuah* (1798): 'In the sect of R. Mordekhai, when he was asked about the purchase of scythes for cutting fodder, he replied . . . that his followers from Lakhovich should not buy them ; so the people of Kletsk bought them and made several thousand profit. And he told one of them to buy honey to send to Vilna, and the man lost on it.' R. Yisrael-Leibel condemns the hasidim for sitting and telling stories 'as [on *Seder* night] about the Exodus from Egypt, whole nights and days and at social gatherings, they all hear and accept as truths all the follies and lies.'

Not only in the 'principal community' of Slutsk, which was close to Lakhovich, did R. Mordekhai have followers ; even in the stronghold of the mithnagdim, in distant Vilna, there came into being a 'Karlin *minyan*' which R. Mordekhai was able to bring under his influence by means of the connections that he established with it through the intermediary of his son-in-law, R. Yitshak the son of R. Wolf. From documents in the government archives in Vilna it transpires that this son-in-law of R. Mordekhai used to visit Vilna and even extend assistance to the *Habad* hasidim there, who were at that time in the forefront of the fierce fight with the mithnagdim. Most probably, R. Yitshak served as the intermediary between R. Mordekhai and his followers in Vilna, bringing the latter their Rebbe's blessing and encouraging them in their struggle for survival. This struggle of the Lakhovich hasidim in Slutsk, and their participation in the religious conflict in Vilna in the period of the third *herem* against the hasidim, recall the struggle waged by the Karlin hasidim in Karlin and Pinsk during the first *herem*. But then the mithnaged attacks marked the beginning of the conflict, whereas now it was virtually over. Even before this bitter inter-sectarian struggle finally ended, we find among the members of the Vilna *kahal* 'a representative of the Karliners' (R. Yehudah ben Eliyahu) ; and after it had ended, we find—in 1812—a house of 'Lakhovich hasidim' mentioned in 'the register of mortgages' in Vilna.[9] So great was R. Mordekhai's authority in hasidic circles that one of the emissaries from the Holy Land, R. Meir of Bykhov, the personal envoy of R. Avraham of Kalisk, thought fit to place R. Mordekhai at the head of the fund-raisers for *Erets Yisrael* ; and R. Avraham of Kalisk wrote from Tiberias to '. . . the people's willing helpers in the province of Lithuania and Reissen. . . . Your eyes behold your teacher . . . who is famed for his charity and trustworthiness, the holy and distinguished R. Mordekhai of Lakhovich. . . . By his light they shall behold the light, that they may be guided in the true way. . . . Just as a man fastens on his belt, so the sons of the living God shall be fastened to him.'[10]

R. Mordekhai left no collection of writings. The religious teachings which are found attributed to him here and there in hasidic apocryphal literature express the same ideas as those in *Beth Aharon* by R. Aharon of Karlin ; for example, his views on prayer, on education for perfection, on melancholy, and the like.[11] His disciple, R. Moshe of Kobrin, is reported to have related of himself: 'My master, R. Mordekhai of Lakhovich, taught me to pray and told me that whoever says the word "Lord" and at the same moment intends to say "of the world" has not said anything. When he is saying "Lord" he must devote himself entirely to the word "Lord," even if his spirit departs on "Lord" and it is never granted him to say "of the world." The word "Lord" is sufficient for him. This is rightly called prayer.' A hasidic legend relates that, once, one of R. Mordekhai's lungs was torn while he was praying. The hasidim hastily brought him to the doctors in the city of Lvov,who found that the tear was so serious that it could not be healed. Then R. Mordekhai prayed and said: 'Lord of the Universe. I did not want to utter only one prayer ; I want to utter many more prayers.' And he recovered. Some time later, when R. Mordekhai was again in Lvov and a large crowd of hasidim had gathered round his house, one of his doctors passed by. On seeing the large crowd, he asked the reason for the concourse and was told by the hasidim that the Rebbe from Lakhovich was staying in the house. 'What, is he still alive ?' the doctor asked in astonishment. 'If so, he is living without one lung.' R. Noah of Lakhovich used to quote his father as saying: 'He who fears the Holy One Blessed Be He with the fear of a man that is afraid of a sharp sword laid on his neck has not yet attained to the degree of perfect awe.' On the talmudic saying: 'Make me a single opening for repentance like the point of a needle' (*Midrash Shir ha-Shirim Rabbah*), R. Mordekhai used to comment: 'Like the point of a needle —provided that it is sharp and pierces right through.'

On the power of the *Tsaddik* to help in worldly matters, R. Mordekhai is reported to have said: 'We [the *Tsaddikim*] did not come into the world to help with worldly needs, but to instill the belief in the Divine Name and the fear of Heaven into Jewish hearts. Nevertheless, when a Jew in need of material help comes to us, we order him to stay with us. And on the holy Sabbath we fill his heart with the belief in the Divine Name, and then all his other wishes are auto-matically fulfilled.'[12] This explanation, even though it is only a hasidic tradition, can be regarded as a kind of apologetic reply to the attacks of the mithnagdim, and perhaps also as evidence of differences of opinion between R. Mordekhai and R. Shneur-Zalman. From the instances quoted by R. Yisrael-Leibel in his *Sefer ha-Vikkuah*, it is clear that R. Mordekhai attached great importance to the *Tsaddik's* task of helping his hasidim in their physical needs, too. The following statement is attributed to him: ' A *Tsaddik* who wishes to be the leader of his generation must feel and be aware of the vicissitudes and needs of the one that seeks his help, and must know the remedy that he requires even before the man enters the *Tsaddik's* room, while he is still standing outside the door. If he does not feel this, he is not fit to be the leader of the community.' It is further related that he once said to his followers: ' The *Tsaddik* cannot deliver any religious teaching, unless his soul is first bound to the soul of his dead Master, which is in turn bound in heaven to the soul of *his* Master, and so on up to the Kabbalists, the Prophets, and right up to our Teacher Moses, and then back again: from Moses to Joshua to the Elders, right down to his Master, and from his Master to the *Tsaddik*. Only then can he teach his followers to understand the Law.' R. Mordekhai of Lakhovich also had a strong feeling for *Erets Yisrael* and used to make large financial contributions to the welfare of the Jewish community there.

The hasidim relate that he used to put aside sums of money for the Holy Land at all times—when he rose from his bed, before and after the blessing for the dawn, before and after study, before and after meals, indeed throughout the whole day. To prevent this from becoming generally known, he used to add his contribution to that of his hasidim. When-ever R. Avraham of Kalisk (the hasidic story continues) received the money in Tiberias and looked at the names of the donors which were attached to the contributions, he used to smile and say: ' Here there is also something of the Lakhovich *Tsaddik*, and here, too, there is something from the Lakhovich *Tsaddik*!' The hasidim also relate that when R. Mordekhai was given the honour of being the *sandek* ['godfather'] at the circumcision of the son of his fellow-*Tsaddik* and friend R. Asher the First of Stolin (i.e., of R. Aharon the Second of Karlin, the author of *Beth Aharon*) he was requested to pronounce a blessing over the new-born child. R. Mordekhai placed his two hands on the infant's head and said: 'Do not deceive the Lord, do not deceive your fellow-men, and do not deceive yourself.'

In addition to his organisational work and his active participation in the struggle with the mithnagdim, R. Mordekhai of Lakhovich performed another great service for the Lithuanian hasidic movement by adding three of his disciples to the ranks of its influential personalities: his son and successor, R. Noah of Lakhovich; R. Mikhal of Lakhovich, and R. Moshe of Kobrin. R. Mordekhai's closest friend was R. Asher the First of Stolin. Through the marriage of their children, the two men became the forbears of a new dynasty of *Tsaddikim*, that of Koidanov, which was founded by their grandson R. Shelomo-Hayyim (the son of R. Mordekhai's son, R. Aharon, who died in 1807, and of R. Asher's daughter).

The situation prevailing in Lakhovich in R. Mordekhai's time is reflected in a letter from the *Tsaddik* R. Moshe-Leib of Sasov which was found among 'the holy writings' in the Stolin *genizah*. R. Moshe-Leib writes as follows:

'In the year [5]556 [= 1796].

'To all the Jews and to the revered, pious and perfect *Rabbanim*, every one according to his excellence. I write to reply out of reverence and awe. Who am I, the smallest of the small, that has never truly feared the Lord of Lords. If I have committed no other sin, it is enough that I say a hundred blessings every day without awe and dread whereby in my iniquity I anger the Holy One Blessed Be He a hundred times a day. Woe to me and woe to my soul for the faults I commit every day in addition to that! For if there is no awe, there is nothing. Hence a base creature like myself would do well to keep his mouth closed. Man sees into the eyes, but God sees into the heart. . . . Everyone that restrains himself from dissension, etc. Therefore I write to request that there should be peace in the world, for without peace there is nothing. For through Isaac shall your pure descendants be named. As for the concern that you express about my kinsman, the learned and pious *Rav*, the delight of God and men, the Teacher R. Feivish, the Lakhovich *Av Beth-Din*, the Almighty will help him. A broken and contrite heart God will not despise.

'Written by the lowly and contemptible creature, Moshe Yehudah-Leib of Brod.'

The self-deprecating and self-abasing style of the letter is typical of R. Moshe-Leib of Sasov's whole character. This letter was written in 1796, the year in which the mithnagdim renewed their attacks on the hasidim. This is what the *Tsaddik* is alluding to when he writes: 'Everyone that restrains himself from dissension. . . . Therefore do I write to request that there should be peace in the world, for without peace there is nothing.' Assuming that R. Moshe-Leib's kinsman, R. Feivish, was a hasid, it follows that in the year when the mithnaged harassment of the hasidim in Lithuania was at its height, not only was a hasid officiating as the *Av Beth-Din* in the small Lithuanian town of Lakhovich, but the leaders of the *kahal* were actually concerned for his welfare. All this was almost certainly due to the influence of R. Mordekhai of Lakhovich. When R. Moshe-Leib writes 'For through Isaac shall your pure descendants be named,' he is apparently referring to the son of R. Feivish. Because of the topographical closeness of Lakhovich to Stolin, and as a result of the family ties between the two *Tsaddikim*, the letter found its way from Lakhovich to the Stolin *genizah*.

R. Mordekhai died in 1810, while on a visit to Stolin to attend the wedding of his grandson, R. Shelemo-Hayyim. He was buried in Stolin. [13]

R. Noah, the son of R. Mordekhai (b. 1774), was the leader of the Lakhovich hasidim from 1810 to 1832.[14] He succeeded in preserving the autonomy of the Lakhovich branch and keeping it independent of Karlin. In 1821 he published an appeal on behalf of the hasidim in the Holy Land in which he declares that his father and his teachers, R. Shelomo of Karlin and R. Barukh of Mezhibozh, made a practice of supporting the needy in *Erets Yisrael*,[15] but he makes no mention of R. Shneur-Zalman. This proclamation gives

expression to the great importance attached by the
Lakhovich *Tsaddikim* to the hasidic support of the Jewish
community in Palestine, and describes all R. Mordekhai's
efforts to this end. Below are excerpts from it:

'To all our dear brethren and loyal followers . . . and
especially to those who of their own free will support the
community of the dwellers in the Holy Land . . . and who
are closely bound to the great ones among our holy teachers,
and in particular to my revered Father, Teacher and Rebbe
of blessed memory. It is well known to all that the righteous
ones of the generation charged my Father . . . with the
burden of this *mitsvah,* which he took upon himself . . . out
of affection and holy love, to support the inhabitants of the
Holy Land. It was thereby vouchsafed him to be one of the
upholders of the *Torah* in the Holy Land, and in particular
of the holy community [sc. the hasidim] which is supported
by all the righteous ones of our times. My revered Father,
Teacher and Rebbe, of blessed memory, all his life not only
preached, but also performed this *mitsvah* [of supporting
the Jewish settlers in the Holy Land]. . . . Day and night he
did not cease or rest from awakening men's hearts, to
accustom them and strengthen them in the performance of
this *mitsvah.* As on weekdays, so on holy days: he did not
rest from his work [on behalf of the Jews of the Holy Land]
on Sabbaths or Festivals, and even on the Day of Atonement he preached and himself fulfilled the commandment
of never forgetting Jerusalem . . . according to the Divine
gift he possessed of bringing men's hearts nearer to the pious
awe of God ; and in particular in this *mitsvah,* he would
demand of them more than they could give. . . . He implanted
this *mitsvah* in their hearts . . . and appointed regular times
for them to bring their contributions to the prayer-house,
devoting special attention to this *mitsvah* even before their
study of the *Torah* and their prayers . . . that no one should
miss a single Sabbath in the regular weekly payment of his
contribution. And even those that had a mere pittance—he
would exhort them to make their contribution before the
kiddush on the Sabbath eve. . . . He often expounded to us
secret passages in the *Torah* concerning this *mitsvah.* . . .
Moreover, we had heard from my Teacher and Father of

blessed memory, and from the holy Rebbe . . . Shelomo Halevi [of Karlin] of blessed memory, and from the holy Rebbe . . . Barukh (may his soul be blessed!) [of Mezhibozh], that . . . they were in the habit of generously supporting the poor of *Erets Yisrael*, and especially the holy community [sc. the hasidim]. . . . Therefore, my beloved brethren, do not wrongly neglect this *mitsvah* (Heaven forbid!), but keep it like the apple of your eye . . . abating nothing of the regular contribution fixed for every one [of you].

'I have heard some say . . . that all these injunctions [to contribute to the Holy Land] were for the generations before ours, when the people of *Erets Yisrael* were great men, but not for these times. They speak idle words ; for why do they not take note that we, too, have declined by ten degrees, as everyone knows ? Nay, our woeful decline . . . is greater than theirs. . . for, thank God, they occupy themselves with the study of the *Torah* and the performance of *mitsvoth*, and with praying for our fellow-Jews, each one according to his degree. . . . Therefore, my dear brethren, take thought for your bodies and souls, and strengthen yourselves in the performance of this *mitsvah*, for it comprises the several *mitsvoth*: of charity, of supporting those that study the *Torah*, and of love of the Holy Land. . . .'

The flourishing condition of Lakhovich hasidism in the time of R. Noah is evident from the following entry in the communal records of the small town of Radoshkovich (north of Minsk), dated the 12th *Iyyar*, 1826: 'Before us, the leaders of the *kahal*, there appeared several distinguished persons, the leaders of the hasidim who are followers of the *Rav* of Lakhovich, and showed us a written undertaking from the leaders of the *kahal* to give the leaders of the hasidim . . . 20 roubles for the building of a *beth midrash* for them. And now . . . we, the leaders of the *kahal*, have given the sum to the above-mentioned leaders of the hasidim . . . and the leaders of the hasidim have undertaken, under solemn oath and on pain of excommunication [*herem*], never from this day on to request any tallow for their *beth midrash* or to request any allocation from the leaders of the *kahal* towards the expenses of a Rabbi for them. . . .'[16] Thus, not only did the Lakhovich hasidim receive money from communal funds for the building of their own house of prayer, but they also had their own Rabbi.

R. Noah left no collection of writings. However, hasidic tradition gives us a good idea of the character of his leadership and of his considerateness and kindness to ordinary simple people. Thus, it is related that R. Noah once heard one of his followers reciting the Thirteen Principles [of Judaism] in the *beth midrash* and stopping after every 'I believe with perfect faith' to say to himself: 'I don't understand that! I don't understand that !' R. Noah went out of his room, entered the *beth midrash*, and asked the hasid: 'What is it that you don't understand?' The hasid answered him: 'I don't understand what I am saying. Either one thing or the other: If I believe with perfect faith, how can I be a sinner? And if I do not believe with perfect faith, then I am uttering a lie!' R. Noah replied: 'The words "I believe" are a prayer, meaning "I want to believe; May it be Thy will that I should believe."' Thereupon, the hasid excitedly began proclaiming with joyful fervour: 'I believe! Lord of the Universe, may it be Thy will that I should believe!' Another hasid complained to R. Noah that his intelligence was limited and his good deeds few in number, and his fear that his prayers were not being accepted caused him even to be afflicted with melancholy. 'It is not so,' replied R. Noah, 'You have seen a mortal monarch who, though he has a group of musicians that can play all kinds of instruments skilfully, yet likes to hear the twittering of a little bird in his palace. So it is with the Holy One Blessed Be He. Although He has troops of angels praising and glorifying Him in clear voices and melodious tones, He is more delighted by your heartfelt prayer.' One of R. Noah's followers used to make clothes for Russian aristocrats and ministers. Once R. Noah asked him what his practice was with regard to the 'remainder' of the material which the tailors were in the habit of taking as their perquisite. The tailor answered that he did what all the others did. R. Noah explained to him that, in so doing, he was deceiving his customers. From that day onwards the tailor made a point of not leaving any 'remainders,' and told his customers that he had learnt a new way of cutting

159

M

whereby he could make the garment with less cloth. But he added that he was increasing the price to cover the cost of learning the new method.

Apart from R. Moshe of Kobrin, who has already been mentioned and who was also at one time a pupil of R. Noah's father, R. Noah had another distinguished disciple— R. Avraham of Slonim, the founder of the Slonim hasidic dynasty. R. Noah had no son to succeed him, and after his death the Lakhovich hasidim split into two camps. One of them chose as its leader R. Noah's son-in-law, R. Mordekhai the son of R. Moshe-Baer (called R. Mordekhai the Second, to distinguish him from 'the holy grandfather,' R. Mordekhai the First), who remained in Lakhovich.[17] The other group chose R. Shelomo-Hayyim, the grandson of R. Mordekhai the First, who settled in the small town of Koidanov (close to Minsk).[18]

R. Mordekhai the Second, the son of the sister of R. Aharon the Second of Karlin, was not a public figure and was content to recognise the authority of R. Aharon of Karlin, thus considerably reducing the independent power of Lakhovich hasidism. For example, the Lakhovich hasidim, led by R. Mordekhai, used to go to R. Aharon in Karlin for New Year and the Day of Atonement ; and R. Aharon used to visit the Lakhovich hasidim like any Rebbe visiting his followers.[19] Matters reached such a pitch that even the prayer-house in which R. Mordekhai habitually prayed was called ' the Stolin *shtiebel*.'[20]

As a result of the split within its ranks, which resulted in the rise of Koidanov hasidism, and in consequence of its dependence on Karlin, Lakhovich hasidism went into a sharp decline, after flourishing for forty years (1793-1832). Its influence was now confined almost entirely to the town of Lakhovich and its immediate environs. R. Mordekhai the Second, who is depicted as a scholar of lofty character and simple humanity, died in the middle of the 1860s.[21]

In the time of his son and successor, R. Aharon (Malovitski), the Lakhovich hasidim threw off the authority of Karlin and regained their independence. This was a unique event in the history of Lithuanian hasidism. A group of hasidic elders, who still remembered the time of

R. Mordekhai the First, rebelled and succeeded in restoring the independent status of the Lakhovich *Tsaddikim*.[22] Since then Lakhovich hasidism has remained independent. In the time of R. Aharon (d. 21st *Sivan*, 1881),[23] and still more in the days of his son, R. Noah (d. 20th *Tammuz*, 1920), it was weakened and reduced in numbers by the *Haskalah* movement, and at a later date by the political movements which influenced the younger generation. R. Noah was a vehement opponent of Zionism.[24] though at the same time he supported the Lakhovich *kolel* in Palestine.

The historical importance of Lakhovich hasidism lies in the fact that it spread hasidic doctrines in the north-eastern part of Lithuania, just as the Karlin dynasty did in the southern part. It was thanks to the Lakhovich hasidim that hasidism penetrated into 'the principal community of Lithuania,' Slutsk and even into Vilna. During the difficult period of the third *herem* and afterwards, when hasidism was under violent attack, the Lakhovich hasidim had a hard struggle to maintain their existence. They were saved by the skill and tenacity of R. Mordekhai of Lakhovich who enabled them to hold their own in this corner of the border between Lithuania and White Russia, even though they were at all times a minority in the midst of the prevailingly mithnaged population. Some of R. Mordekhai's disciples, as already stated, were influential in Lithuanian hasidism. Under his descendants, however, the influence of this branch of hasidism declined, under the pressure of internal and external factors.

B. *Koidanov Hasidism*

Koidanov hasidism is in fact a continuation of Lakhovich hasidism, partly because of the family ties between the two dynasties and their adherence to the same hasidic doctrines and practices, but even more because most of the Lakhovich hasidim -actually joined the Koidanov dynasty. As already stated, R. Noah of Lakhovich (d. 1832) left no son to succeed him. One section of the Lakhovich hasidim, consisting mainly of those in Lakhovich itself, chose as their Rebbe R. Noah's son-in-law, R. Mordekhai the Second, who for all practical purposes submitted to the authority of R. Aharon the Second of Karlin. But the choice of the majority of the Lakhovich hasidim was R. Shelomo-Hayyim (Perlov), a grandson of R. Mordekhai the First of Lakhovich and R. Asher of Stolin. Born in 1797, this R. Shelomo-Hayyim was, as noted above, the son of R. Mordekhai's son, R. Aharon, who died young in 1807.[25] After his marriage in 1810, [26] R. Shelomo-Hayyim continued to live in the house of his grandfather, R. Asher of Stolin. Later, he was chosen —according to a hasidic source[27]—to be a *Rav* in Stolin, presumably through the good offices of R. Asher, and afterwards a *Rav* in the small town of Turov (close to Stolin) where the influence of the Stolin hasidim was strong. He remained in this town until he was chosen as Rebbe after the death of R. Noah. He then took up residence in the small town of Koidanov, not far from the provincial capital of Minsk.

Koidanov hasidism's main sphere of influence was in the region between Lakhovich-Minsk and Baranovich. Even in Lakhovich itself there was a Koidanov *shtiebel*.[28] Consequently, R. Shelomo-Hayyim was able to play an influential part in the propagation of hasidism in the northern section of Polesia, and even outside its confines, and Koidanov was in those days the northernmost centre of hasidism in Lithuania, R. Shelomo-Hayyim, the old Rebbe of Koidanov, maintained friendly relations with the *Tsaddikim* of the dynasties of Neskhizh, Zlochov and Chernobil, and in particular with his uncle, R. Aharon the Second of Karlin.[29] He left no written work.[30] However, appended to the Koidanov prayer-book *Or ha-Yashar,* which was published after his death, there is a special supplement describing the customs of R. Shelomo-Hayyim. Included among the Sabbath hymns in this prayer-book is the liturgical poem composed by R. Aharon the Great of Karlin, ' Lord, I yearn for the Sabbath's delight' (though with no mention of the author's name).[31] The supplement on R. Shelomo-Hayyim's customs lists with an almost legalistic precision every single detail of his daily life, including the white clothes that he wore on the Sabbath and the hasidic melodies that he sang (liturgical poems, hasidic verses).[32] In the ' day's programme' printed in his name on the title-page of the prayer-book, time is allocated for the daily study of the *Gemara* and the *Shulhan Arukh,* and it is laid down that every Jew must every morning undertake 'in the language of *Ashkenaz*' [i.e., Yiddish], to guard against idle talk, gossip, levity, and slander, that he may be granted God's help. Of R. Shelomo-Hayyim's disciples mention is made of R. Benjamin of Lida. R. Shelomo-Hayyim died on the 17th *Av,* 1862.[33]

His son and successor, R. Barukh-Mordekhai (Perlov), was born in 1818.[34] He is described by his own son as a man who 'studied the *Torah* in poverty and hardship . . . became very harsh to his children, paid no attention to what his wife and children said, but gave himself up entirely to the revealed lore and wisdom. He would study patiently, reading every word separately, like a man counting coins, and concentrating on it with all his might. And when he prayed, he prayed from the heart, while his hands and whole body trembled for fear of the Lord and of the glory of His majesty. . . . In those days, when the true believers split into various groups each one of which sought to discredit the others, we heard nothing of this kind from him. He expressed neither contempt nor esteem for any *Tsaddik* or great man in Israel, for he never used to speak about these things. . . . My revered Grandfather, my Teacher and Master R. Shelomo-Hayyim . . . in his own lifetime made him the general supervisor of funds for the Holy Land, with responsibility for our *kolel* in Tiberias.'[35] The dispute mentioned here by the writer between the hasidic dynasties is typical of the state of hasidism in those days. Concern for the welfare of the Jewish community in Palestine was one of the basic characteristics of the Karlin *heder.* Its first manifestations, displayed in the time of R. Asher of Stolin and of R. Mordekhai and R. Noah of Lakhovich ('the Lakhovich *kolel*'), had been continued by R. Aharon the Second of Karlin (the purchase of the house of R. Mendel of Vitebsk, and the like) and by the Kobrin hasidim, and even more vigorously by the Slonim hasidim. Now this same tradition was carried on by the Koidanov dynasty ('the Koidanov *kolel* in Tiberias'). R. Barukh-Mordekhai left nothing in writing, and the thoughts subsequently published in his name by his son are simply a repetition of previously known hasidic ideas.[36] He died on the second day of *Rosh Hashanah*, 1870.

At the same time as R. Barukh-Mordekhai succeeded his father as *Tsaddik* in Koidanov, one of his brothers, R. Noah, settled as Rebbe in the small town of Horodishch (close to Navarodok), and the other brother, R. Avraham-Aharon, became a Rebbe in the small town of Pukhovich (in the district of Igumen).[37] Though they enjoyed the good will and support evoked by their family name, they had only a limited influence. R. Noah died in 1904.

The Koidanov dynasty was continued by R. Aharon, the son of R. Barukh-Mordekhai.[38] Unlike his father, R. Aharon was endowed with great energy. While his father was still living, in 1866, he drew up a public appeal in his father's name to the Koidanov hasidim on behalf of the 'Koidanov *kolel* in Tiberias.' This public appeal contains important information about the situation in Palestine at that time. R. Aharon writes, *inter alia*: 'We have received several letters from the Holy Land from our *kolel* in the holy city of Tiberias . . . informing us of the hardships . . . that they are suffering . . . all manner of troubles, sickness and locusts (Merciful Heaven preserve us!). . . . They were forced to leave the holy city of Tiberias and to make their painful way to the holy city of Safed. . . . All the time the epidemic grew steadily worse, until they were obliged to place guards over the houses and courtyards . . . and keep watch over the wretched and weak, and they spent large sums on the drugs and medicines that they required, until now they have not sufficient money left for their needs and food. . . . Therefore . . . people of the Lord let us all be strong and strengthen each other on behalf of the cities of our God, on behalf of our kinsmen! . . . Let no one of our followers change his contribution . . . from every couple one gold piece ; let the poor not give less than that, apart from the regular yearly contributions to *Erets Yisrael*. . . .'[39]

Various religious teachings handed down in R. Aharon's name were published in book form by one of his followers.[40] R. Aharon also wrote an introduction to the Koidanov prayer-book, *Or ha-Yashar*, which was published in 1877

Printed on the title page of this prayer-book are his eight
principles which, when carried out by eight of the body's
organs, lead to perfection. He further saw through the press
R. Moshe Cordovero's book *Or Neerav*, with an appendix of
his own, *Nireh Or* (published posthumously, Vilna 1899).
Printed together with the work of R. Moshe Hagiz, *Sefath
Emeth*, is a collection of writings by R. Aharon, including
passages from kabbalistic and hasidic literature on the
importance of *Erets Yisrael* (Vilna 1876). R. Aharon's
personality and his extensive knowledge of the *Kabbalah* and
the *Talmud* helped to establish Koidanov hasidism on a firm
basis.

An eye-witness description of R. Aharon of Koidanov and
of a single event in the life of the Koidanov 'court' is given
in the memoirs of a mithnaged *maskil*, who writes as
follows: 'The Rebbe R. Aharon of Koidanov was famous
throughout the district. Since my own father and grandfather were mithnagdim, I very rarely went to the prayer-
house of the hasidim (the *shtiebel*). But it occasionally
happened that I would pray together with the hasidim in
the "tailors' synagogue," since they were in the habit of
coming to pray in this synagogue on weekdays, when they
did not have the time to draw out their prayers as was their
custom in their own prayer-house. There were three *batei
midrash* standing side by side in the "synagogue court"
(*Shulhof*), and on weekdays the hasidim presumably used to
pray in all of them. The prayer-house of the hasidim stood
in the farthest corner of this large court. . . . The hasidim and
mithnagdim were on good neighbourly terms, but they did
not intermarry. The Rebbe's family lived in its own "royal
court." The Rebbe himself, a man of short stature, used to
appear before his hasidim only on rare occasions, mainly
during the prayers in his own prayer-house. In the Rebbe's
house there was an "iron box" which served as a repository
for the scanty savings of the inhabitants of the small town.
Widows used to deposit in the "iron box," coin by coin, the
small sums that they put aside from their meagre livelihood
to provide a dowry for their growing daughters. Not only
the hasidim, but the mithnagdim, too, used to deposit their

savings in the " iron box," for they all believed in the Rebbe's integrity.

Once . . . the rumour spread abroad that the Rebbe had gone bankrupt. There was a great uproar, until it transpired . . . that it was not the Rebbe, but his son that had gone bankrupt. . . . Nevertheless, the Rebbe was prosecuted by one of his creditors . . . and was obliged to appear in the district court in Vilna. He was defended by well-known lawyers. On the day of the trial, which took place in Vilna. the hasidim assembled outside their prayer-house. Throughout this day telegrams were received from Vilna with instructions about which prayers they were to say. All the instructions were punctiliously carried out. What I saw on that day made a tremendous impression on me. I had the feeling that here under my very eyes there was a direct link, both visible and invisible, between the Rebbe in the district court in Vilna, the hasidim in Koidanov, and the Holy One Blessed Be He in Heaven. Fascinated, I followed the prayers, which were uttered with ecstatic fervour. This was one of the rare occasions when I, a mithnaged youth, was able to see the hasidim at their worship of the Creator. The bottle of brandy, which was there for all the congregation to drink from, added a special liveliness to the atmosphere. The news coming from Vilna was alternately encouraging and discouraging. The mood of the " public " fluctuated in accordance with the contents of the telegrams, and all the time it was clear that these were experiences which affected the hasidim to the depths of their being. After a day of great emotional tension, the last telegram arrived: the Rebbe had been acquitted and the hasidim were to sing the song of praise *Az Yashir* [the song sung by Moses over the Egyptians drowned in the Red Sea]. This instruction was carried out with tremendous enthusiasm. The singing of the hasidim could be heard all over Koidanov; and when it ended, the barrel of liquor was found to have been drained dry. The mithnagdim, too, joined in the rejoicing. The dispute with the Rebbe was a purely internal Jewish matter. . . . Perhaps even a vengeful man would have been pleased with the verdict, for if the Rebbe had not been acquitted, his court expenses would have been greater than the sum of money that he owed to the creditors.'[41]

R. Aharon of Koidanov died on the 26th *Elul*, 1897.

The younger son of R. Barukh-Mordekhai, R. Shalom (Perlov) of Brahin, distinguished himself by his literary work. It was he who edited and published the teachings of 'the Koidanov dynasty.' Born in 1850,[42] he lived in Lida ;[43] then in 1884, he was appointed *Rav* in the small town of Berezna (Volhynia), and in 1890 in the small town of Brahin (in the province of Minsk).[44] He published the following books: *Divrei Shalom* (Vilna 1882) which contains, in addition to various teachings of the Koidanov *Tsaddikim* and others, important biographical information about the Koidanov dynasty ; *Mishmereth Shalom* (two parts, Warsaw 1912 ; 2nd edition, no place or date of publication, 1959 ?), comprising religious laws and customs, especially those followed by the author's father, together with the author's own explanatory comments, and also quotations from the *Gaon* of Vilna and R. Akiva Eger, side by side with quotations from the *Tsaddikim* of Karlin, Lakhovich, Slonim, from R. Shneur-Zalman of Ladi, and others ; *Atereth Shalom* (Warsaw 1895), a commentary on the liturgical poem 'Lord, I yearn for the Sabbath's delight' by R. Aharon the Great of Karlin. Mention should be made of two booklets: *Midrash Pinhas he-Hadash* (Warsaw 1910) and *Shem Aharon* (Warsaw 1910) which present the views of various *Tsaddikim* (R. Aharon of Koidanov, R. Noah of Horodishch, the Karlin *Tsaddikim,* and others) on human affairs (including an instruction to teachers of young children [*melammedim*] not to strike their pupils), on the effectiveness of various charms, prayers, and the like. The short will left by R. Shalom of Brahin consists mainly of details about the arrangements for his funeral and burial, and about the annual prayers and studying on the anniversary of his death —all in accordance with the kabbalistic and hasidic spirit. Appended to the will are descriptions—'copied from the author's manuscript'—of the exorcising of a *dybbuk* [evil spirit] and of the transmigration of souls, stories which have no parallel anywhere else in Lithuanian hasidic writings. The will also bears witness that, at that time (1922), there were Koidanov hasidim living in Palestine, and that R. Shalom left writings in manuscripts.[45] R. Shalom of Brahin died at the age of seventy-five on the 26th *Heshvan*, 1925.

R. Aharon of Koidanov was succeeded by his son, R. Yosef. Like the later Karlin and Slonim *Tsaddikim*,[46] R. Yosef also founded a *Yeshivah* [*Talmud* school] in which about one hundred and fifty pupils studied. During the general decline of the hasidic movement, this *Yeshivah* played a role of some importance in the education of part of the Jewish population in that region. In R. Yosef's time, Koidanov was still a centre to which his followers flocked, especially on the Penitential Days, on *Shavuoth*, and on *Hanukkah*. The Koidanov hasidim were in the habit of starting their prayers early and of not praying lengthily or noisily, in contrast to the Karlin practice. In 1890 R. Yosef wrote an 'approval' of the Koidanov prayer-book. In his day, there were still hasidic prayer-houses (*shtiebelakh*) outside the limits of the province of Minsk, for example in Vilna. In America, too, the Koidanov hasidim set up their own *shtiebelakh* (*Beth Aharon, Beth Yosef*), the members of which later merged with the Kobrin hasidim. R. Yosef died at the height of the First World War, in 1915.[47]

After this war, part of the region, including Koidanov, was detached from Poland and came under Russian rule. Those of the Koidanov hasidim that remained in Poland were led by R. Yosef's brother, R. Nehemyah. He settled in the town of Baranovich and devoted himself to preserving the tradition of his forefathers.[48] He died in 1927.[49]

Koidanov hasidism came into existence after the struggle with the mithnagdim had already ended, though there was still tension between the two camps in Lithuania. R. Shelomo-Hayyim, the founder of the dynasty, had stones thrown at him ; and in the days of his grandson, R. Aharon, the mithnagdim were still not prepared to intermarry with the hasidim. Just as Karlin hasidism strove to gain a foothold in the 'principal community' of Pinsk, and Lakhovich hasidism did the same in Slutsk and Amdur hasidism in Grodno, so Koidanov hasidism endeavoured to penetrate into the nearby provincial capital of Minsk. However, its influence in Minsk remained limited, as did that of all the other branches of Lithuanian hasidism in the nearby large and important communities. Unlike the non-Karlin dynasties originating in Volhynia which arose in Lithuania at the same time—the first quarter of the nineteenth century (Liubeshov or Libeshei, Berezna, Horodok) and which confined themselves to deepening and developing the individual hasid's belief in his *Tsaddik*, the Koidanov *Tsaddikim* endeavoured to mould the lives and conduct of 'those that found shelter in their shade' [i.e., their followers] in the spirit of hasidic doctrine. To this end they drew up a hasidic code of conduct and published 'the Koidanov prayer-book,' as well as manuals of customs, all of them bearing a kabbalistic and hasidic stamp (R. Shelomo-Hayyim, R. Aharon). At a later stage still, they also turned their attention to rabbinical learning (R. Yosef's setting up of a *yeshivah*), though in this field they did not reach the level attained by Polish hasidism. Their interest in revealed lore gradually displaced their inclination to mysticism. The typically 'Lithuanian character' of the Koidanov movement expressed itself in the form of more *Torah* [i.e., study of the Law] than in Volhynia and the Ukraine, and less mysticism than in Poland.

C. *Kobrin Hasidism*

After the death of R. Noah of Lakhovich in 1832 (at the time when his son-in-law, R. Mordekhai the Second had succeeded him in Lakhovich and his nephew, R. Shelomo-Hayyim, was founding Koidanov hasidism), his father's former disciple and later also his own pupil, R. Moshe, was chosen Rebbe. R. Moshe took up residence in the small town of Kobrin and there became the founder of the Kobrin dynasty of *Tsaddikim*.[50] Through the Lakhovich branch of the movement Lithuanian hasidism spread northwards in Polesia; through the Koidanov dynasty it reached as far as the provincial capital of Minsk; and through the Kobrin dynasty it pushed out westwards, close to the Polish border.

R. Moshe was a unique character in Lithuanian hasidism who has not yet been properly appreciated. He had something of the quality of the first leaders of the hasidic movement. He called for the spiritualisation of the individual not only at prayer-time, but in all the affairs of daily life, too, and he demanded that his followers' aspiration to holiness should be as strong on weekdays as on Sabbaths and Festivals. The ideas which he is reported to have expressed also recall hasidic sayings from the earliest period of the movement. 'If I were truly God-fearing,' R. Moshe used to say, 'I ought to walk through the streets of the town, shouting: "Why are you transgressing the words of the Holy Book, Ye shall be holy ? " ' [51]

R. Moshe the son of R. Yisrael (Poliyer) of Kobrin was born in 1784, in the small town of Piesk which lies close to Grodno, between Amdur and Slonim. His father was a baker. In his youth he was attracted to hasidism and went to study hasidic doctrine with the *Tsaddik* R. Moshe of Shershov (near Kobrin), who was a disciple of R. Hayyim-Heikel of Amdur. For two years R. Moshe travelled regularly to his teacher. In the end, however, he felt that 'this place was not suited to his deepest nature,' since the *Tsaddik* of Shershov's way of attaining to sanctity was by fasting, self-mortification, and constant study of the Law day and night. R. Moshe therefore left him and went to study with R. Mordekhai of Lakhovich whose enthusiastic disciple he became. R. Moshe used afterwards to say that all the rest of his life he did penitence for those two years.[52] When R. Asher of Stolin upbraided him—so hasidic tradition relates—for recognising the authority of Lakhovich, which was far away from Kobrin, rather than that of Stolin, which was nearer and of better hasidic 'lineage,' R. Moshe's eyes filled with tears as he replied: 'What is my offence and what is my sin, if my soul yearns and longs for a way that is suited to its deepest nature ? '[53] After the death of R. Mordekhai in 1810, R. Moshe became the disciple of his son, R. Noah. Hasidic tradition relates that R. Moshe travelled regularly to R. Noah for seven whole years, but to his sorrow received no illumination. Once, on a Sabbath eve after the 'table' [festive meal], R. Moshe was so overcome by grief that he laid his head on his arms and wept bitterly till sleep overcame him. Suddenly he dreamt that he saw R. Mordekhai who asked him: 'My son, why are you weeping?' R. Moshe replied: 'How shall I not weep, when it is now seven years since you set your dwelling in the secret place of the All Highest and I have not seen the light?' R. Mordekhai said to him: 'If I were now in the world I would do as my son Noah does. Submit yourself and it will be well with you.' And R. Moshe continued to study with R. Noah.[54] When R. Noah died, some of his followers chose R. Moshe as their Rebbe. At first he absolutely refused, since he considered himself unworthy of the honour. Only after they pressed him and assured him that 'his strength was great enough to rule the Lord's people' did he finally consent.

R. Moshe's strength did not lie so much in the extent of his personal influence, which was restricted in the main to the town of Kobrin and its environs, but rather in his sincere endeavours to give practical expression to the teachings of hasidism in the daily affairs of life. To this end, he used to address himself to his followers in letters of exhortation and encouragement.[55] In one such characteristic letter we read:

'Strengthen yourselves with perfect faith and may you live and wherever you turn may you succeed and prosper. The best advice for every matter is strength and unity through love, fellowship, and true affection. When there is any resentment or harshness in the heart of anyone of you, even against a simple man, he is far removed from the true essence of human nature; and there is nothing worse or more bitter than turning away from the Blessed Lord. Therefore each one of you must avoid this like a man fleeing from an arrow. No more need be said on this. Each one must do his utmost to strengthen his worship (that is his prayer), joyfully and gladly. Be not downcast by the treachery of the time, for salvation is the Lord's and He will never desert his pious ones. Guard yourselves and trust in the Lord and do what is good, every one according to his manner as the Lord has blessed him. Conduct yourselves with joy and gladness and the Lord will surely help you and you will succeed and prosper in all your physical and spiritual doings. . . . The Father of Mercy will have mercy on a sorely laden people. . . .'

In another letter, written (half in Hebrew and half in Yiddish) in reply to an appeal from his followers that he should pray for them during an epidemic which had then broken out, R. Moshe exhorts them to be strong and confident in spirit, 'for trust in God is the most important part of healing.' After advising them to send redemption money to the *Tsaddik* of Savran, he ends his letter as follows: 'Let not fear master you (Merciful Heaven protect us!), and the Holy One Blessed Be He will surely help you. For His whole desire and wish is to preserve you from all evil talk and to reward you with every good. And I, too, will not fail (Heaven forbid!) to mention you wherever I am. My dear brethren, be strong and of good courage and keep up your spirits; only have no fear. I shall be granted to behold your deliverance and well-being, both spiritual and physical. . . . From him who is bound to you by strong bonds of true and everlasting love, Moshe Poliyer.'

Both these letters were found in manuscript in the Kobrin 'court,' marked only with the day of the week and the Portion of the Law for the week. The same Kobrin archives also contained a letter from the *Tsaddik* R. Noah of Lakhovich to R. Moshe, requesting him to use his good offices to collect the *halukkah* funds 'on behalf of our brethren in the Holy Land.' Apparently then, R. Moshe was well known in hasidic circles already in the lifetime of R. Noah his Master, although from a deed of sale in the prayer-house in the small town of Drohichin close to Kobrin it appears that R. Moshe's followers still in 1849 called themselves 'Lakhovich hasidim.' R. Moshe passed the whole of his life in Kobrin. A hasidic source relates that towards the end of his days, he used to travel to R. Yisrael of Ruzhin just like a hasid making the pilgrimage to his Rebbe.[56]

R. Moshe wrote no book. It is related that, when asked the reason for this, he replied: 'I have written my books on the hearts of Israel.'[57] After his death, his followers collected together his teachings and *obiter dicta* and published them under the title *Amaroth Tehoroth*. This volume also contains a description of R. Moshe's conduct as a hasidic leader. Unlike other *Tsaddikim*, R. Moshe lived modestly: he used to travel without attendants, once apologised to a friend for not being able to send him a *Purim* present,[58] and even wrote to his followers (in the letter quoted above) that they should pay their redemption money to another *Tsaddik* (from Savran). Once, when lighting the *Hanukkah* candles, he said: 'Our Father in Heaven knows that it is all the same to me whether I pronounce the blessing over the candles, as once, in a clay candlestick, or as now, in a silver one ; and that it is all the same to me whether I eat, as once, with a wooden spoon, or, as now, with a silver one.'[59] Unlike those *Tsaddikim* (such as R. Shelomo of Karlin) who expressed the opinion that God counted the miles traversed by the hasid on his journey to the Rebbe and recorded them to his credit, R. Moshe used to say that he would be called to account for every step that a Jew took to come to him.[60] At the same time, however, he attached great importance to the hasid's adherence to his *Tsaddik*. The *Tsaddik,* he said, is like a tree and his followers—the hasidim—are like its branches.

The tree may have dry branches, but even so, as long as the branch is attached to the tree, there is hope of its obtaining sap from the tree and producing fruit. But if the branch is completely severed from the tree, then even if it contains sap it will nevertheless soon dry up and be thrown away. So it is with the individual Jew's soul: if it is closely bound to the *Tsaddik*, there is still hope ; but Heaven forbid that it should be severed from the *Tsaddik*.[61] Yet, when a hasid from Poland came to see him, R. Moshe asked him : 'Why have you come to me, when you have already been to your own Rebbe ? Your Rebbe is a *Tsaddik* who is the son of a *Tsaddik*, whereas my father was just a villager.'[62] Once he said to his followers : 'Let not the leader in Israel think that the Holy One Blessed Be He has chosen him because he is greater and more worthy than other men. If a mortal king were to hang his crown on a simple wooden peg, would this simple peg thereby become of greater worth ? Even so, every leader must know that he is merely a simple peg on which the King has hung His crown.'[63] He even forbade his followers to say of him that he was a *Tsaddik* : 'If anyone says any words of praise about me, calling me a *Tsaddik* or the like, I shall never forgive him.

The only thing that I permit to be said about me is that I love Israel with all my heart and soul, without any distinction between hasidim and others.'[64] This request of R. Moshe was written in the structure [ohel] over his grave at Kobrin.[65] He gave the following injunction to his grandson and successor, R. Noah-Naftali: 'If, after my death, someone comes and says, " I shall enjoy the reward of R. Moshe's merits," do you give that man to understand that I am displeased by such words. The only thing that may be said of me is that I loved Israel.'[66]

Once, towards the end of his life when, old and feeble, he was sitting at his 'table' on the holy Sabbath with his followers, his servant urged him to go and rest a little. R. Moshe replied: 'Stupid man ! I go to rest ? What is rest for ? My only rest is when I am sitting together with other Jews. This, and nothing else, is my rest.'[67] On another occasion, before the blowing of the shofar, he called to the assembled congregation of his followers: 'Fellow-Jews, do not place your trust in me. Let each one of you do what is required of him.'[68] On still another occasion, he said to them: 'If only I knew for certain that I had helped one of our adherents in the worship of the Divine Name, I should not worry at all. But I see that there is not one of you that has accepted the words that I have spoken to you at the "table" in the course of my life. If you ask how I know this, I shall tell you. As you know, words spoken from the heart go to the heart. And if the words do not go to the hearer's heart, the Holy One Blessed Be He does not let them just remain floating in the empty space of the universe. He shows His graciousness to the man who spoke them by making the words return to his heart. And I see that all that I ever said has returned to my heart.'[69]

The quality of joyfulness—one of the main elements in hasidism, particularly in Karlin hasidism—did not play as important a part in R. Moshe's religious outlook as it did with his contemporary, R. Aharon the Second of Karlin. On the other hand, R. Moshe was filled with a profound sense of religious awe and consumed with a constant desire for repentance. 'When I was a child,' he recounted on one occasion, 'I was once playing with other children in the month of *Elul* [preceding the Penitential Days]. My sister asked me, "Are you playing today, too ? Today is the month of *Elul* when even a fish in the water trembles with fear." When I heard these words I began to tremble, and I remember that fear to this day.'[70] Again, hasidic tradition relates that once, on *Rosh Hashanah* eve, when R. Moshe stood up in front of the congregation to lead the prayers, he was seized with trembling in all of his body, his teeth chattered, and his limbs shook like the trees of a forest in a strong wind. When he took hold of the pulpit, it also swayed to and fro, and he could not stand up because he was trembling so. Until at last he bent backwards and all the congregation saw how he forced the fear back into himself. Only then did he stand firmly in his place and begin the prayer.[71] 'When a Jew says the word " Blessed " —so R. Moshe taught—he must say it with all his strength, till he has no more strength to say " art thou," and then the Holy One Blessed Be He, who desires the prayers of the righteous gives him the strength to say " art thou." So always, with every single word—the worshipper says it with all his strength and the Holy One Blessed Be He fills him with fresh strength to say the word that comes next, till the end of the blessing.'[72] At the same time, R. Moshe used to encourage those of his followers who could not attain to such a degree of intensity in prayer: ' We say in our prayers, " For Thou hearest the prayer of every mouth "—this means that, even if the prayer is only in the mouth, the Holy One Blessed Be He still hears it.' He also used to say: ' It is written, " In your mouth and in your heart to do it " (Deut. xxx, 14)—this means first in your mouth and then in your heart.'[73]

R. Moshe often used to quote the reply made by General Gobin to the Tsar Nicolas. Gobin served as a general for fifty years and continued to hold his commission even when a very old man. Once, when the Tsar was present at a parade of soldiers who were encamped near Kobrin, he asked the old general: ' Does your blood still warm you ? ' ' It is not blood that warms a man but work ' [which in Hebrew also means 'worship '], was the general's reply.[74] R. Moshe once told the following story to his hasidim: 'When I was at the house of my Teacher in Lakhovich for the *Purim* meal, the *Tsaddik* of Lakhovich said: "Now is the time when every beggar is given something. Therefore, if anyone wishes to ask of me the gift of instruction in Divine worship, I can grant it to him." Every one of his disciples received what he asked for. "And you, Moishele, what is your request?" asked the Rebbe. "I do not wish for a free gift," I replied. "I want to be an ordinary soldier and to obtain what I deserve through my own efforts." '[75] He also told them: 'When I was with my Teachers and heard their teachings and their instruction in the hasidic form of worship, I did not wish to hear any new teachings before I had carried out their first instructions.' Once R. Moshe was holding forth on the Sabbath at his 'table' round which some young men were standing. R. Moshe fixed his gaze on one of these young scholars who was one of his followers and a member of his household. Suddenly R. Moshe asked his servant: 'Who is this young scholar?' Surprised that R. Moshe did not recognise the scholar, the servant told him his name and those of his father and father-in-law. But R. Moshe insisted that he did not know the youth. After his servant had helped him with certain recognition aids, such as the young man's place of residence and the like, R. Moshe remembered who he was and said to him: 'Do you know the reason why I did not recognise you today? Because a man is his thought; and where his thoughts are, there is the man. Now, since I saw today, while I was expounding my teaching, that your thoughts were wandering elsewhere, I did not see in front of me anything but a piece of flesh.' It is also related that once, amongst the hasidim standing round him, there was a young scholar whose name was also Moshe. R. Moshe turned to him and said: 'Your name is Moshe, and so is mine. It is therefore only right that both of us, the two Moshes, should repent of our sins together.'[76]

Particularly prominent among R. Moshe's personal qualities was his integrity and the steadfastness of his faith even in suffering. Once one of the followers of R. Yitshak of Vorki came to him after the death of his Master. R. Moshe asked him: 'Have you not enough *Tsaddikim* in Poland that you have come to me?' The hasid replied: 'I heard my Master say that it was a *mitsvah* to get to know the *Tsaddik* from Kobrin who speaks the truth in his heart.' R. Moshe answered: 'Untruth is so powerful that it can lead even *Tsaddikim* astray. For the truth is very hard to attain. It is a free gift from the Almighty Blessed Be He. This is the meaning of the verse, "Thou givest truth to Jacob." For the quality of truth cannot be measured.' Then R. Moshe took a little tobacco between his finger and thumb, showed it to his visitor, and throwing it away, said: 'Even less than this.' Immediately he took another pinch of tobacco and added: 'Let it be even less than this, provided that it is the truth.'[77] Once, when R. Moshe paid a visit to R. Yisrael of Ruzhin, the latter came out to meet him when he was still a good distance from the town, greeting him he said: 'I felt your truth while you were still several miles away.'[78]

Of the way in which he would implant faith in the hearts of his adherents the following story is told: Once, one of his hasidim, who was working on the fortification of the town and had many worries, came in his trouble to R. Moshe to ask his advice. Just as he entered the Rebbe's house, the Rebbe was being served a dish of groats for his breakfast. Although R. Moshe saw the hasid, he did not greet him but said the blessing 'By whose word all things were created' over the groats, while the hasid stood some way off. R. Moshe said to him: 'I used to say that you resembled your father, but now I see that it is not so. I remember that your father, too, once came to me when he was full of care, and he, too, entered just as I was saying the blessing "By whose word all things were created." After the blessing I asked him whether he wanted to ask anything of me. He replied that he did not. He just said farewell to me and went his way, without saying another word. Do you know why? When a Jew hears the blessing "By whose word all things were created," he has received the answer to all his questions and cares. For what is there to ask about or worry about when everything has been created by God's word?' Then R. Moshe bade him farewell, and the hasid, too, said no more but held out his hand to his Rebbe and returned to his business.[79]

On the nature of suffering R. Moshe once expressed himself as follows: When a man is suffering, let him not say that he is an evil case, for the Holy One Blessed Be He does not bring evil on men. He can only say that his plight is bitter. Suffering is like drugs which are given to sick people to heal their bodies. Some of these drugs are bitter, but all of them are given to heal the patient. So it is with suffering. It, too, is given to man only to heal his soul; and though it is bitter, it is still for the sufferer's good.[80] The hasidim were in the habit of chanting in Yiddish the words that R. Moshe used to say on the authority of a certain *Tsaddik*: 'Angel! Angel! It is no wonder that you are an angel. You sit there in the heavenly heights, where you are not obliged to eat or drink, to beget children and support them. Pray come down to us on the earth, where you will have to eat and drink and procreate like us, and then we shall see if you still remain an angel. Then you will have the right to be proud of yourself, but not now.'[81]

R. Moshe of Kobrin is described as follows in the memoirs of a writer and *maskil* from the small town of Motele (between Pinsk and Kobrin):[82] 'My father was a devoted adherent of the *Tsaddik* of Kobrin, the aged R. Moshe (after whose death he stopped travelling to the *Tsaddikim*— " There's no one to go to "...). My father used to tell many stories about his *Tsaddik*. For example, how he set no store by worldly pleasures. When his silk caftan became all creased with age, he refused to have a new one made: " I will not waste Jewish money." So what did the best of hasidim do? They secretly had a new caftan made for him, and on a Sabbath eve they cunningly stole the old one and put the new one in its place. The Rebbe realised what had happened, but he could not help himself—he had to appear for the Sabbath prayer and meal. Once he had said the *She-Heheyanu* blessing over the new garment, the hasidim were confident that the blessing would not become just empty words and that the *Tsaddik* would not refuse to wear it. And so it was. Or the story of the *Tsaddik's* last

Sabbath on earth. He still presided over his "table," sitting however not on a chair, but on a couch, propped up by cushions and quilts. He began chanting "Blessed be the Lord every day," and when he reached the words "therefore with all our heart . . . and all our soul . . . and all our might" (as father told this story he used to chant with the appropriate intonation), he slid down from the cushion and fainted. On recovering consciousness a full two hours later, he concluded his song in a tone of joyful serenity: "Let us crown Him as our one and only King!". . . Three days later he departed this life.'

Evidence of the attitude of the leading contemporary Lithuanian *Rabbanim* to R. Moshe of Kobrin towards the end of his life is provided by two letters written to him on the same subject in 1857.[83] One of these letters is from the Pinsk *Av Beth-Din,* R. Mordekhai Zakheim, who died in Pinsk on 21st *Tishri,* 1857, after holding the office of *Rav* there for thirteen years,[84] and who was known among his fellow-*Rabbanim* as 'the keenest mind of the *Geonim.*'[85] The second letter was written by the Karlin *Av Beth-Din,* R. Shemuel-Avigdor Tosefaah, who was the *Rav* of Karlin in his last years and died there on 18th *Nisan,* 1866.[86]

Here are the texts of the two letters:

'With God's help, on the second day of *Sivan,* [5]617 [1857], here in the community of Pinsk—I address myself to his honour, the distinguished Rabbi, Moshe Poliyer.

'I spoke with your excellency several years ago about my kinsman, R. Avraham the son of R. Dov of this place, who has been living in the Holy Land for the past few years and does not receive support from any *kolel,* because they all say that he belongs to your *kolel.* In consequence of this, he and his dependents are so short of food (Heaven preserve us!), that one of his sons actually died of hunger (may God have mercy on us!). One of the respected citizens of our town being at present here from the Holy Land, I was urged to investigate the matter, which I did thoroughly. I discovered that he quite certainly belongs to your *kolel.* Hence it is your holy excellency's duty to include him in your *kolel,* like all the other members of it. Heaven forbid that you should shut your eyes to this. I trust in your holy

excellency's great sense of justice, that you will give heed
to these sincere words of mine. And also as the *Torah*
commands us. From your friend, that prays for your welfare
and peace, Mordekhai of Rozhinoy, *Rav* of the above-
mentioned community of Pinsk.'

'To his honour, Rabbi and our Teacher, Moshe Poliyer,
Whereas trustworthy witnesses have testified before us,
as commanded in the *Torah,* that the Rabbi and scholar
Avraham the son of the scholar Dov of Sherishov, who used
to live here and is now in the Holy Land, was one of your
learned honour's followers and loyal adherents and always
used to travel to your honour for Festivals, and that he has
now been close on five years in the Holy Land without
receiving support from any *kolel,* but being sent all the
time from one to the other ; we therefore notify your learned
honour that, according to the above testimony, it has been
decided that the above-mentioned R. Avraham's support
devolves upon your holy honour's *kolel,* according to the
amount given to the hasidim like him who are in the Holy
Land. Particularly as we have been clearly informed that
he is very poor and without means of livelihood, and that
his wretched children are suffering from hunger. We therefore further request your honour to exhort the members of
your *kolel* to carry out the above instructions, and we have
no doubt that they will act according to your exhortation, as
is well known. In full confidence that you will fulfil our
request, I will end briefly with greetings to your revered
honour from us the undersigned, on the first day of the week,
Rosh Hodesh Sivan, [5]617 [= 1857], here in Karlin.

'Shemuel Avigdor Tosefaah, *Rav* of the community of
Karlin, and
Avraham-Leib, the son of the scholar Yaakov Weil, and
Yitshak the son of the scholar Yosef of blessed memory.'

'All that is written here we have copied exactly from
the letters of the *Geonim,* the Pinsk and Karlin *Avoth Batei-
Din,* not making the slightest alteration, but copying the
original words letter by letter. In proof of which we here-
under sign our names, together with the official stamp of
the *kahal,* on the above copy. The third day of the week,
the 3rd *Sivan,* [5]617 [= 1857], here in Pinsk.

'Yisrael Yitshak, the son of the late scholar and Master
R. Shemuel-Hayyim of blessed memory, of Pinsk ;
Moshe the son of Zeev-Wolf of Karlin ;
Yehudah the son of the scholar R. Shadar of Pinsk.'

(STAMP OF THE
TAX COLLECTOR OF
THE KARLIN
COMMUNITY)

The war waged by the mithnagdim against the hasidim
in Lithuania had already begun to die down by the end of
the eighteenth century. The deposition of R. Avigdor from
his office of *Rav* in Pinsk in 1793 ;[87] the release of R. Shneur-
Zalman of Ladi from his first imprisonment in St. Petersburg,
together with 'his important associates . . . from amongst
the followers of the Karliner sect,' in 1798 ;[88] the victory of
the hasidim in the elections to the Vilna *kahal* in 1799 ;[89]
the change in favour of the hasidim made, during the years
1800-1808, in the regulations of the various Jewish study
circles[90]—all these facts are evidence of the equality of
status attained by the hasidic community in Lithuania in
this period. The above two letters from R. Mordekhai
Zakheim and R. Shemuel-Avigdor Tosefaah to R. Moshe of
Kobrin show the friendly relations existing in the fifties of
the nineteenth century even *between the Geonim of
Lithuania and a hasidic Tsaddik*. Even in Lithuania, the
Rabbanim granted recognition to the way of life led by
the *Tsaddik* and the hasidic community, and actually turned
to them for help. Both sides—the *Rav* and the *Tsaddik*—
came to realise that there was no place for disputes between
them in religious matters, despite the great difference in
their respective interpretations of Jewish teaching. The days
of the doctrinal polemics between R. Avraham Katzenellenbogen of Brest-Litovsk and R. Levi-Yitshak of Berdichev
were past.[91] These two letters deal with a purely social
problem the solution of which, as requested by the
Rabbanim, is made possible by the social structure created
by the hasidic movement, and by its spirit of mutual
assistance deriving from the relations of the *Tsaddik* with
his hasidim and of the hasidim with each other. The letters

thus illustrate the power of the hasidic *Tsaddik* in providing social assistance where leading *Rabbanim* were unable to do anything.

As regards talmudic learning, however, there is no doubt that the Lithuanian *Rabbanim* continued to have a poor opinion of the hasidic *Tsaddikim*. This is clear from a popular tradition about the attitude of the same R. Shemuel-Avigdor Tosefaah to one of Rabbi Moshe of Kobrin's chief adherents, R. Meir Meirim, the *Rav* of Kobrin, and the author of the volume *Nir*, a commentary on the Jerusalem *Talmud*. This popular story relates that, once, when R. Meir Meirim came to Karlin to enquire after the *Tsaddik* R. Aharon the Second of Karlin, he paid a courtesy call on R. Shemuel-Avigdor Tosefaah, who was at that time the Karlin *Av Beth-Din*. After a while their conversation turned to the study of the *Torah* and hasidism. R. Shemuel-Avigdor said to R. Meir Meirim: 'I am very concerned about you. When, in another hundred and twenty years (may you be granted a long and happy life!) you are called to Heaven, it will be hard to find you a place there. The mithnagdim will refuse to accept you at their table, because you are a hasid and frequent the threshold of their *Tsaddikim*. And the hasidim, for their part, will also refuse to accept you, because you are very learned in the *Torah* after the manner of the mithnagdim. Hence you will be rejected by both tables.' R. Meir Meirim replied with a smile: 'Have no fear, our Rabbi. I am sure that there will be many hasidim like me who are learned in the *Torah*, and that a special table will be laid for us.' The trustworthiness of this story is confirmed by the many similar statements made by the leading Lithuanian *Rabbanim* of the time about their attitude to hasidism and its *Tsaddikim*—for example, the remarks of R. Eisel Harif, the *Rav* of Slonim, on the *Tsaddik* R. Avraham of Slonim, the founder of the Slonim dynasty;[93] and the comments of R. Yosef-Baer Soloveychik, the *Rav* of Brest-Litovsk,[94] of R. Hayyim of Volozhin and his son R. Yitshak,[95] and even of R. Shemuel Mohilever. [96]

R. Moshe of Kobrin died on the 29th *Nisan*, 1858. When, after his death, one of his followers came to the *Tsaddik*

R. Mendel of Kotsk and the latter asked him, 'What was the most important thing in the opinion of your Master, R. Moshe ? ' the hasid answered: 'Whatever he was doing was, at that moment, for him the most important thing.'[97] Another *Tsaddik* said of him, after his death: ' If R. Moshe had had people to speak to, he would have gone on living.'[98]

The most important of R. Moshe's disciples[99] were, first, the above-mentioned *Rav* of Kobrin, R. Meir the son of R. Moshe Meirim, the author of *Nir*, a commentary on the Jerusalem *Talmud* which was highly esteemed by the *Rabbanim* and has also been considered worthy of note by scientific scholars.[100] R. Meir publicly acknowledged the authority of the *Tsaddikim*, even though he himself was a *Rav* in a Lithuanian town. After the death of R. Moshe of Kobrin R. Meir Meirim became a disciple of R. Avraham of Slonim. He died in 1873 and was buried in Kobrin, beside R. Moshe his first Master. R. Moshe's second disciple (who had been, first of all, together with R. Moshe, a disciple of R. Noah of Lakhovich) was R. Avraham of Slonim, the founder of the Slonim dynasty of *Tsaddikim*. Another of R. Moshe's disciples was his grandson and successor, R. Noah-Naftali. Also an adherent of R. Moshe's was the man who subsequently became a member of the Kobrin *Beth-Din* and a *dayyan* [Jewish judge] in the *Beth-Din* of R. Meir Meirim, R. Noah-Hayyim the son of R. Moshe Levin, the author of many works of a biographical and anthologising character which reveal a keen insight into, and detailed knowledge of, halakhic literature. Written approval of his books were given by mithnaged *Rabbanim*, like the Pinsk *Av Beth-Din*, R. Elazar-Moshe Hurwitz, and the Lemberg *Av Beth-Din*, R. Yosef-Shaul Nathanson, as well as by hasidic *Tsaddikim*, like R. Avraham of Slonim, and others.[101]

R. Moshe was succeeded by his grandson, R. Noah-Naftali, the son of his son, R. Yisrael-Yaakov. R. Noah was the Rebbe of the Kobrin hasidim for more than thirty years. Just as Lakhovich hasidism was weakened by the Koidanov and Kobrin dynasties, so Kobrin hasidism was now weakened by the Slonim dynasty which came into being after the death of R. Moshe. The small volume of teachings

attributed to R. Noah-Naftali, which was published under
the title *Maamarim Tehorim* together with the collection
of his grandfather R. Moshe's sayings, *Amaroth Tehoroth*
(Warsaw 1910), does not consist only of expository comments
on biblical verses. R. Noah-Naftali also makes use of parables
and illustrations from daily life and nature, as his grandfather R. Moshe had done before him, apparently with the
object of making it easier for their supporters, who were
not all scholars, to understand their ideas. The small volume
also contains a letter, undated, from R. Noah-Naftali to the
Kobrin hasidim in Palestine, to 'those who have been
dwelling in the Holy Land for a long time and those who
have recently arrived,' dealing with the sanctity of the
Land.[102]

Another grandson of R. Moshe of Kobrin, and also the
brother-in-law of R. Noah-Naftali, was the important writer
of the *Haskalah* period, Yehudah-Leib Levin, better known
by his pen-name Yahalal. In his autobiography *Zikkaron
ba-Sefer* (Zhitomir 1910), Yahalal describes the life in the
Kobrin 'court,' giving very instructive details about the
atmosphere there in those days. He refers to R. Moshe of
Kobrin as 'the most famous *Tsaddik* of his generation.' He
gives an eye-witness account of how R. Moshe's adherents
split into rival factions after his death, one group following
his disciple, R. Avraham of Slonim, and the other his grandson, R. Noah-Naftali of Kobrin. R. Moshe had a band of
followers even in the provincial capital Minsk, whom he
used to visit twice a year. Of R. Moshe's spiritual character
Yahalal relates the following two details. Once, when the
hasidim complained to him that his grandson—Yahalal—
was not devoting himself seriously to his studies, R. Moshe
replied: 'Do not stir up or awaken love until it please.'
Later, when Yahalal distinguished himself as a scholar, his
father would relate R. Moshe's remark to everyone that
entered his house. 'When I was thirteen years old,' Yahalal
continues, 'I knew "by page" eight hundred pages of
Gemara and my father took me to Kobrin at *Rosh Hashanah*
to begin laying *tefillin* in my grandfather's house. On the
day when I first laid *tefillin*, there assembled in my grandfather's house all the leading hasidim, and also the Kobrin

Gaon and *Av Beth-Din*, R. Meir Meirim. They examined me on the eight hundred pages of *Gemara* that I knew . . . correctly, and I felt very proud of myself. Noticing this, my grandfather asked me: "Do you know where it is written: 'Do not say there is no humility as long as I am alive?'" "Yes," I replied at once. "It is at the end of *Sotah,* page 49b." "And what do the words mean?" asked my grandfather. I gave him the usual explanation. He shook his head and exclaimed: "No! The meaning is: Where there is I—the egoism of man—there is no humility." His words pierced my heart like arrows and made me blush with shame.' When Yahalal took up secular studies 'my mother kept on proving to me that a man did not need to know how to write. The strongest proof of all was that the *Tsaddik* our Teacher and Master, her father and my grandfather, also did not know how to write. What could I reply?'

When Yahalal's secular learning showed signs of undermining his faith, his parents were deeply distressed. 'I told my parents that I agreed to go to Kobrin, but I wanted to travel by way of Slonim in order to see the *Tsaddik* R. Avraham, my grandfather's disciple, because my brother-in-law would not be able to answer my questions. . . . I visited the *Tsaddik* R. Avraham, who recognised me because when I had been there, too, as a hasid visiting his Rebbe for *Rosh Hashanah*. . . . When I stood before his "table," with a large group of his adherents all around me, the *Tsaddik* began to expound the story of the snake and the tail, as related in my book *Elhanan.* I was very much offended, and on the evening of the same day . . . I forced my way into his private room. Since I felt sure of myself, being the grandson of his Master, the *Tsaddik* R. Moshe, and having been freed by the *Haskalah* of the customary religious reverence for the *Tsaddikim,* I took him to task for publicly humiliating me. He apologised and told me to ask him all my questions. . . . I evaded the point by saying that I had no questions, and after much idle talk he put on a very serious look and said: "My friend, I have heard bad things about you, but I will not believe such things about the offspring of our revered Teacher and Master." . . .' In the course of further conversation, he spoke most insultingly about my brother-in-law [R. Noah-Naftali] from Kobrin: I was incensed and answered him with such violent effrontery that he was taken aback. For he was not used to hearing such words. When I turned to go . . . he asked me to come the next day to his midday meal. I did so and found him surounded by a very large crowd of hasidim. On seeing me, the *Tsaddik* began to deliver a homily which was all about effrontery. When he had finished his exposition, which consisted mainly of pointed allusions to me, he looked at me and said with a bitter smile: 'And you, Yehudah-Leib, you are insolent even to a good Jew!' . . . But I . . . answered him: '. . . Perhaps the accursed devil appears in the guise of a good Jew.'

On his meeting with the *Tsaddik* R. Noah-Naftali of Kobrin, Yahalal writes: 'My brother-in-law the *Tsaddik* would sit alone with me in his room and remonstrate with me. To his credit, it must be said that he did not try to argue with me, since he knew very well that he was no match for me, as he openly admitted: "It is not for me to try to convince you with quotations from writers and books, since you are far better versed than I am both in *Gemara* and in hasidism." All that he said was simply to entreat me not to bring dishonour on our grandfather.' Yahalal left Kobrin 'without yielding to the entreaties of my brother-in-law and the tearful requests of my sister that I should remain with them.'[103]

The appearance of a *maskil* poet and writer in the closely knit family circle of a hasidic Rebbe was a sign of the times, and Yahalal's literary activity heralds the opening of a new era. R. Noah-Naftali was sadly aware of this historical process and—according to hasidic tradition—expressed his opinion about it in the form of a parable: 'The *Tsaddikim* of today are greater than the first *Tsaddikim*. For it is the way of the world, when the house is shaky and dilapidated, to prop it up with ordinary supports; but if the house is actually about to fall down, it must be strutted with strong supports. . . . So in these days, when the whole world is collapsing, the supports—that is, the *Tsaddikim*, who are sent to prop it up and hold it ... must be ... very great and strong.'

R. Noah-Naftali died in 1889.[104]

After his death a split occurred in Kobrin hasidism. One of R. Noah's sons, R. David-Shelomo, remained as Rebbe in Kobrin. The other, R. Aharon, settled as Rebbe in Doma-chevo (near Brest-Litovsk), where, in the words of an eye-witness, 'he established his authority ... gathering round him distinguished and learned adherents, and ruling his court high-handedly.' He died, according to hasidic tradi-tion, in 1907. At that time there was still a 'Lakhovich *kolel*' in Palestine, supported by the Kobrin *Tsaddikim*.[105] R. David-Shelomo died in 1918.

Those of the Kobrin hasidim who emigrated to the United States sent for the son-in-law of the Rebbe R. David-Shelomo, R. Barukh-Yosef [Zhak], who was living in Palestine, and installed him as their Rebbe. He was the author of several books, such as *Birkath Yosef* (New York 1919) which comprises, inter alia, allegorical commentaries in the hasidic spirit on the weekly Portion of the Law. In hasidic circles he was known as 'the Rebbe of Kobrin.' He had a loyal following of Kobrin hasidim till his death, on the 15th *Sivan*, 1949.

Unlike the Karlin, Koidanov and Slonim dynasties, Kobrin hasidism produced no written work. While it is true that this branch of the movement gained adherents for hasidism in the western part of Lithuania, it is also true that even before its existence there were hasidim in Kobrin,[106] and that its influence in the nearby 'principal community' of Brest-Litovsk was extremely limited. The real glory of Kobrin hasidism was the personality of R. Moshe. In contrast to the *Tsaddikim* of his generation and to the *Rabbanim* of his native land who preached and wrote about the way of life commanded in the *Torah*, R. Moshe endeavoured to live according to the *Torah*. At a time when hasidism had given way to the cult of the *Tsaddik*, he sought to revive the ancient splendour of the movement by returning to the pristine practices of its early days which were directed to the personal spiritual purification. For this he was admired and venerated by two such opposite types as the talmudic scholar and *Rav*, R. Meir Meirim, and the *maskil* poet, Yahalal. The radiance of hasidism, which was fast being dimmed in that period, shone out with renewed splendour in R. Moshe. His descendants owed their leadership to his reflected glory.

D. *Slonim Hasidism*

If R. Moshe of Kobrin was the truly righteous man among the *Tsaddikim* of Lithuanian hasidism, his disciple and friend R. Avraham, the founder of the Slonim dynasty, was their outstanding scholar and kabbalist. Whereas his Master, R. Moshe, sought to put the doctrines of hasidism into practice in daily life, R. Avraham turned back to the study of the written word. With his great learning and intellectual acumen he gave added depth to hasidic thought. It was probably through his influence that Slonim hasidism adopted a positive attitude to the settlement of Jews in Palestine, in practice as well as in theory. While he was still living, several of his descendants and followers went to live in the Holy Land and R. Avraham kept up an active correspondence with them. After his death, his adherents in Tiberias and Jerusalem established *yeshivoth* which are still in existence today.

R. Avraham, the son of R. Yitshak-Matithyahu (Weinberg), was born in 1804.[107] On account of his great talmudic learning—so a hasidic source relates—he was chosen head of a *yeshivah* in Slonim.[108] He was influenced by hasidic doctrine and became one of the outstanding disciples, first of the *Tsaddik* R. Noah of Lakhovich and, after his death (in 1832), of R. Moshe of Kobrin.[109] On the latter's death (1858), many of his followers chose R. Avraham to be their Rebbe in Slonim. This, as already noted, resulted in the weakening of Kobrin hasidism and the strengthening of the movement in the Jewish communities between Kobrin and Baranovich, i.e., in the north-western part of Polesia, although here too the hasidim remained a small minority in the midst of the mithnagdim. After R. Aharon the Second of Karlin, whose influence extended over a wider area, R. Avraham was the most distinguished of the *Tsaddikim* of his generation in Lithuanian hasidism, even though the mithnagdim relate that the well-known *Rav* of Slonim in those days, R. Eisel Harif, dismissed R. Avraham, with his usual contemptuousness, as a person of no account.[110] In or about 1870, R. Avraham's grandson, R. Shemuel, who was to succeed him after his death, visited Palestine, accompanied by his brother, R. Noah, and family who settled permanently in Tiberias. This was the beginning of the special position that Slonim hasidism established for itself in the history of hasidism in Palestine at the end of the 19th century.

The large published collection of letters from R. Avraham to his followers in Tiberias shows how frequently the latter used to appeal to him, especially in time of trouble. In these letters, written both to the whole community and to separate individuals, we find hints of various dissensions between his followers.[111] His letters deal only with spiritual matters, such as the holiness of the Land of Israel, the sanctity of the Sabbath, the importance of unity, and the like, no mention at all being made of the settlers' difficult economic situation and their need for financial assistance—subjects which were so much written about by other *Tsaddikim* before and during his time (*Kolelim*, fund-raising, etc.). In these letters R. Avraham quotes teachings propounded by R. Shelomo of Karlin, R. Mordekhai and R. Noah of Lakhovich, R. Moshe of Kobrin, and also by R. Avraham of Kalisk. He refers to R. Moshe of Kobrin as 'Our Revered Master and Teacher,' the title given by hasidim to their Rebbe.

Of the books written by R. Avraham, the first was *Hesed le-Avraham* (in three parts, Yuzefov 1886), containing comments on the Portion of the Law dealing with the Creation, and kabbalistic views on the tenets of Judaism. R. Avraham knew that this kabbalistic work was intended only for those versed in mystic doctrines, and he therefore expressed the wish, as testified by his grandson and successor R. Shemuel in his foreword to the volume, that in his own lifetime 'only about thirty copies should be published and they should be placed only in the hands of specially qualified readers.' This particular book was first published posthumously. Quite different in content was R. Avraham's second book, *Yesod ha-Avodah* (in two parts, Warsaw 1892), which also contains R. Avraham's letters to his followers in Palestine. This work is written in an easy style, full of parables and illustrations taken particularly from ancient Jewish history, but also from everyday life. The author quotes freely from the Babylonian and Jerusalem *Talmuds,* Maimonides' *More Nebukhim,* the *Zohar,* R. Yitshak Luria, R. Hayyim Vital, Nahmanides, the *Kuzari, Hovath ha-Levavoth, Sefer Mitsvoth Gadol* and *Sefer Mitsvoth Katan* [13th century collections of halakhic rules], and various Jewish commentators. R. Avraham's doctrine is based on the following axioms : the study of the *Torah* for its own sake, the supreme importance of prayer, love and awe of the Creator, humility and faith.[112] He also regards self-mortification and mourning as ways to repentance : ' Let him conduct himself in the opposite way—mourning and grief in place of delight and joy, neglect of his dress in place of fine raiment, and other signs of suffering which are opposite of the pleasure that he derived from his transgression.'[113] At the same time, however, he advises his followers ' to keep far away from melancholy, for this quality causes a man to fall into the power of the evil impulse '[114] ; and ' a man must always hold on to the quality of joyfulness, for if anyone is melancholy the Divine Presence departs from him.'[115] R. Avraham lays special stress on the importance of ' the righteous man [*Tsaddik*] as the foundation of the world ' (Prov. x, 25). ' For everyone can raise himself up spiritually and attain to repentance by binding himself to a righteous man, since the righteous man is the soul of the generation. . . . It is in the power of the righteous man to raise up the people of his generation by repentance and worship. . . . The *Tsaddik* is like a man's head or heart which ensures that all his organs and sinews function in peaceful harmony, because they are all bound to his heart. . . . So, when the people of any generation are bound to the *Tsaddik,* who is their heart, they live peacefully together, because everyone feels the pain of his fellow, which is not so when (Heaven forbid !) there is no peace between them. This is a sign to them that they have spurned the righteous man of their time and gone far away from their roots, so that they have lost their creative vitality and therefore hate each other. . . . All the influence of the time must come from the *Tsaddik* . . . " the foundation of the world." '[116]

The *Tsaddik* is thus the unifying agent who binds his adherents together into a single close-knit, harmonious society 'free of groundless mutual hatred.' In this work R. Avraham makes no mention at all of the *Tsaddik's* power in material matters, a power in which the hasidim believed so strongly that this belief became the main tenet of contemporary hasidism. Nor, following his custom in his letters, does R. Avraham here quote from the rich collection of hasidic writings or refer to any previous *Tsaddik*. The hasidim explain: 'He followed this principle, so that even the mithnagdim should read his books.' In one place he uses the expression 'I heard from my teacher,' but he does not mention the teacher's name.[117] For all these reasons, the volume *Yesod ha-Avodah* is an unusual hasidic work.[118] In addition to the above two books, the one kabbalistic and the other hasidic, R. Avraham also wrote an allegorical commentary on the *Mekhilta* [a collection of midrashic homilies on Exodus], entitled *Beer Avraham* (Warsaw 1927).[119]

An eye-witness reports that R. Avraham ruled his band of followers with a firm hand and was feared by them.[120] In contrast to the noisy form of prayer favoured by the Karlin hasidim, R. Avraham himself worshipped quietly without any outward signs of religious ecstasy. His followers, however, used to pray with great outward fervour. Once, when asked, 'What is the Lakhovich way of prayer ?' R. Avraham answered: 'The Lakhovich way is that when a man utters a word [before God], it issues from his heel'— that is to say, the prayer penetrates the worshipper's whole body.[121]

R. Avraham died on the 11th *Heshvan,* 1883, and was succeeded by his grandson, R. Shemuel.

One of R. Avraham's disciples was R. Menahem-Nahum,

o

the son of R. Yehudah-Leib Epstein, who was born in 1846
and became an adherent of R. Avraham while living in
Kobrin. After R. Avraham's death, R. Menahem-Nahum was
chosen as Rebbe by a section of the Slonim hasidim. He had
his own prayer-house (*shtiebel*) in Kobrin, which continued
in existence till the Nazi holocaust. In 1895 he left Kobrin
and settled in the city of Byalistok, whence his followers
were called ' the Byalistok hasidim.' He used to pay regular
visits to his followers in Kobrin, Brest-Litovsk and other
towns. He died in 1918.

R. Shemuel (Weinberg) of Slonim was born in 1850. His
father, R. Mikhal-Aharon, was not a Rebbe.[122] R. Shemuel
maintained his grandfather's spiritual legacy both in Slonim
and its environs, and in Palestine. He was a man of great
energy and an active public worker. Realising the growing
extent of the influence of secular movements on the younger
generation of his day, he set to work to strengthen religious
institutions and religious life (he was a member of *Mahazikei
ha-Dath* and other similar associations),[123] and did a great
deal for the Jewish community in Palestine by fund-raising
in the Karlin-Lakhovich-Kobrin tradition. In 1900, one of his
most important followers in Tiberias, R. Moshe Kliers,
together with members of R. Shemuel's own family who
were living in the town, founded the *Or-Torah* [' Light of
the Law '] *yeshivah*, beside the The Tomb of R. Meir *Baal
ha-Nes*, and next to it a soup kitchen for the poor. Here sit
mainly aged Jews, studying *Mishnah* tractates ' for the
ascension of the souls of the departed,' and the like. The
institution is supported by contributions from those who, on
account of its sanctity, come there to pray in time of trouble.

Although the institution is directed and managed by the
descendants and followers of the Rebbe of Slonim, the name
of Slonim does not appear on it. R. Shemuel kept in touch
with his followers in Palestine.[124] The house of prayer of the
Slonim hasidim in Tiberias and its Karlin counterpart were
the only places of worship established by Lithuanian
hasidism in that town. In R. Shemuel's day, Slonim hasidism
produced melodies which became famous even outside
hasidic circles. According to his son, R. Avraham, R. Shemuel
taught his followers this parable : ' The whole matter of this

world is like . . . a man who moves from one dwelling to a better and more beautiful one. But, in the process, he has to cross a road full of mud and dirt, and must put on high boots in order to get through the mud. . . . The soul does not belong at all to this lower world. . . . It has to rise to a higher degree, but must descend to this world and clothe itself in the body, in order to pass through the mud and thereby eventually attain its goal.' He is also reported to have said that the *mitsvah* of dwelling in a booth [on the Feast of *Sukkoth*] was equal to all the other *mitsvoth*, because in no other case did a Jew attain to the degree of entering into the performance of the *mitsvah* with his whole body. But the sanctity of the Sabbath was greater even than that of the *sukkah* [booth]. 'For it is also possible to go out of the *sukkah*, whereas on the Sabbath, wherever a man happens to be, the observance and sanctity of the Sabbath is spread over him.' R. Shemuel left no written work. A volume of teachings attributed to him was recently published by the Slonim hasidim.[125] R. Shemuel died on the 19th *Shevat*, 1916.

After the death of R. Shemuel in Slonim,[126] the majority of the Slonim hasidim chose his son, R. Avraham the Second, as his successor. The hasidim relate that, when this R. Avraham was chosen to the position previously occupied by his great-grandfather, R. Avraham, and his father, R. Shemuel, he described the nature of his task in the following parable : 'Our forefather, Abraham, dug down and found wells of water. After him came Isaac, who also dug down and found new wells of water. But of Jacob it is not said that he dug, but that he took care that the water should not stop flowing and that the wells dug by his fathers should not become blocked. So I too—continued Avraham—have not come to make innovations, but only to preserve the legacy of my fathers.' This description actually applies very well to many of the *Tsaddikim* of Lithuanian hasidism in the 19th century.

After residing for some time in the city of Byalistok, R. Avraham moved to Baranovich. Here, in 1918, he established a *yeshivah* called *Torath Hesed* in which, as in all the *yeshivoth*, the main subjects were *Gemara and Posekim*. Hasidism made itself felt here chiefly on Sabbaths and Festivals. It imbued the *yeshivah* students with a sense of joyfulness and faith, and fostered in them a deeper understanding of allegory and mysticism and a belief in the sanctity of the *Tsaddik*. As in all the other hasidic *yeshivoth*, here too there was opposition to the *Musar* method of teaching which prevailed in many Lithuanian *yeshivoth*. R. Avraham the Second visited his followers in Palestine twice (1929 and 1933)[127] and kept up a regular correspondence with them, as he did with his followers in America, Roumania and other countries.[128] Among his correspondence we even find letters of consolation and encouragement that he wrote to followers of his in the Soviet Union (Minsk).[129] A collection of teachings based on the Portions of the Law for Sabbaths and Festivals, attributed to R. Avraham the Second, were published by the Slonim hasidim in Israel under the title *Beth Avraham* (Jerusalem 1958).[130] This bulky volume consists mainly of restatements of well-known ideas and principles from earlier hasidic writings, with frequent use of acronyms. It also contains sayings of the Lithuanian *Tsaddikim* and their disciples (R. Shalom of Vileyka, R. Yehiel of Mush— the disciples of R. Mordekhai of Lakhovich who have already been mentioned), and of many other *Tsaddikim*. In contrast to the practice of R. Moshe of Kobrin—as related by hasidic tradition—and to *Yesod ha-Avodah* of R. Avraham the First of Slonim, there are here hardly any parables or illustrations from life and history such as might appeal to the simple reader.

R. Avraham the Second died on the 1st *Iyyar*, 1933.

The eldest son of R. Shemuel, R. Yissakhar-Aryeh, officiated as Rebbe in Slonim. He died in this town, in the midst of his followers, in 1928.[131] His son and successor, R. Avraham, emigrated to Palestine in 1935 and settled in Tel Aviv, where he founded a modest institution for the study of the *Torah*, called *Midrash Shemuel* after his grandfather.

We see, then, that before the Nazi holocaust Slonim hasidism had two main centres—the one in Lithuania, and the other in Palestine.

NOTES TO CHAPTER IV

1 Kleinman, *Mazkereth Shem ha-Gedolim*, p. 108.
2 Dr. A. Grynspan, 'R. *Mordekhai mi-Lakhovich*,' *Sefer Zikkaron*, ed. Dr. Y. Rubin, p. 191, Tel-Aviv 1949.
3 *Sefer ha-Vikkuah* by R. Yisrael-Leibel, supr., p. 51.
4 Quoted by Dubnow, *Toledoth ha-Hasiduth*, p. 457.
5 V. supr., p. 57.
6 V. supr., p. 72 ; A. Y. Braver, '*Al ha-Mahloketh bein R. Shneur-Zalman mi-Ladi ve-R. Avraham-Hacohen mi Kalisk*,' *Kiryath Sefer*, Vol. I, p. 237, Jerusalem 1924 ; Heilman, *Beth Rabbi*, Pt. I, pp. 83, 87.
7 *Sefer ha-Vikkuah* by R. Yisrael-Leibel, quoted by Dubnow, *op. cit.*, p. 222.
8 Kleinman, *Mazkereth Shem ha-Gedolim*, p. 102-108 ; Idem, *Or Yesharim*, pp. 3-36, Petrokov 1924.
9 Dubnow, *Yevreyskaya Starina*, Vol. III, p. 267 ; Idem, *Toledoth ha-Hasiduth*, p. 223 ; Klausner, *Vilna bi-Thkufath ha-Gaon*, p. 24ff., 45.
10 Yaari, *Sheluhei Erets Yisrael*, p. 625, Jerusalem 1951 ; Braver, *op. cit.*, p. 237 ; Hilman, *Iggeroth Baal ha-Tanya*, pp. 117, 182.
11 Kleinman, *Mazkereth Shem ha-Gedolim*, p. 102ff ; Idem, *Or Yesharim*, p. 3 ff ; Buber, *Tales of the Hasidim, Later Masters*, p. 153-158, New York 1966 ; Lipson, *Mi-Dor Dor*, passim ; Grynspan, *op. cit.*, pp. 187-193 ; *Iggereth ha-Kodesh, Helek 2 mi-Sefer Likkutei Amarim . . . R. Menahem-Mendel mi-Vitebsk . . . Avraham . . . mi-Kalisk, Hanhagoth ha-Rav ha-Kadosh mi-Lakhovich ve-R. Hayyim-Heikel . . .* p. 48, Lemberg 1911. In all these sources it is difficult to distinguish historical fact from legend.
12 Kleinman, *Mazkereth Shem ha-Gedolim*, p. 104.
13 *Divrei Shalom* by R. Shalom of Koidanov, p. 13, Vilna 1882. Other disciples of R. Mordekhai were: R. Yehiel, the *Av Beth-Din* of the small town of Mush ; R. Shalom, the *Av Beth-Din* of Vileyka, and others. For hasidic traditions about them, and also about his most distinguished disciple, R. Mikhal of Lakhovich, see Kleinman, *Or Yesharim*, pp. 11, 12, 37, 44. The letter from R. Moshe-Leib of Sasov was reproduced, in a somewhat different version, at the end of the book *Tsavvaath ha-Ribash*, p. 61, Jerusalem 1948. R. Feivel (Feivish) and R. Yitshak, his son, are mentioned, s.v., by Valden, *op. cit.*, Warsaw 1880.
14 Kleinman, *Mazkereth Shem ha-Gedolim*, pp. 153-155.
15 *Divrei Shalom* by R. Shalom of Koidanov, p. 25.
16 Y. Halpern, '*Havuroth la-Torah ve-la-Mitsvoth ve-ha-Hasiduth be-Hithpashtuthah*,' *Zion*, 22nd year, p. 205, Jerusalem 1957. Sayings attributed to R. Noah are found in popular and hasidic writings: Kleinman, *Mazkereth Shem ha-Gedolim*, ibid.; Idem, *Or Yesharim*, pp. 36-49. Buber, *op. cit.*, pp. 157-158 ; Lipson, *op. cit.*, passim ; *Divrei Shalom* by R. Shalom of Koidanov, passim ; Grynspan, 'R. *Noah (ha-Zaken) Ben ha-Rav R. Mordekhai mi-Lakhovich*,' *op. cit.*, p. 193 ff.
17 Grynspan, 'R. *Mordekhai Ben R. Moshe-Hayyim*,' *op. cit.*, p. 195. The name of R. Mordekhai the Second's father was actually R. Moshe-Baer; v. Hausman, *op. cit.*, p. 244 ff ; and on R. Moshe-Baer, v. supr., Chap. Two, n. 147.
18 *Divrei Shalom*, pp. 13, 14.
19 Grynspan, *opt. cit.*, *ibid.*
20 Y. M. Tukchinski, '*Lakhovich mi-lifnei 70 Shanah*,' *Sefer Lakhovich*, p. 16 ; also as reported by a descendant of the Lakhovich dynasty.
21 Grynspan, *op. cit.*, p. 198.

[22] Idem, ' Ha-Admur R. Aharele Malovitski,' Sefer Lakhovich, p. 198.

[23] Idem, op. cit., p. 200 ; and as reported by a descendant of the dynasty.

[24] Idem, op. cit., p. 213.

[25] Divrei Shalom, p. 13 ; Kleinman, Mazkereth Shem ha-Gedolim, p. 108.

[26] Divrei Shalom, p. 13.

[27] Op. cit., p. 14.

[28] Tukchinski, op. cit., p. 16.

[29] Divrei Shalom, p. 15 ; Zikhron Tov by R. Yitshak of Neskhizh, published by Y. Landa, p. 72. Petrokov 1892.

[30] In Divrei Shalom, his grandson, R. Shalom, quotes sayings attributed to his grandfather, R. Shelomo-Hayyim ; and his second grandson, R. Yitshak Perlov, prints a ' Testament' and ' Declaration of Faith' (said to have been written by his grandfather) in his book Erez ba-Levanon, p. 52 ff., Vilna 1899.

[31] This liturgical song was subsequently printed, as stated above, in various prayer-books.

[32] Seder Tefillath Yisrael. . . . Or ha-Yashar, Nusakh . . . Rabbi [Shelomo-Hayyim] mi-Koidanov . . . ve-Rabbi [Asher] mi-Stolin. The prayer-book was published by R. Shelomo-Hayyim's grandson, R. Yitshak of Vileyka, as printed at last in Fuerth in the year 1764.' The Koidanov prayer-book went through three editions ' because it sold well' : in 1877, 1903, and 1928. I have here used the last of them (Vilna 1928).

[33] Divrei Shalom, p. 15 ; Levi [Ovchinski], Nahalath Avoth, Pt. I, p. 28, s.v., Benjamin of Lida, Vilna 1894. The Tsaddik, R. Aharon of Koidanov, used to relate that, when his grandfather, R. Shelomo-Hayyim, came for the first time to the Lithuanian city of Novogrudok, the mithnagdim threw stones at his carriage, but eventually they became his devoted adherents. R. Shelomo-Hayyim used to call them ' my precious stones.' Cf. S. E. Stamm, Zekher Tsaddik, p. 10, Vilna 1905.

[34] Divrei Shalom, p. 17. The family name ' Perlov'—like the family name of the Karlin dynasty—is derived from the first name of R. Shelomo-Hayyim's mother, ' Perl.'

[35] Op. cit., p. 16.

[36] Op. cit., pp. 22, 23 ff.

[37] Grossman, Sheerith li-Sheerith, p. 8, a supplement to the volume Shem u-Sheerith, and as reported by a descendant of the Koidanov dynasty. The son of R. Shelomo-Hayyim's daughter, R. Yaakov (Perlov), founded a separate dynasty in the small Polish town of Novominsk, which branched out into Poland, Galicia and the United States. Cf. the volume Shufra de-Yaakov (Jerusalem 1964), published by his grandson, R. Nahum-Mordekhai Perlov, which contains teachings attributed to R. Yaakov of Novominsk and biographical details about him.

[38] Ovchinski, op. cit., p. 21, s.v.: Aharon of Koidanov.

[39] Stamm, Zekher Tsaddik, at the end. Cf. Yaari, Sheluhei Erets Yisrael, p. 823 ff.

[40] Stamm, op. cit.; 'Which I heard with my own ears from . . . our Revered Teacher and Master of Koidanov . . . R. Aharon.' Some of his allegorical comments on the Bible are printed in Erez ba-Levanon, by R. Yitshak Perlov, p. 55-57.

[41] Yosef Schlosberg, ' Hasidim un Misnagdim Amol in Mein Stetel,' in the 4.12.1957 issue of the Yiddish paper Tog-Morgen Jurnal, New York ; Stamm, op. cit., p. 14 ; M. Ivenski, ' Der Koidanover Rebbe, R. Aharele,' Koidanov, Memorial Volume, New York 1955.

42 *Mishmereth Shalom* by R. Shalom of Koidanov, in the introduction, Warsaw 1912.

43 *Divrei Shalom*, pp. 7, 8, and on the title-page ; *Atereth Shalom*, by the same author, p. 68, Warsaw 1895.

44 S. N. Gottlieb, *Oholei Shem*, p. 26.

45 Attached to the volume *Atereth Shalom* is a supplement entitled *Ha-Tsevi Yisrael* which contains letters from his father, R. Barukh-Mordekhai, an exchange of letters with his brother, R. Aharon, and selected teachings of his brother, R. Yisrael-Tsevi-Hirsch, together with a hasidic allegorical commentary by R. Shalom. Hasidic ideas, kabbalistic statements and minutiae of religious observance are all casuistically combined in his commentaries. His booklet *Tikkun Lag ba-Omer*, or *Hillula Rabba ha-Hadash* (mentioned by Gottlieb, *op. cit.*) contains selected passages from the *Zohar*. *Kuntres Dover Shalom* 'the last testament of . . . R. Shalom . . . of the city of Brahin,' New York (no date of printing).

46 V. infr., pp. 195, 220, 222.

47 Grossman, *Shem u-Sheerith*, p. 55 ; also as reported by a descendant of the dynasty.

48 M.B. '*Beth ha-Rav ha-Tsaddik R. Nehemyah Perlov, ha-Admur shel Hasidei Koidanov be-Baranovich,' Baranovich, Sefer Zikkaron*, p. 248 ff, Tel Aviv 1953.

49 Reported by descendants of the dynasty.

50 The sources of the historical information and legends about Kobrin hasidism are as follows : Two letters from R. Moshe of Kobrin found in ms. among 'the holy writings' in the Kobrin 'court'; the *pinkas* of the Kobrin Burial Society (in the present author's possession); *Amaroth Tehoroth, Likkutim . . . mi-Pi . . . R. Moshe mi-Kobrin . . . Maamarim Tehorim mi-Pi . . . R. Noah-Naftali mi-Kobrin*, brought to print by Yaakov-Yehudah Hacohen of Kobrin, Warsaw 1910 ; Kleinman *Or Yesharim* pp. 50-167 ; Idem, *Mazkereth Shem ha-Gedolim*, pp. 189-198 ; *Sefer Kobrin*, ed., B. Schwartz and Y. H. Biletski, pp. 20 ff, 211 ff., Tel Aviv 1951 ; Buber, *Tales of the Hasidim, later Masters*, pp. 159-173 ; Lipson, *Mi-Dor Dor*, Vols. I-III, passim ; Yahalal [Yehudah-Leib Levin] *Zikkaron ba-Sefer*, p. 5 ff, Zhitomir 1910.

51 Kleinman, *Or Yesharim*, p. 155. The author of this work, which is to be regarded as in part apocryphal, was close to the Kobrin 'court,' since he was one of R. Avraham of Slonim's followers.

52 Kleinman, *Or Yesharim*, p. 136.

53 Idem, *op. cit.*, p. 45.

54 *Op. cit.*, p. 46, n. 18.

55 *Amaroth Tehoroth, mi-Pi R. Moshe mi-Kobrin*, pp. 51, 52.

56 Kleinman, *Or Yesharim*, pp. 63, 64, 152 ; Drohichin, ed. D. B. Varshavski, p. 168, Chicago 1958.

57 Meirson, '*Ha-Shosheleth ha-Kobrinaith*,' in *Sefer Kobrin*, p. 221 ; Kleinman, *Or Yesharim*, introduction, note.

58 *Amaroth Tehoroth*, pp. 43, 48, 49.

59 Kleinman, *Or Yesharim*, p. 142.

60 Idem, *op. cit.*, p. 143.

61 *Amaroth Tehoroth*, p. 33.

62 Kleinman, *Or Yesharim*, p. 144.

63 Idem, *op. cit.*, p. 56, n. 19.

[64] *Op cit.*, p. 56, n. 18.

[65] Meirson, *op. cit. Sefer Kobrin*, p. 222.

[66] *Amaroth Tehoroth*, p. 49.

[67] Kleinman, *op. cit.*, p. 56, n. 18.

[68] Idem, *op. cit.*, p. 139.

[69] *Op. cit.*, p. 164; *Amaroth Tehoroth*, p. 34.

[70] Kleinman, *op. cit.*, p. 50, n. 1.

[71] *Op. cit.*, p. 142.

[72] *Op. cit.*, p. 52, n. 8.

[73] *Amaroth Tehoroth*, p. 25. Similar remarks are also attributed to R. Asher the First of Stolin (*Beth Aharon*, p. 285, Selections) and R. Uri of Strelisk (*Imrei Kadosh ha-Shalem*, p. 48). Cf. supr., p. 77.

[74] *Amaroth Tehoroth*, p. 40.

[75] *Op. cit.*, p. 49.

[76] Kleinman, *op. cit.*, pp. 144, 164; *Amaroth Tehoroth*, p. 48.

[77] Kleinman, p. 57, n. 21.

[78] *Ibid.*

[79] *Amaroth Tehoroth*, p. 51.

[80] Kleinman, *op. cit.*, p. 57, n. 22.

[81] *Amaroth Tehoroth*, p. 49.

[82] H. Chemerinski, *Ayarathi Motele*, pp. 67, 68.

[83] A ms. copy of the letters is in the National Library in Jerusalem (No. 1069-4°). W. Z. Rabinowitsch, 'Mikhtevei Bakkashah,' *Zion*, 33rd year, p. 180-189. Jerusalem 1968.

[84] S. M. Rabinowitsch, '*Al Pinsk, Karlin ve-Yoshveihen*,' *op. cit.*, p. 9.

[85] Barukh Epstein, *Makor Barukh*, p. 1185, Vilna 1928. The author of this volume of memoirs, a native of Pinsk who is best known for his book *Torah Temimah* (1st ed., Vilna 1902), calls R. Mordekhai Zakheim 'the most famous intellectual genius of his time' and recounts his outstanding virtues; *ibid.*, pp. 1185, 1186, n. 1.

[86] Heikel Lunski, '*Dos Yiddishe Slonim in Biographies*,' in the newspaper *Slonimer Wort*, p. 272, Slonim 1935.
R. Shemuel Tosefaah devoted himself to the interpretation of the *Tosefta* and is best known for his work *Tanna Tosefaah*. He was called by this name by the talmudic scholars, and used to sign' himself '*Tosefaah*' on his approvals of books and on his letters, such as the one under discussion here, and the like. His *Tanna Tosefaah* contains a commentary on the *Tosefta* to the mishnaic 'Orders' Nashim (Vilna 1837), *Zeraim and Moed* (Vilna 1841), *Kodashim* (Warsaw 1849), and was appended to all the parts of the *Tosefta* included in the '*Vilna Talmud*' (such as the edition of 1866 and those of other years) and to the *Tosefta* attached to the edition of *halakhoth* by *Rav* Alfasi (Vilna 1861 and subsequent years).— Rabbis used to appeal to R. Shemuel-Avigdor Tosefaah as an authority on *halakhah*. His 'responsa' were published by him in his book *Sheeloth Shemuel* (no date or place of publication). Another work of his, *Sheerith ha-Peleitah* (Warsaw 1887), contains exegetical comments on the Five Books of Moses, and similar material. He also published comments from a ms. of the *Gaon*, R. Eliyahu of Vilna, which were appended to most parts of his own commentary on the *Tosefta*.
R. Shemuel-Avigdor's *ohel* [structure over the grave] stands in the Karlin cemetery beside the graves of the Karlin Rabbanim who preceded him : The *Av Beth-Din*, R. Yitshak, the son of R. Aharon Minkovski, the

author of *Keren Orah* (Vilna 1852, and many other eds.) ; and his brother, also the *Av Beth-Din* R. Yaakov Barukhin, the author of *Mishkenoth Yaakov* (Vilna 1837, Jerusalem 1960) and *Kehillath Yaakov* (Vilna 1847). Also buried in this Karlin cemetery are the *Tsaddikim*, R. Aharon the Great of Karlin and his son, R. Asher the First of Stolin : S. M. Rabinowitsch, *op. cit.*, p. 15 ; H. Lunski, *op. cit., ibid.*

87 V. supr., p. 44.

88 V. supr., p. 57.

89 V. supr., p. 58.

90 V. supr., Chap. Two, n. 122.

91 V. supr., p. 41.

92 Lipson, *Mi-Dor Dor*, Vol. I, p. 56. *Toyzend Yor Pinsk*, ed. Hofman, p. 268.

93 K. Lichtenstein, '*Toledoth ha-Yishuv ha-Yehudi bi-Slonim*,' offprint from *Pinkas Slonim*, Vol. I, p. 61, Tel Aviv 1962 ; Lipson, *op. cit.*, Vol. I, p. 53, No. 134, and Vol. II, p. 32, No. 925, Tel Aviv 1937. A variant of R. Eisel Harif's contemptuously anti-*Tsaddik* interpretation of the proverb ' A lie has no legs,' which is quoted by Lipson, *op. cit.*, Vol. I, p. 52, No. 133, was popularly supposed to be directed particularly at the *Tsaddik* R. Avraham of Slonim : Maimon, *Sarei ha-Meah*, Vol. III, pp. 21, 22, Jerusalem 1961.

94 Maimon, *op. cit.*, Vol. V, pp. 211, 212 ; Lipson, *op. cit.*, Vol. I, p. 54, Nos. 136, 137 ; p. 55, Nos. 138, 139 ; Vol. II, p. 32, No. 972, and Vol. III, p. 106, No. 2052.

95 Lipson, *op. cit.*, Vol. I, p. 47, No. 120 ; p. 48, Nos. 121, 122 ; Vol. II, p. 30, No. 918 ; Maimon, *op. cit.*, Vol. II, pp. 156-158 ; Vol. III, pp. 22-24, 172.

96 Lipson, *op. cit.*, Vol. I, p. 56, No. 144.

97 Kleinman, *op. cit.*, p. 55, n. 17.

98 *Amaroth Tehoroth*, p. 34. R. Moshe of Kobrin's grandson, Y. L. Levin (Yahala, v. infr., p. 185), writes that R. Moshe died on the day after Passover (*Zikkaron ba-Sefer*, p. 7). However, we should accept the traditional hasidic date of the death—the 29th *Nisan*—since the hasidim make a practice of observing the anniversary of their ' Rebbe's ' death as *Yoma hillula* [' solemn day ']. Y. Levinstein (*Dor va-Dor ve-Dorshav*, p. 97) also gives the 29th *Nisan* as the date.

99 Kleinman, *op. cit.*, pp. 59-62, gives precise details about all of R. Moshe's disciples.

100 M. Tsinovets, ' *Le-Toledoth ha-Rabbanuth be-Kobrin*,' *Sefer Kobrin*, pp. 29, 30.

101 Idem, *op. cit.*, p. 35 ; *Encyclopaedia Judaica*, Vol. X, s. voc.; *Masekheth Avoth im . . . Peirusheihen . . . Nikbetsu . . . al-Yedei . . .R. Noah-Hayyim . . . mi-Kobrin*, Warsaw 1878.

102 *Maamarim Tehorim* by R. Naftali of Kobrin, a supplement to *Amaroth Tehoroth*, p. 74, published by Y. Y. Hacohen, Warsaw 1910.

103 Yahalal, *Zikkaron ba-Sefer*, p. 5 ff.

104 *Maamarim Tehorim*, p. 72 ; Kleinman, *Or Yesharim*, p. 60, n. 27.

105 Meirson, ' *Ha-Shosheleth ha-Kobrinaith*,' *op. cit.*, p. 222 ; Grossman, *Shem u-Sheerith*, p. 82.

106 V. infr., Chap. Five: The Libeshei Dynasty.

107 Kleinman, *op. cit.*, p. 230 ; *Hesed le-Avraham* by R. Avraham of Slonim, Yuzefov, 1886.

[108] Kleinman, *op. cit.*, p. 167, n. 1.

[109] Idem, *op. cit.*, p. 167.

[110] Lipson, *op. cit.*, Vol. I, p. 53, No. 134 ; Vol. II, p. 32, No. 925

[111] *Yesod ha-Avodah* by R. Avraham of Slonim, Pt. II, pp. 56, 74, 84, Warsaw 1892 ; only on one letter (p. 90) is a date given—1881.

[112] *Op. cit.*, Pt. I, p. 136 ff. Cf., *Kelalei Emunath Hakhamim me-Amdur* . . . R. Avraham. . . . See also: *Kithvei Kodesh* . . . *me-Rabbotheinu* . . . Slonim, p. 2-6, published by Slonim hasidim, Germany 1948.

[113] *Yesod ha-Avodah*, Pt. I, pp. 218, 219.

[114] *Op. cit.*, p. 248 ff.

[115] *Op. cit.*, p. 185.

[116] *Op. cit.*, p. 276.

[117] *Op. cit.*, p. 260.

[118] When the Slonim hasidim were in China, in Shanghai, after fleeing from Russia, they published a new edition of *Yesod ha-Avodah*.

[119] R. Avraham left mss. which have never been published: original comments on passages from the *Mishnah* and on the talmudic commentators, and his own kabbalistic commentary on the Books of Moses, Kleinman, *Or Yesharim*, p. 168, n. 3.

[120] Kleinman, *op. cit.*, p. 168. This is confirmed by the eye-witness account of the poet Yahalal ; cf. supr., p. 186.

[121] Kleinman, *op. cit.*, p. 211.

[122] *Op. cit.* introduction ; Grossman, *Shem u-Sheerith*, p. 74, and as recounted by his descendants ; see *Hamelits* (daily paper), 13th *Adar*, 1885.

[123] Kleinman, *op. cit.* introduction in the note.

[124] *Hamishah Mikhtavim* . . .*mi-R. Shemuel* . . . *Slonim*, p. 7-20.

[125] *Kuntres Beth Avraham*, Vol. III, on the title-page and pp. 21-25, published by the *Beth Avraham Yeshivah, Jerusalem* 1951 ; *Sefer Beth Avraham* by R. Avraham of Slonim, pp. 199, 212, Jerusalem 1958.

[126] In his comprehensive monograph ' *Toledoth ha-Yishuv ha-Yehudi bi-Slonim* ' (offprint from *Pinkas Slonim*, pp. 38 ff., 48, 58 ff., 87, 138 ff., 243, Tel Aviv, 1962), the historian of the Slonim community, K. Lichtenstein, takes the view—on the basis of an oral tradition known to him—that hasidism started in Slonim in the eighties and nineties of the 18th century with an influential group of *Habad* hasidim, whose *shtiebel* continued in existence right down to the Nazi holocaust. In the nineties, with the rise of the hasidic centre in Lakhovich, R. Mordekhai of Lakhovich's influence reached to Slonim, which was not far away. In his time there came into being a group of Lakhovich hasidim in Slonim, side by side with the *Habad* group. On the death of R. Mordekhai's son, the *Tsaddik* R. Noah, the Lakhovich hasidim transferred their allegiance to R. Moshe of Kobrin ; and after his death, R. Avraham the First established the Slonim branch of hasidism.

Lichtenstein's monograph contains important biographical details about the *Tsaddik*, R. Avraham the First of Slonim, and about the whole history of Slonim hasidism.

The complaint of the Minsk community (1796) clearly implies that the hasidim had increased in numbers at that time in the province of Slonim (v. supr., p. 55), but it does not explicitly state to which particular branch of the movement these hasidim belonged. The mithnaged spirit was still very much alive in this Lithuanian town even in the second half of the 19th century. Here, in 1860, was made a ' *Copy of Kerekh Mafteah Mahshavoth*

Kesilim,' a mithnaged tract 'about the sect of the hasidim, by the holy *Geonim*, may their souls rest in bliss,' which contains documents of great historical value from early sources (cf. Dubnow, '*Kithvei Hithnagduth al Kash ha-Hasidim*,' *Devir*, Vol. I, pp. 289 ff., Berlin 1923). The polemical tract *Metsaref ha-Avodah* or *Vikkuha Rabba*, in which a Jew of Slonim is made to appear as a mithnaged in the year 1786, is of more literary than historical value (cf. Dubnow's remarks on the subject in *Toledoth ha-Hasiduth*, pp. 381 ff.).

[127] *Kuntres Beth Avraham*, Tract No. 1, pp. 19-24, Jerusalem 1950, and Tract No. 3, p. 36.

[128] *Sefer Beth Avraham, Maamarei Kodesh . . . Mikhtvei Kodesh . . . me-eth R. Avraham mi-Slonim*, p. 252 ff., Jerusalem 1958.

[129] *Op. cit.*, p. 256 ff.

[130] *Kuntres Beth Avraham*, Tract No. 2, Jerusalem 1951, and Tract No. 3, on the title-page, and p. 25-37; *Sefer Beth Avraham*, by R. Avraham of Slonim; M.B., '*Ha-Rav ha-Tsaddik R. Avraham Weinberg*,' Baranovich, *Sefer Zikkaron*, p. 265 ff., Tel Aviv 1953.

[131] Cf., K. Lichtenstein, *op. cit.*, passim; Grossman, Sheerith li-Sheerith, p. 12.

Chapter V

Other Hasidic Dynasties in Polesia

THE LITHUANIAN HASIDIM were, for the most part, connected with Karlin or with one of its four offshoots. However, there were in Polesia three hasidic dynasties that did not owe allegiance to the Karlin *heder* (or school). These were the dynasties of Liubeshov (popularly called 'Libeshei'), Berezna and Horodok, all of which originated in Volhynia. The first two of these were genealogically related.[1] The founder of the Libeshei dynasty was the son-in-law of R. David Halevi of Stepan, the well-known Volhynia *Tsaddik* and *Maggid* and author of the volume *Hanhagath Adam*, and the disciple and son-in-law of one of the Besht's disciples, R. Yehiel-Mikhal of Zlochov. And the founder of the Berezna dynasty was this same R. David Halevi's son.

A. The Libeshei Dynasty

The founder of the Libeshei dynasty, R. Shemaryahu (Weingarten), was the son of R. Avraham-Abba-Yosef of Soroka (in Bessarabia), a disciple of the Great *Maggid*, R. Baer of Mezerich.[2] At the beginning of the 19th century (according to hasidic tradition, in 1802), R. Shemaryahu was Rebbe in Liubeshov—Libeshei, a small town close to Pinsk, and at the same time officiated as *Rav* in Libeshei and Kobrin.[3] He had adherents in the small towns round about Pinsk (Yanovo, Telekhan, Homsk, Motele and others). His sphere of influence stretched between Pinsk and Kobrin, and even in these two towns themselves there were "Libeshei tables.' In the terms of the official rabbinical appointment which, according to hasidic tradition, R. Shemaryahu obtained from the Jews of Kobrin, the position of *Rav* in Kobrin was vested in him and his sons in perpetuity, and he was also empowered to appoint *dayyanim* [Jewish judges] and ritual slaughterers in the town as he thought fit. Consequently, the *dayyanim* and slaughterers of Kobrin were hasidim, even though most of the Jewish population were mithnagdim. R. Shemaryahu's following was also swelled by some of the mithnagdim from the neighbouring small towns. In this way hasidism spread, to a limited extent, in this part of Polesia.

The appointment of the *Tsaddik* of the Libeshei dynasty as *Rav* of all the neighbouring small towns—the only instance of its kind in Lithuanian hasidism—is confirmed by the writer Hayyim Chemerinski in his memoirs. His eyewitness accounts throw light—albeit from the satirical standpoint of a *maskil*—on the spiritual state of Libeshei hasidism, and on the attitude adopted to it by the hasidim of the Kobrin branch of the Karlin movement. Chemerinski writes as follows:[4] 'The old *Tsaddik* of Libeshei . . . had wide powers, with rabbinical authority over all the surrounding small towns, an authority vested "in him and his seed after him till the coming of the Messiah." Hence, no real *Rav* was appointed in these towns, but only *dayyanim* "in place of *Rabbanim*"; and even today [1917] in some of the small towns around us there are *dayyanim* and religious teachers, etc., but no *Rav*. The first of them to revolt against this state of affairs was Motele, in the time of . . . R. Itsikel [sc. the *Tsaddik* R. Hayyim-Yitshak, who will be mentioned below], and the leader of the revolt was—my father. Father, too, was a hasid, only he was a loyal follower of the *Tsaddik* of Kobrin. . . . The *Tsaddik* R. Itsikel hardly ever uttered any words of teaching. His followers were ignorant commoners from the lowest classes, "the dregs of society." All the carpenters were Libeshei hasidim . . . the tax-collectors and inn-keepers were Libeshei hasidim. . . . The hasidim that remained loyal to other *Tsaddikim*, with my father at their head, waged "a war to the death" against R. Itsikel. . . . I have already said that R. Itsikel hardly ever uttered any words of teaching. This "hardly" is meant to exclude "obscurantist doctrine." On rare occasions, when the spirit moved him, he would deliver some "saying" from his holy mouth, and even that only at the "third meal," as darkness fell. When he was in Motele, he used to stay in the house opposite ours; and when R. Itsikel sat down at sunset to eat the "third meal," father would hasten to say *havdalah*, and then light many candles and suddenly place them in all the windows of our house, so that those sitting in the house opposite were flooded with light and the "saying" was stopped in the middle. In the matter of the appointment of a *Rav* in Motele, specifically a *Rav* and not a *dayyan*, father, as representative of the community, got the better of R. Itsikel.'

R. Shemaryahu died in 1846. Hasidim from the surrounding region used to visit his grave to kindle a memorial light over it.

R. Shemaryahu's successor was his son, R. Yehiel-Mikhal, and after him his second son, R. Avraham-Abba, who was *Rav* of the nearby small town of Yanovo (between Pinsk and Kobrin) and in Libeshei.[5] At this time, after the death of R. Shemaryahu, the influence of the Libeshei dynasty in Kobrin itself passed, as a result of dissension, to the Kobrin 'court' (R. Moshe of Kobrin, R. Meir Meirim).[6] After the death of R. Avraham-Abba in Pinsk (1861), the position of Rebbe was held first by his son, R. Hayyim-Yitshak (from 1861 to 1879), and then by his grandson, R. Yaakov-Leib (from 1879 to 1922). According to information from hasidic sources, the Libeshei hasidim in those days numbered up to two thousand. The fact that his son-in-law, R. Eliezer-Lippa Klepfisch, was *Rav* in Libeshei[7] shows the extent of R. Yaakov-Leib's influence over the whole Jewish population. At the same time (1886), another son of R. Hayyim-Yitshak's, R. Abba, took up residence as Rebbe of the small town of Yanovo. The small area of Libeshei hasidim was thus split between two factions, with consequent dissensions and conflicts. Of these, and of the general social situation in that time and region, we can read in the satirical description written in 1886 by a native of Yanovo, Yisrael Levin.[8] He writes: 'Our small town has long been known as the "capital city" of the *Tsaddik* of the hasidim that are named after it, and it prides itself on his honoured presence. But till now our town has borne this honourable name only for the holy dead, whereas the living righteous left it several years ago and transferred their residence to Liubeshov, the town near to it; and already in the time of the grandfather of the R. Leibele, who is living today, its glory had declined.

But now the ancient splendour of our city has been restored, for it is now half a year since the Lord raised up an adversary to R. Leibele from his own house, his younger brother, who broke away from him and established his own independent kingdom, choosing our town as his residence, and thereby bringing blessing to our home; but not the blessings of heaven above, since poverty, which has also chosen our town as its dwelling, is just as prevalent now as it ever was and even increased in intensity throughout the past winter; rather, the blessings of the deep that couches beneath, for Satan has started his devil's dance in our midst and even the poor inhabitants of our town, who have not enough food to keep themselves alive, now dance with all their might and are divided into rival bands, the one under the standards of the mithnaged Rabbanim (for the mithnagdim, who number more than a hundred souls, have two Rabbanim . . .), and the other under the standards of the two Rebbes. Naturally, each of these factions harasses the other as much as it can, and we have no lack of quarrels and disputes; and the hasidim, who are men of action, even come to blows and great is the uproar amongst them, with son rising up against father, brother against brother, and wife against husband. If a man remains loyal to his old Rebbe, his wife says: "No, I want to follow his younger brother, R. Abbele [sc. the Rebbe, R. Abba of Yanovo]; he will be my Rebbe and from his lips I will receive blessings all my life."

In this wise did the mithnagdim and hasidim, men and women, spend the past winter all singing praises in their homes till the time of the Feast of Passover arrived, the time when a Jew cleans out his house and finds something to do. And the Lord blessed our poor with everything—with *matsoth* [rounds of unleavened bread] and *maror* [bitter herbs], meat and wine, and they were all happy and glad at heart. Then it was that they found the time that they needed for their desire, and they devoted it to a day of " slaughter." As soon as it came to the ears of the Leibele hasidim [the followers of the Rebbe, R. Yaakov-Leib in Libeshei] that the young Rebbe had made a mistake in the order of the *haggadah* and had eaten the unleavened bread and bitter herbs together, without saying aloud " in memory of the temple, after the manner of Hillel, etc.," they were all filled with joy and became drunk with victory, and they spoke mockingly of R. Abbele and his followers and called him a psuedo-Rebbe who was not fit to wear the Rebbe's crown or the glorious *streimel* [hasidic fur hat]. But their joy lasted only for a moment, for the rumour speedily spread abroad that the same terrible thing had happened to their own Rebbe, too, that he, too, had made a mistake in the order of the service on the second *Seder*-Night, forgetting to divide the round of unleavened bread into two, so that when he later came to the distribution of the *afikoman* he did not find anything, and all the hasidim were abashed.

One of Leibele's followers, S.K., was filled with such zeal for the honour of his Rebbe that he spoke offensively about R. Abbele in the presence of the town governor; and when R. Abbele's followers heard this, they fell upon him at a prayer-meeting intending to kill him. When S.K. saw that the crowd of his enemies who had set themselves around him were determined to kill him, he remembered a *halakah* that he had learnt at school, " For the *Torah* is my protector and deliverer," and he snatched up the Scroll of the Law from the table and thereby succeeded in saving himself from the blows prepared for him by the enraged crowd, for they did not dare to come close to him. But the following day, too, their wrath had not yet abated, and they fell upon each other with wicked fists and murderous blows; nor did the battle cease until the town clerk was hastily summoned to the *beth midrash* to put an end to these scandalous acts. But he washed his hands of them, saying : " To the devil with you, you vile hasidim ; Today is a holiday for me and I have no time for you ! "

In the end, the *beth midrash* was locked up, to our shame and disgrace.'

According to this source, the Libeshei dynasty was originally founded in the small town Yanovo, and its hasidim were originally named after this town. It was R. Avraham-Abba, the son of the founder of the dynasty, R. Shemaryahu, that transferred his place of residence to Libeshei.

R. Abba died about 1924. His prayer-house in Yanovo was known, till the Nazi holocaust, as 'the prayer-house of R. Abbele' (possibly in memory of his grandfather, R. Avraham-Abba).

Although Libeshei hasidism originated and developed in the centre of Lithuanian Polesia, it was essentially an offshoot of the hasidism of Volhynia, the home of the founders of its dynasty. In character it belonged to the whole hasidic movement of the time, in giving the cult of the *Tsaddik* predominance over all the other principles of hasidic doctrine. The Libeshei *Tsaddikim* left no written works. They were opposed to fasting and stressed the importance of joyfulness, though they did not know how to realise this principle in their lives as Karlin hasidism did. They also had their own hasidic melodies. A characteristic phenomenon of Libeshei hasidism was that its *Tsaddikim* held the office of *Rav* in Lithuanian towns (Kobrin, Yanovo and Libeshei). This is evidence of the good relations prevailing between them and their predominantly mithnaged environment, and also of the authority wielded by the founder of the Libeshei dynasty, R. Shemaryahu. This is further demonstrated by the fact that R. Shemaryahu's son married the daughter of the then famous Pinsk *Rav* R. Hayyim, the son of R. Perets Hacohen, who settled in Palestine and became the leader of the mithnaged community there.[10]

B. *The Berezna Dynasty*

Unlike the Libeshei dynasty which arose in Polesia, the Berezna dynasty came into being in Volhynia—where there were Karlin hasidim—and penetrated into Polesia from there.

P

The founder of the Berezna dynasty, R. Yehiel-Mikhal, known amongst the hasidim as R. Mikhele (Pichenik), was the son of the *Tsaddik* and *Maggid,* R. David Halevi of Stepan in Volhynia. He at first lived at Stolin in the house of his father-in-law, R. Leib.[11] Later, presumably after the death of his father (1809),[12] he took up residence as one of his father's successors, in the small town of Berezna not far from Stepan (between Sarny and Rovno). According to hasidic sources, he settled in Berezna on the invitation and with the support of the local *poritz* [Gentile aristocrat and estate-owner] who hoped, by establishing a hasidic ' court ' in Berezna, to develop the town to his own material benefit.[13] The ties formed by R. Mikhal with the Jews of Stolin during his residence there continued after his departure, and both in Stolin itself and in the surrounding district (Pinsk, Luninyets and other towns) there were ' Berezna houses of prayer,' even though the actual number of Berezna hasidim in these towns was small. It is quite possible that R. Mikhal was helped in making a name for himself in Stolin by the fact that this was the time (after 1810) when R. Asher the First left Stolin and moved to Karlin.

R. Mikhal died in 1848.[14]

His son and sucessor, R. Yitshak, was the leader of the Berezna hasidim till 1865.[15] He gained a reputation as a wonder-worker and his main influence was with the simple masses. Even Christians frequently turned to him for advice or to obtain his blessing.[16]

After R. Yitshak's death, the dynasty split into two. One group, including the Berezna hasidim living in Polesia, recognised R. Yitshak's son, R. Yosef, as their leader ; while the others chose his son-in-law, R. Hayyim (Taubman), who was also the son of the Libeshei Rebbe, R. Yehiel-Mikhal. R. Hayyim founded his own dynasty in Berezna. He died in 1907.

R. Yosef died young in 1870.

His eldest son and successor, R. Avraham-Shemuel, faithfully preserved the heritage of his fathers for forty years, till 1917. He won the esteem of the mithnagdim, and used to pay regular visits to his supporters in the towns of

Polesia (Stolin, Pinsk, Luninyets) in order to maintain his links with them.

Here is an eye-witness description of R. Avraham-Shemuel himself and of the life led by the Berezna hasidim: 'R. Shemuel was a faithful leader and good father to the hasidim of Berezna and the surrounding district, up to Pinsk and Luninyets. . . . He was a short, broad-shouldered man, with fiery eyes, penetrating and wise. He had a long whitish-yellowish beard, and wore a silk or satin caftan and white trousers. All this gave him a dignified appearance. On *Simhath Torah*, the Berezna hasidim flocked to the Rebbe's house where the "court" musicians competed. . . . And on *Hanukkah* nights, hasidim of all classes flocked to his house —merchants and artisans, every one of whom, according to, and even beyond, his means, gave *Hanukkah* money to the Rebbe and enjoyed *Maoz tsur* [the *Hanukkah* hymn] sung in the special Berezna fashion. On Sabbaths they came, towards evening, to the "third meal" to obtain the privilege of a crumb or a piece of ' gefilte ' fish. . . . When the Rebbe began the *havdalah* prayer in a low voice with " Behold God is my salvation," the hasidim listened intently to these words and firmly believed in the God of salvation. . . . Prayers and supplications in the town: the Rebbe is ill ! For whole nights Psalms were read, and on the last night the people of Berezna did not close their eyes. As the reports on the Rebbe's condition came in one after the other, the foreboding grew that he was about to depart this life. Berezna mourned his death for a whole year."[17]

The Berezna dynasty left no book or other written record. Like the Libeshei dynasty, that of Berezna was the product of the Volhynia hasidic movement and resembled it in character, being free of the tendency to talmudic scholarship which was found in other branches of hasidism at the time. Most of the Berezna hasidim were simple people whose unquestioning belief in their Rebbe strengthened their trust in God and gave added joy to their lives.

C. *The Horodok Dynasty*

At the beginning of the 19th century, an independent

hasidic dynasty was established in the small town of David-Horodok, near Pinsk and close to Stolin. The adherents of this dynasty were known in Polesia, and particularly in the neighbourhood of Pinsk, as 'the Horodok hasidim' (not to be confused with the followers of R. Menahem-Mendel of Vitebsk, who were also called by this name). This was the smallest of the offshoots of the hasidic dynasties in Lithuania, its followers being confined to the small area stretching between David-Horodok, Lakhva, Luninyets, Pinsk and Kozhan-Horodok. While the Libeshei hasidim gained a foothold west of Pinsk, between Pinsk and Kobrin, the small Horodok branch established itself to the east, between Pinsk and Lakhva.

The founder of this dynasty was R. Wolf, known to the hasidim as Wolfche (Ginsburg), the son of the *Tsaddik* R. Shemuel Halevi of Koshivka (a small town in Volhynia not far from the well-known hasidic centre of Neskhizh).[18] R. Shemuel was the close friend of a well-known Volhynia *Tsaddik*, R. Mordekhai of Neskhizh.[19] From a letter written by R. Asher the First of Stolin to R. Wolf (between 1802 and 1826) it transpires that there were friendly relations, and also marriage connections between these two *Tsaddikim*.[20]

We do not know exactly how R. Wolf managed to establish an independent dynasty in the heart of 'the Karlin domain.' The only hasidic source that mentions R. Wolf describes him as 'the *Rav* and *Av Beth-Din*.'[21] There was also a popular tradition that R. Wolf was first chosen as *Rav* in David-Horodok and only afterwards, apparently on the strength of his distinguished ancestry, was also appointed Rebbe in the same town. Precise information about his personality, his life, and the date of his death is lacking, but the various popular legends about his death are evidence of the extent of his renown and influence.

His successor as Rebbe was his son, R. David, who, according to popular tradition, was not a person of much consequence. Thus, for example, his name is not mentioned at all in the short family biography of hasidic provenance.[22] In contrast to this, his son, R. Yisrael-Yosef Halevi, was one of the chief figures in this branch of hasidism. He made a name for himself as an erudite talmudic scholar, and kept firm control of his followers. He was feared and respected by the inhabitants of his town, and also by those of the surrounding district. Unlike the Berezna hasidim, who were mostly simple people, R. Yisrael-Yosef's followers included Jews of high social standing, and even some from mithnaged homes. Thus, for example, whenever he visited the Horodok house of prayer in Pinsk, the official (government) Rabbi of Pinsk, the public worker and *maskil*, Beilin,[23] would come to his 'table,' as would other leading local figures. R. Yisrael-Yosef was a personal friend of the well-known Volhynian *Tsaddik*, R. Yitshak of Neskhizh, with whom he was also connected by marriage. His dependence on R. Yitshak is clear from his letters to him (from the years 1856, 1861, 1864). When he writes 'I entreat and beseech . . . that he should not forget us . . . that I may be able to dwell in my house in peace and quiet,'[24] he is apparently referring to the quarrel that arose at that time between his own followers and the Stolin hasidim, who regarded the Horodok hasidim as their inferiors. The form of prayer followed in his place of worship in Horodok, popularly known as 'the Rebbe's house of prayer,' was close to that of Volhynia.

When R. Yisrael-Yosef died in c. 1899, a common structure [*ohel*] was erected over his grave and those of his father and grandfather in the Horodok cemetery.

On the state of Horodok hasidism after the death of R. Yisrael-Yosef, and on the difference between the hasidim of Horodok and those of Karlin-Stolin, we find the following first-hand account in a book of memoirs written by a native of the town:[25] 'David-Horodok had its own dynasty of *Tsaddikim*. The sons and grandsons of the old Rebbe . . ., R. Yisrael-Yosef, still dwell in the town . . . His sons and daughters lived in the street in which stands the *beth midrash* of "the old Rebbe." They lived in poverty, but enjoyed general respect reflected from the cold, distant light of the star that had gone out—their grandfather, "the old Rebbe." It was otherwise in the prayer-house (*shtiebel*) of the Stolin hasidim. Here all was happiness and joy, especially when the Rebbe from Stolin came to the small town. On those days even the mithnagdim used to go to their prayer-house in secret and pressing themselves to the side of the roads, for fear of a blow on the neck or back from some drunken Stolin hasid. Still worse was the plight of the followers of " the old Rebbe " who were downcast and depressed in spirit. David-Horodok was the " capital " of the Rebbe, R. Yisrael-Yosef, just as Stolin was the " capital " of R. Aharon.'

On the difference between the spiritual and social life of Stolin hasidim and Horodok hasidim in this period, another eye-witness, a native of the town of Luninyets, writes as follows: [26] 'The large prayer-house known to the Jews as " Die Alte Shul " was the centre of the Stolin hasidim, while " Die Horodoker Shul" was the centre of the Horodok hasidim. . . . The old *beth midrash* was the first one built in the town, in 1895. Here prayed the *Rav*, the leading members of the Jewish community and the wealthy citizens. This *beth midrash* was a fine, large building, with a well-stocked talmudic library. Most of the Stolin hasidim prayed according to their own special form of prayer and with the fervour characteristic of the Stolin-Karlin hasidim. They were not fond of *hazzanuth* [cantillation], and were not eager to have a prayer-leader that knew Hebrew grammar. Neither did they approve of preachers and sermonisers. . . . The Stolin hasidim prayed at the top of their voices and with great fervour, to the accompaniment of hand-clapping, beating on the bench, stamping or running from place to place and from corner to corner of the *beth midrash*. They were not particular about correct accentuation. What they mainly paid attention to was the *kavvanah* [intensity of the prayer], and some of their prayers truly made a tremendous impression. Whosoever has heard the prayer of the Stolin hasidim . . . especially the " May it be thy will " in the " Counting of the *Omer*," will never forget this passionate supplication . . . as if every single one of them were giving expression to his own character and qualities. The " third meals " that they conducted in the prayer-house after the *minhah* [afternoon prayer] are a chapter in themselves. The singing of the *zemiroth* [liturgical poems] by the unconducted hasidic choir rose to ever greater heights of ecstasy. . . . And how intense was the hasidic rejoicing after the blessing over the wine, when the slight intoxication of the body gave rise to the " exaltation of the spirit " ! Then the hasidim stood up from the tables, formed a ring, and began to dance around the pulpit, their arms linked or their hands on each other's shoulders. Here all distinctions and contrasts disappeared : rich and poor, scholar and simple man, old and young—they all merged into a single mass of dancing Jews. In the pause at the end of every dance, the leader would proclaim: " May it be granted us to celebrate again next year, may we live to see salvation and solace for the Jews, and may our just Messiah come speedily in our days!'

The *beth midrash* of the Horodok hasidim was the second in the town, and was built in 1903. In the old *beth midrash* most of the worshippers were from the " the town's high society "—rich timber merchants ; here most of them were artisans. . . . The founders and builders were simple folk . . . and this *beth midrash* had a popular character. Here the prevailing atmosphere was not one of " family snobbery " . . . but of modesty and simplicity. The Rebbe of the Horodok hasidim also conducted himself with simple modesty. . . . The Horodok hasidim did not have just one Rebbe, but the whole of the Ginsburg family: R. Bobele (R. Wolf), R. Alterke, and later the young Rebbe, R. Velvele, the son of the Rebbe R. Itsikel [R. Yitshak]. Most of the Horodok hasidim were artisans—cobblers, carters, carpenters and the like. . . . Their prayers were not noisy but restrained, the words and tunes well known and moderate. The *gabbaim* [wardens] were simple men. The first *gabbai* . . ., one of the founders of the *beth midrash,* did not even know how to sign his name properly, yet he managed the affairs of the prayer-house to the worshippers' satisfaction and was re-elected *gabbai* every year. The second *gabbai* was . . . a barber and musician by profession. Here, too, " third meals " were held, but in a more modest manner. . . . The Horodok hasidim had their own *zemiroth* and melodies. They, too, danced, but without the ecstatic fervour of the

Stolin hasidim. Here they besought not only the national blessing of "salvation and solace," but also such more personal boons as: "May we soon drink at your daughter's wedding ! " or "May your son be released from military service ! " and the like. If the *gabbaim* were not scholars, the *shamash* [usher] of the prayer-house was an enlightened Jew. . . . For a long time certain prayers used to be sung in the *beth midrash* to his melodies. . . . In the prayer-house of the Horodok hasidim a liberal spirit prevailed. For example, they permitted . . . a secular school to be opened in the adjoining room ; and we were always allowed to hold Zionist meetings here. . . . There was always general rejoicing amongst the Horodok hasidim during the traditional visit to the town [Luninyets] of one of the Horodok *Tsaddikim* (R. Bobele, R. Alterke or the young Rebbe, R. Velvele). The rejoicing went on for a whole week. . . . R. Bobele made a deep impression [on those who knew him] by his remarkable good-heartedness and modesty. He was greatly loved and revered by his followers.'

These reminiscences give us a picture of the relations prevailing between these different branches of hasidism in Lithuania and of the way of life characteristic in those days of each separate branch, as seen through the eyes of 'enlightened' [*maskilim*] contemporaries.

Of R. Yisrael-Yosef's descendants, his grandson, R. Yitshak, (d. 1908) still had a certain influence.

Apart from the letters of R. Yisrael-Yosef, which have already been mentioned, the Horodok *Tsaddikim* left no written records. The dynasty came into being, it would seem, with the choice of the son of a *Tsaddik* as *Rav*, who thus became both *Rav* and Rebbe at the same time. In this respect, the rise of this dynasty was similar to the rise of the Libeshei dynasty. In the small Horodok branch of hasidism, the only outstanding personalities were the *Tsaddikim* R. Wolf and R. Yisrael-Yosef, who somewhat increased the number of hasidim in this corner of Polesia.[27]

¹ Gottlieb, *Oholei Shem*, p. 103 ; Grossman, *Shem u-Sheerith*, pp. 31, 51 ; Tsinovets, '*Le-Toledoth ha-Rabbanuth be-Kobrin*,' *Sefer Kobrin*, pp. 26, 27.—Information provided personally by the last Libeshei Rebbe, R. Yitshak-Aharon, about the dates of the *Tsaddikim* of the dynasty. Gottlieb, the author of *Oholei Shem*, was a native of Pinsk and closely acquainted with the *Tsaddikim* of the dynasty in Polesia. His book is therefore to be regarded as a reliable source of information.

² Grossman, *op. cit.*, p. 51.

³ Gottlieb, *op. cit., ibid.; Jewish Encyclopedia*, Vol. VII, p. 526, s.v.: Kobrin.

⁴ Chemerinski, *Ayarathi Motele*, p. 67 ff., Tel Aviv 1951 ; Cf., Y. Z. Vilenski, '*Zikhronoth*,' *Sefer Kobrin*, p. 283. Even in a very small town in Polesia like Motele we find a 'mixed population'—mithnagdim, Kobrin hasidim (like the father of H. Chemerinski, the writer), Libeshei hasidim and Stolin hasidim (like the maternal grandfather of the first President of Israel, Dr. Chaim Weizmann). H. Weizmann-Lichtenstein, *Be-Tsel Korathenu*, p. 34, Tel Aviv 1948.

⁵ Gottlieb, *op. cit., ibid.*, and statements by the descendants of the dynasty.

⁶ Vilenski, *op. cit., ibid.* The author mistakenly wrote 'R. Asher' for R. Avraham-Abba.'

⁷ Gottlieb, *op. cit., ibid.* Eliezer-Lippa Klepfisch was later a member of the Rabbinate in Brest-Litovsk. *Brisk de-Lita, Entsiklopediyah shel Galuyoth*, ed. A. Steinman, p. 342, Jerusalem 1954.

⁸ Printed in *Hamelits* (daily paper), Year 26, 1886, pp. 544-545; see also: B. Fishko, *Gilgulei Hayyim*, p. 9 ff., Tel Aviv 1948.

⁹ A. Shisha, *Ha-Darom* (journal), Nos. 5-6, p. 178, New York 1958 ; A. L. Frumkin, *Toledoth Hakhmei Yerushalayim*, additions . . . by A. Rivlin, Pt. III, Supplements, p. 57, n., Jerusalem 1929.

¹⁰ A. Yaari, *Sheluhei Erets Yisrael*, pp. 769, 777. Amongst the *kolelim* that existed in Palestine in the last quarter of the 19th century was also a '*Libeshei kolel*' (*Otsar Yisrael*, ed. Y. D. Eisenstein, Vol. IV, p. 286, s.v.: *Halukkah*, London 1935).

¹¹ Grossman, *op. cit.*, pp. 31, 51. According to family tradition, R. Leib was a disciple of R.Shelomo of Karlin.

¹² In Dubnow's 'Hasidic Archives' in the *YIVO Institute* in New York there is a reproduction of the epitaph of R. David, the son of R. Yehudah Halevi of Stepan, who died on the night of the Day of Atonement, 1809.

¹³ A. Pichenik, '*Ha-Shoshaloth ha-Hasidiyoth be-Vohlyn*: Berezna, *Yalkut Vohlyn, Osef Zikhronoth u-Teudoth*, No. 5, Tel Aviv 1946.

¹⁴ Grossman, *Shem u-Sheerith*, p. 31.

¹⁵ Pichenik, *ibid.*

¹⁶ Pichenik, *ibid.*

¹⁷ Dr. D. Beigel, *Ayarathi Berezna*, p. 143, Tel Aviv 1954 ; A. Avatihi, *Ha-Shosheleth ha-Bereznaith*,' *Sefer Stolin*, p. 151 ; Y. Zeevi, '*Lunin-yetser Botei-Midroshim*,' *Yizkor Kehilloth Luninyets-Kozhan-Horodok*, pp. 140, 142, Tel Aviv 1952.

¹⁸ Kleinbaum, *Shema Shelomo*, Pt. II, p. 21.

¹⁹ *Zikhron Tov* by R. Yitshak of Neskhizh, published by Y. Landa, p. 94. R. Shemuel was the founder of an independent hasidic dynasty which was forgotten even in hasidic circles. His successor as Rebbe in Koshivka was his son, R. Mikhal, followed in 1892 by his grandson, R. Shemuel (*Zikhron Tov*, p. 94).

[20] *Beth Aharon*, by R. Aharon of Karlin, p. 294. In this letter 'my son Aharon, long may he live!' is R. Aharon the Second, who was born in 1802. R. Asher the First died in 1826.

[21] *Zikhron Tov*, p. 93. This source implies that R. Wolf died before the month of *Tammuz*, 1859, since his grandson and successor in Horodok, R. Yisrael-Yosef, mentions him in connection with the blessing over the dead, in a letter that he wrote at that date to R. Yitshak of Neskhizh.

[22] *Zikhron Tov, ibid.*

[23] On this person, see *Toysend Jor Pinsk*, pp. 270, 329.

[24] *Zikhron Tov, ibid.*

[25] M. Slutski, '*David-Horodok mit fuftsig Jor zurik*,' *David-Horodok, Sefer Zikkaron*, ed. Y. Edan and others, p. 405 ff, Tel Aviv (no date of publication).

[26] Y. Zeevi, '*Iskei Kahal*,' *Yizkor Kehilloth Luninyets-Kozhan-Horodok*, p. 36 ff., 138 ff.

[27] The reminiscences and legends about the *Tsaddikim* of the Horodok dynasty quoted here have been published in the volume *David-Horodok, Sefer Zikkaron*, pp. 92, 95, 153, 155, 209, 412 ; in an article written by one of the descendants of the dynasty, Ts. Kunde-Ginsburg, '*Zikhronoth*,' *ibid.*, p. 97-99 ; and in the memorial volume *Yizkor Kehilloth Luninyets-Kozhan-Horodok*, pp. 36 ff., 139, 194, 207, 218 ff.

The Horodok dynasty, like its Koshivka origin, was evidently forgotten even by the hasidim themselves, since neither of them is mentioned in the genealogical table of the hasidic dynasties (*Ilana de-Tsaddikaya*, Warsaw 1927).

Chapter VI

The Final Tragedy (1921-1966)

AFTER THE DEATH of R. Yisrael of Stolin (*Rosh Hashanah*, 1921), the Karlin hasidim gathered together in Stolin. R. Yisrael had six sons. After considerable argument[1] it was decided that one of them, R. Moshe, should remain as Rebbe in Stolin ; a second son, R. Avraham-Elimelekh, should take up residence as Rebbe in Karlin ; a third, R. Yohanan, should settle in Lutsk (Volhynia) ; while a fourth, R. Yaakov, received a call from the Karlin hasidim who had emigrated to America. However, the association between hasid and Rebbe was not determined by place of residence, but—and this was characteristic of the hasidic movement—by the personal attachment of the individual hasid to the Rebbe, 'according to the deepest needs of his soul.' Hence, there were Karlin hasidim in Stolin, and Stolin hasidim in Karlin. In this way, Karlin hasidism lost some of its homogeneity and unity. Thus, for example, of the two hasidic houses of prayer in Pinsk, one belonged to the Stolin hasidim (the followers of R. Moshe), and the other to the Karlin hasidim (the followers of R. Elimelekh). The same phenomenon recurred much later —in the thirties of the present century—in Tel Aviv ; while R. Yohanan in Lutsk and R. Yaakov in America used both names—Stolin and Karlin—of themselves. Another son of R. Yisrael's, R. Asher, lived in Stolin. A talented musician, his gifts won the acclaim of musical authorities, and he went to study at the conservatory in Berlin.

A special place among the sons of R. Yisrael was reserved for R. Aharon (R. Aharele). Despite the requests of many of the hasidim, R. Aharon refused to become a Rebbe. A completely unworldly man, he settled in Warsaw (where, too, there were Karlin hasidim) and lived a life of austerity, devoting himself to helping the sick, the poor and the wretched. His selflessness was known and admired not only in hasidic circles. He died a martyr's death in Warsaw during the Nazi holocaust (apparently in 1942). The stories told of his martyrdom have a legendary ring which bears eloquent testimony to the nobility of his spirit and the loftiness and purity of his self-sacrificing saintliness. His character has also been commemorated in verse.[2]

R. Moshe of Stolin, a qualified *Rav* and a man of general education, made a name for himself by his practical energy. He also showed sympathy for the idea of Jewish nationalism. He visited Palestine twice (in 1933 and 1937), and expressed himself in favour of the partition of the country between Jews and Arabs—the question of the moment then—in order to make the free immigration of Jews immediately (1938) possible.[3] He had a way with young people and concerned himself for their education, founding (in 1922) a *yeshivah* in Stolin. This was a new phenomenon in the history of Karlin hasidism. The *yeshivah* was called *Beth Israel* and the main subject taught was *Gemara,* the aim being to achieve a synthesis of Lithuanian talmudic scholarship with the spirit of Karlin hasidism. The *yeshivah* quickly became a centre of religious learning for the whole district, with as many as a hundred pupils. R. Moshe himself bore the burden of running the institution,[4] which continued in existence until the Nazi holocaust.

R. Moshe's last years were tragic indeed. In 1939, when Stolin was occupied by the Russians, the Soviet authorities evicted him from his house.[5] He used to wander like a shadow about the streets of Stolin, beloved of his fellow-Jews whose sufferings he shared, until he was killed three years later, together with all the Jews of Stolin, when the town was destroyed by the Nazis (29th *Elul,* 1942). Of his last days we have the following account by an eye-witness :
' The last time I saw the Rebbe and his family . . . was the day before the great deportation. . . . The ghetto was plunged in dreadful darkness. . . . Everyone felt that the end was approaching. . . . The angel of death hovered over Stolin. . . . We (my husband and I) went to the Rebbe's house. It was after midnight. In the Rebbe's house all was dark. In the hall we found the Rebbe's wife and her

daughter-in-law, Perele, and heart-rending cries rose from the courtyard. . . . We entered the Rebbe's room through an open doorway. There in the darkness we made out the shadows of men sitting at a table, wrapped in *talithoth* [prayer-shawls] and swaying rhythmically to and fro. I could just recognise the Rebbe R. Moishele and his eldest son, Nahum-Shelomo. . . . Now, the Rebbe went up to the prayer-desk and his whispered words reached our ears (my husband caught several expressions and explained to me afterwards that they were part of the *vidduy* [confession of sins]). Suddenly, the Rebbe raised both his arms and called out with great emotion: " Our Father, Our King, have mercy upon us and upon our children ! " He then broke out into bitter sobbing. . . . On the morning of the eve of *Rosh Hashanah*, 1942, when all the Jews of Stolin were collected in the market-place to be sent to the slaughter, peering at the terrible spectacle from our hiding-place through a crack in the wall, we did not see the Rebbe and his family there. . . . When I visited Stolin in 1945, I asked the local Gentiles what had happened to the Rebbe. They, and also the Ukrainian policemen who had been there on that grim day in the market-place, told me that they had not seen the Rebbe among those sent to their death. Some of them reported that, according to one story, the Rebbe and his brother, R. Asherke, and also their brother-in-law, R. Yaakovele, had hidden themselves with their families in the bath-house in the Rebbe's courtyard. Three days after the slaughter, a fire mysteriously broke out there and all of them were burnt alive. The faithful shepherd followed his flock : the beloved and the lovely, in life and in death they were not divided.[6]

Thus was the Stolin centre of Karlin hasidism ravaged and destroyed.

R. Elimelekh's taking up residence in Karlin led to the revival of the hasidic community there, though its influence did not extend beyond the limits of its own narrow circle. On the days of *Rosh Hashanah*, when the *shofar* was being sounded or when R. Elimelekh was being escorted to *tashlikh* [the ceremonial purification from sin], and on

Simhath Torah, when the hasidim used to dance in *hakkafoth* ['circuits'] with the Scrolls of the Law until late into the night, almost till dawn, after spending the whole of the eighth day of *Sukkoth* in song and dance in the Rebbe's *sukkah* [booth] on those days it was still possible to see in Karlin something of past hasidic glories and to hear an echo of former days.[7]

Amongst R. Elimelekh's guests in Karlin on the Jewish Festivals were hasidim from Polesia, Volhynia, Poland and Palestine. R. Elimelekh also took an interest in political and cultural problems connected with Jewish life. Thus, for example, he was well versed in modern literature about hasidism (Buber and similar writers), and treated both the writers and their works with respect. Like R. Moshe in Stolin, R. Elimelekh, too, founded a *yeshivah*—in the neighbouring town of Luninyets (between Pinsk and Stolin) —and raised the necessary funds for its maintenance. In contrast to the heavily philosophical spirit of the *Musar* [morality] movement prevailing in the mithnaged *yeshivah* in Karlin, near to the Rebbe's house, his own *yeshivah* was dominated by the spirit of Karlin hasidism, with its joyous affirmation of life. This contrast brought out the essentially hasidic character of the *yeshivah,* though its primary purpose, like that of its mithnaged counterpart, was the teaching of the *Talmud.* R. Elimelekh won the special esteem of veteran hasidim, and the elders of the Jerusalem community—both in the Old City and in *Meah Shearim*—as well as inhabitants of Tiberias and Safed, were among his followers.

Between 1922 and 1939, R. Elimelekh paid several visits to his followers in Palestine. On one such visit to Jerusalem, he inaugurated there—as commemorated by a special tablet—the Karlin *yeshivah* bearing the name *Beth Aharon ve-Yisrael.* R. Elimelekh kept up a regular and frequent correspondence with his Palestinian followers, for whom his visits to the Holy Land were occasions of festive rejoicing.[8] R. Elimelekh visited Palestine for the last time in the summer of 1939, shortly before the Second World War. Returning to Karlin, he met a martyr's death there in the Nazi holocaust. Here are eye-witness reports of his last years: 'On a grey morning in *Elul*, 1940 [at the time of the Bolshevik occupation of Pinsk], I happened to visit the house of the Rebbe [of Karlin], of blessed memory. The Rebbe was not at home. He had not yet returned from morning prayers in the *beth midrash*. When I entered the house a most distressing picture of poverty met my eyes, wherever I turned. Particularly stark was the total absence of any kind of furniture in the room, apart from a long, narrow, uncovered table which had once been used for the festive hasidic gatherings on Sabbaths and Festivals, especially for the "third meal" and the *melavveh malkah*, when the hasidim used to sit after the meal singing *zemiroth* and other tunes. In the doorway of the kitchen stood a thin woman, clothed in a ragged dress, with a torn kerchief over her head. This was the Rebbe's wife, of blessed memory. Her face was so haggard and sunken that I had difficulty in recognising her. In great pain and distress she told me of "the fresh trouble" that had come upon them : they had been ordered by the Housing Department of the Town Council to take in a non-Jewish tenant, a government official, and to share their kitchen with him. This meant that the Rebbe's family was in fact deprived of the use of the kitchen, since the new tenant, a pure Russian from Greater Russia, naturally paid no heed to matters of *kashruth* . . . and even used to roast a small pig in the oven. Moreover, he was intending to bring the rest of his family to live with them. . . . I left the house greatly depressed. . . . On the intermediate days of *Sukkoth*, 1940, when I was working as the director of the stores of the government consumers' association in the province of Pinsk, some of the Rebbe's followers came to me. . . . After repeated representations, they succeeded in getting the Rebbe registered for work as a night-watchman for the stores. . . . They did this in order to "qualify" the Rebbe as a citizen possessing the full rights of a permanent local employee, and thus ensure that he would not be forced to leave the Pinsk province, like the other "non-productive elements" in Pinsk who were expelled by order of the authorities to remote small towns, a distance of fifty kilometres from the city's boundaries. . . . Presumably, the Rebbe R. Elimelekh did not himself perform the duties of watchman late into the night, but the few of his loyal adherents that remained used to take his place in turn, all through the night till the morning. This went on, to my knowledge, until the 6th November, 1940 . . . and perhaps the Rebbe continued to hold this post for a long time after this.'

'My friend, Mr. Nathan-Note Weiner, of Vladimirets near Visotsk . . . one of the long-standing followers of the Rebbe, also told me that, on the eve of *Purim*, 1941, he visited the Rebbe at his home in Pinsk in connection with some family matters of his own, and found him in a state of great depression and looking very ill and distraught. The Rebbe told him that he had stopped receiving his followers in his usual manner, since every day brought new and even greater exactions, miseries and persecutions upon him, and matters had reached such a pitch that he was afraid even of the members of his own circle. " My life is so bitter, because I do not know who the people dancing around me are "— such were the Rebbe's words, as reported by the above-mentioned Mr. Weiner.'[9]

We do not know any details of how R. Elimelekh lived during the Nazi occupation of Pinsk or of how he met his martyr's death. But we have an eye-witness account of the tragic end of his daughter, Hannele. To save herself from a shameful death at the hands of the Nazis, she took her own life by swallowing poison.[10] The same eye-witness does not remember whether he saw R. Elimelekh in the Pinsk ghetto. The 14th *Heshvan*, 1942, is considered by the hasidim to be the date of R. Elimelekh's death ; whereas the Pinsk-Karlin ghetto was destroyed on the 18th-20th *Heshvan*, 1942.

R. Yaakov, the son of R. Yisrael, was called to the United States in 1923 to become the spiritual leader of his father's followers. He, too, displayed an interest in general Jewish problems. There were in New York originally four *shulkhens* [prayer-houses] of the Stolin hasidim. One of these, which was close to the Rebbe's house and had been purchased by the Stolin hasidim, was called *Beth Aharon*. In Detroit, too, there was a Stolin *shtiebel* [hasidic prayer-house], founded by Stolin hasidim working as mechanics in the city's factories. On the Penitential Days, the Rebbe's followers from various towns used to come to him to pray together with him for a good year. R. Yaakov, for his part, used also to visit his followers in the towns where they lived. His personality provided a rallying point for the faithful adherents of Karlin hasidism. He died in 1946, while visiting his followers in Detroit, and was buried there.

The youngest of R. Yisrael's sons, R. Yohanan, was the spiritual leader or the Karlin hasidim in Volhynia and its environs up to the outbreak of the Second World War. It is related that, when the Nazi forces advanced on the town where he was living, Lutsk, R. Yohanan, together with his wife and two daughters, escaped with the partisan fighters to Russia, where his wife and elder daughter died. After many hardships on the long journey from the Soviet Union through Germany, R. Yohanan and his surviving daughter finally reached Palestine in 1946, thanks to the intercession of his followers, and settled in Haifa. Practically all the Karlin and Stolin hasidim, who had been left leaderless by the deaths of R. Moshe and R. Elimelekh, recognised him as their Rebbe. In addition to the already existing Karlin houses of prayer in Safed, Tiberias and Jerusalem, another one was built in Tel Aviv, and a Karlin *minyan* came into being in Haifa. Next to the Karlin *yeshivah* which had previously been established in Jerusalem, R. Yohanan set up another, smaller *yeshivah* for beginners. On the Penitential Days and on *Simhath Torah*, the Karlin hasidim used to come to their Rebbe in Haifa where it was still possible to hear the traditional Karlin melodies. In 1948, R. Yohanan went to the United States, in response to a call from the Karlin hasidim there, and took up residence in the same house in which his brother, R. Yaakov, had lived previously. He established a *yeshivah* there and sent regular contributions to the *yeshivoth* in Jerusalem. The Karlin hasidim living in America looked to him as their spiritual leader.

R. Yohanan published the *Siddur Beth Aharon ve-Yisrael* (New York, 1952), incorporating the rites and customs of the Karlin dynasty of *Tsaddikim*. Included in this prayer-book are sayings and homilies of the Karlin *Tsaddikim,* taken from the original *Beth Aharon* and arranged according to the order of the prayers. At the end of the book there are ' holy letters ' written by the Karlin *Tsaddikim,* also taken from the original *Beth Aharon.* This *siddur* is intended to make the religious teachings of Karlin hasidism more widely known. It is still used daily by the Karlin hasidim.

For *Rosh Hashanah,* 1955, R. Yohanan paid his third visit to his followers in Israel (his previous visit had been in 1938), and spent the Festivals of the month of *Tishri* with them. Now a *Karlin Yeshivah* is being built in Jerusalem, a large edifice financed by contributions from R. Yohanan's followers in Israel and the United States. R. Yohanan himself went back to America, intending to return to Israel and settle there permanently. But shortly after reaching America, he fell ill and died on the 21st *Kislev,* 1955—the last representative of the Karlin-Stolin dynasty. After his death, the Karlin hasidim brought out the volume *Beth Aharon* ' in a third edition by . . . our Teacher R. Yohanan of blessed and pious memory ' (Brooklyn 1952, as printed in Brody 1875). On the 18th *Adar II,* R. Yohanan's followers brought his body from the United States to Israel and chose Tiberias as his final resting place—the city in which the Karlin hasidim had first settled in the Holy Land, and which had exercised a spiritual influence on the whole Karlin dynasty. When R. Yohanan died, the last remaining Karlin hasidim were left leaderless.[11] The Karlin melodies still sung here and there in Jerusalem and New York by the still surviving Karlin hasidim are the last flickerings of the bright ray of light which, for six generations, illuminated the darkness of the *galuth* for the Karlin hasidim.

The Nazi extermination of the Jewish people in Europe devastated all the branches of Lithuanian hasidism.

The son of R. Noah the Second of Lakhovich,[12] R. Yohanan, died a martyr's death, together with his faithful followers, in the exterminaton of the Jewish community of Lakhovich, in 1942.

After the death of R. Nehemyah, the brother of R. Yosef of Koidanov, who had settled in Baranovich,[13] the Koidanov hasidim were led by his son, R. Shalom-Alter, until the latter's death at Nazi hands in the Vilna ghetto in 1941.[14]

The son of R. David-Shelomo of Kobrin,[15] R. Moshe-Aharon, led the community of the Kobrin hasidim until his death in the holocaust in 1942.

R. Avraham the Second of Slonim[16] was succeeded by his son, R. Shelomo, who also lived in Baranovich. R. Shelomo led his band of followers for ten years. A few of his sayings, written in his father's style, are found appended to the teachings of his ancestors.[17] He, too, was in close touch with his followers in Palestine and wrote them letters of encouragement, as at the time of the Arab riots in 1936. His last letter before the holocaust, which arrived in Palestine on Passover Eve, 1941, deserves to be reproduced in full:

'My dearly beloved friends,

With God's help. Even though there is, of course, nothing for us here to say and the wise man will keep silent . . ., yet those that call upon the Lord will not be silent. Be not silent, and do not let Him be silent, until He make Jerusalem a glory on earth, for it is impossible to describe [the sufferings of Eastern Jewry]. . . .

Perhaps I was wrong to remain here, but what can I do when my children [i.e., followers] are dependent on me? I need say no more. May the Merciful One have mercy and behold the sufferings of His people, who stand before Him and are trampled under foot here [Lithuania and White Russia] and in Poland. May the Lord have mercy on us and on them, and on all His people who are in distress as never before. I send you all good wishes for a *kasher* [ritually pure] and happy Festival.

S(helomo) D(avid) Y(ehoshua).'[18]

He died a martyr's death, together with all his fellow-Jews in Baranovich, on the 6th *Heshvan*, 1943.[19]

In 1955, the Slonim hasidim chose as their Rebbe R. Avraham (the son of the R. Noah mentioned above), who had immigrated to Palestine as a boy and settled in Tiberias. He continues the dynasty as R. Avraham the Third.

In 1942, the year of the destruction of European Jewry, the Slonim hasidim in Jerusalem founded the Slonim *yeshivah—Beth Avraham*—which is considered one of the finest *yeshivoth* in the city. It now has about a hundred students, from settlements in various parts of Israel. Attached to the *yeshivah* there is a large soup kitchen and boarding-house for the students. The syllabus of the institution is like that of the Slonim *yeshivah* of a hundred years ago, in the time of the author of *Hesed le-Avraham* and *Yesod ha-Avodah,* and its teachers and students imbibe the doctrines of the Slonim dynasty of *Tsaddikim* and publish their teachings.[20]

R. Meir-Shalom (Shchedrovitski), the son-in-law and successor of R. Menahem-Mendel in Byalistok,[21] began his public life as a *dayyan* in Byalistok and was the head of his father-in-law's hasidim in this mithnaged city—Byalistok—in western Lithuania. He died in 1939.[22]

R. Yitshak-Aharon, the son and successor of R. Yaakov-Leib in Libeshei,[23] also lived in Pinsk and in Kobrin, where he had followers. In the period between the two World Wars, he several times visited his adherents in America. He died a martyr's death in the extermination of Polesian Jewry.

R. Avraham-Shemuel of Berezna[24] was succeeded by his three sons. The first, R. Yitshak the Second, also held the position of *Rav* in Berezna,[25] and used to visit his followers in Polesia. He died in the autumn of 1939. The second son, R. Nahum, was *Rav* and Rebbe in the small Volhynian town of Dombrovits (between Berezna and Stolin). He was killed by the Nazis in 1942. The third son, R. Yosef, settled in Sarny.[26] The successor of R. Yitshak the Second, R. Aharon, settled in Rovno. He died of cold and hunger while hiding with the partisans in one of the forests of Polesia, and his grave was dug there by his two daughters.

The parallel branch of the Berezna dynasty was headed first by the sons of R. Hayyim, R. Gedalyah and R. Aharon, and, after R. Aharon, by his son, R. Hayyim. R. Gedalyah and R. Hayyim died as martyrs, together with their followers.

One of the grandsons of R. Avraham-Shemuel of Berezna, R. Ben-Zion Rabinovich, emigrated to America and founded a synagogue there named, after his grandfather, *Beth Shemuel.*

Of the latter-day descendants of R. Yisrael-Yosef of Horodok,[27] mention should be made of R. Aharon who lived in nearby Luninyets. He is described as follows by one of the local inhabitants:

'R. Aharele came to Luninyets during the First World War and took up permanent residence. . . . He was not an official *Rav*, but he spent all his days in the neighbourhood prayer-house studying *Torah* with great earnestness. He was supported by the local inhabitants and the Horodok hasidim. He was a handsome man, with a dignified and upright bearing, his long, black beard and elegant dress giving him an aristocratic appearance. His sensitive face had a special charm. When he walked along the street, Christians would look at him and say, "A good-looking Rabbi." However, R. Aharele was not only physically handsome but also spiritually noble, a modest and retiring man who lived in poverty and want, as prescribed by the *Talmud.* In the neighbourhood prayer-house he was the acknowledged spiritual leader. He did not preach or expound, but taught the *Torah* to all and sundry and exercised an uplifting influence over the members of the community. He was killed by the Nazis, together with all the Jewish population of our town [Luninyets].'[28]

R. Aharon's brother, R. Moshe, was the last Rebbe of the Horodok dynasty. R. Moshe studied *Torah* and *Talmud* in the *yeshivoth* of Volozhin and Lida. A gifted preacher, he became a supporter of Zionism and won general esteem. His tragic death at the hands of the Nazis is described by eyewitnesses: 'Three weeks after the mass murder of the men in Horodok, a women's ghetto was created. . . . Amongst the women there were several men disguised in women's clothes, one of them being the Rebbe, R. Moshe, the son of R. Velvele Ginsburg. He was recognised by the Gentile citizens who were examining the faces of the women on the transports, taken off and killed.'[29]

Together with the destruction of the Karlin-Stolin dynasty and all the offshoots of Lithuanian hasidism in the Nazi holocaust went the loss of the Stolin *genizah*, the great store of hasidic historical documents. These archives, which served as a basis of this present study and which have been frequently mentioned in this work, were referred to by the hasidim themselves as ' the holy writings.' They were housed in the cellar of the old Rebbe's residence (the ' court ') in Stolin and comprised the following items: the correspondence of the Karlin *Tsaddikim* and of the *Tsaddikim* of other important dynasties, from every period of the hasidic movement ; regulations governing various associations ; wills ; manuscripts published and unpublished ; a pledge of loyalty (*shetar hithkashruth*) given by R. Yitshak Luria's and R. Hayyim Vital's disciples in 1575 ; old books ; a talmudic compendium of Alfasi, printed in Venice in 1522 ; *Sefer ha-Tsoref* (1,400 pages, 22 x 35)—a manuscript written by the Shabbatean, R. Yehoshua-Heshel Tsoref ; a manuscript of a small volume by R. Hayyim Vital ; a manuscript, said to have been written by R. Yehuda Liva (Maharal) of Prague ; and other writings.

' Accompanied by the granddaughter [of the Rebbe's wife] '—so wrote the late David-Tsevi Bakhlinski in 1930—' I went down to the cellar and took out several files full of various letters. I now discovered that, when I had entered the cellar for the first time the year before, I had seen only the tenth or twentieth part of all the treasure hidden there. I estimate that there are there about a thousand letters and other writings of the leading hasidic figures of all periods.'

Thus were lost important original documents which could have provided valuable source-material for the study of Jewish history.

[1] Y. Benjamini, 'Hilluf Mishmaroth be-Hatsar ha-Rebbe,' Stolin, Sefer Zikkaron, p. 176.

[2] S. Shalom, Dodi Reb Aharale, Shirim, p. 349, Tel Aviv 1949; H. Zeidman, 'R. Aharon Perlov be-Geto Varshah,' Stolin, Sefer Zikkaron, p. 209; Y. Ben-Zakkai, 'Ha-Keter she-Nuppats,' Or Zarua, ed. A. Avatihi and Y. Ben-Zakkai, p. 45; Dr. S. Shazakh, 'Simhath R. Aharele,' in Hatsofeh (daily paper), Tel Aviv, 14.10.1951; Y. Feingold, 'Gilgulo shel Niggun,' in Davar (daily paper), Tel Aviv, 28.12.1945—the writer gives the date of R. Aharon's death : 25.7.1942.

[3] In a private communication.

[4] M. Kopelovich, 'Ha-Yeshivah,' Stolin, Sefer Zikkaron, p. 83.

[5] B. Kempinski-Lieberman, 'Yamav ha-Aharonim shel ha-Rebbe Moshele Perlov,' Stolin, Sefer Zikkaron, p. 226.

[6] Op. cit., ibid.

[7] I have myself witnessed these hasidic celebrations.

[8] M. Bunim, 'Aharon ha-Admorim be-Karlin,' Stolin, Sefer Zikkaron, p. 227; A. Shakh, 'Yeshivath Beth Yisrael,' Yizkor Kehilloth Luninyets-Kozhan-Horodok, edited by Y. Zeevi and others, p. 45, Tel Aviv 1952; Y. Kule, 'A Hasidisher Shabbes in Luninyets,' Yizkor Kehilloth Luninyets-Kozhan-Horodok, p. 152. Cf. n. 11.

[9] Feivel Ginzburg of Pinsk, now of Ramat Gan, in a letter in his own name and that of Nathan-Note Weiner of Vladimirets (Volhynia), also now in Ramat Gan.

[10] A. Dolinko, Kakh Nehervu Kehilloth Pinsk ve-Karlin, pp. 73, 83, 84 stencil, Tel Aviv, (no date of duplication); B. Ben-Porath, 'Ha-Admor mi-Karlin,' in Hatsofeh (daily paper), Tel Aviv, 22.6.1945. Reminiscences and legends about the Tsaddikim of the Karlin-Stolin Dynasty have been published in the above-mentioned memorial volume, Or Zarua.

[11] R. Yohanan of Karlin was survived in the U.S.A. by a grandson, Barukh-Yaakov-Meir, his daughter's child, who was born just a year before R. Yohanan's death. Karlin hasidism once again passed through the same crisis as it had known eighty years previously, when the Tsaddik R. Asher the Second had died leaving no other heir than Ha-Yenuka—'The Child' (v. supr., p. 102). Only this time the situation was even worse; for meanwhile the movement's centre in Stolin had been destroyed and there was now nothing but the Tsaddik's personality to hold together the surviving remnants of the Karlin hasidim who were scattered about in the U.S.A. and Israel. In contrast to the first crisis, when the overwhelming majority of the Karlin hasidim decided to continue their loyal support of the Karlin dynasty, there was this time a split in their ranks. Some of them, particularly the older generation, who felt that they could not live without a Rebbe and did not want to wait until the young heir grew to manhood, installed as their Rebbe, on 15th Av, 1962, the Tsaddik of the Lelov dynasty, R. Moshe-Mordekhai Biedermann. This R. Moshe-Mordekhai, who like his forefathers was close to Karlin hasidism, now received the title of 'Tsaddik of Lelov-Karlin hasidim.'

Below is the text of the declaration made by the hasidim at R. Moshe-Mordekhai's investiture: 'With God's help and on behalf of the Karlin hasidim in the holy city of Jerusalem and all the cities of our Holy Land and the Diaspora, we hereby undertake to regard you as our Master, Teacher and Rebbe—our divinely appointed leader. We trust that you will guide the holy congregation in the way of the holy forefathers of the

Karlin-Stolin dynasty. We pray to Him that dwells on high that we may all be granted to advance, together with our Rebbe, to meet our righteous Messiah.'

However, a large section of the hasidim—consisting mainly of the younger generation but including also some older men—considered that the installation of the Lelov Rebbe meant the end of the Karlin dynasty and its role in history. They strongly opposed the investiture of a 'foreign' *Tsaddik* as their Rebbe and swore allegiance to 'The Child.' Even individual families were rent by this dissension, with the grandfather, for example, joining the supporters of the Lelov *Tsaddik*, while the son and grandson remained .loyal to 'The Child.' The Jerusalem prayer-houses were also divided by the schism. The Lelov-Karlin hasidim prayed in the old prayer-house of the Karlin hasidim. But the building of the large *yeshiva, Beth Aharon ve-Israel*, in Jerusalem, which was the main centre of the Karlin hasidim, became the stronghold of the loyal supporters of 'The Child.' These were joined by the Karlin hasidim in Tel Aviv, the Karlin *minyan* in Haifa, and of course the Karlin hasidim in the U.S.A.

The future of Karlin hasidism—from which the whole of Lithuanian hasidism sprung—will be decided by history. (See the following Hebrew newspapers : *Maariv*, 16.8.1962 ; *Haarets*, 19.8.1962 and 3.2.1964 ; *Heruth*, 18.2.1963 and 1.3.1963 ; *Yedioth Aharonoth*, 14.8.1964.)

In his work *Divrei Aharon* (v. supr., Chap. Two, n. 161), A. Hausman published sixty letters from R. Elimelekh (pp. 125-186), and thirty-two from R. Yohanan (pp. 187-208), which provide first-hand evidence for the opinions of these two Karlin *Tsaddikim*. Most of R. Elimelekh's letters were written to his followers in Jerusalem for the various Festivals. He encourages them 'to be strong in joyfulness and not to pay too much regard to " Frumkeit," . . . for the way of hasidism is to be always joyful and this is the quality that delivers a man from everything evil. Whereas, through excessive " Frumkeit," we may fall (Heaven forbid !) into melancholy, which was greatly abhorred by our holy forefathers. . . . Let us band together . . . in unity and affection, to implant in Jewish hearts love and pious awe, and to pluck out the irreligion that has spread like a plague. . . . Everyone must guard against dissension . . . for you have all bound yourselves to me . . . although by my deeds I am unworthy of this.'

Most of R. Yohanan's letters—nearly all of them dated only by the Portion of the Week—were written while he was in the United States to students of the Karlin *yeshivah* in Jerusalem. Like his brother, R. Elimelekh, he, too, stresses the principles which were characteristic of hasidism as a whole, and particularly of its Karlin branch: '. . . To live in unity and brotherhood, to raise oneself up above the darkness . . . to exalt the *Torah* and hasidism . . . to study constantly . . . and to do everything with enthusiasm, as we have always desired. . . .' Particularly interesting is the pledge of allegiance from the 15th *Shevat*, 1948, entitled *Ahavath ve-Ahduth Haverim* [' Love and Brotherhood of Fellow-Members '], which is signed by twenty Karlin hasidim and proclaims their allegiance to their Rebbe, R. Yohanan, and to each other.

[12] V. supr., p. 162.

[13] V. supr., p. 169.

[14] Dr. M. Dvorzhezki, *Yerushalayim de-Lita ba-Meri u-ba-Shoah*, p. 279. Tel Aviv 1951. The teaching of the *Tsaddikim* of the Koidanov dynasty is presented in a recent publication, *Siah Avoth* (Tel Aviv 1963), an anthology

compiled by R. Mikhael Erlich. To the hasidic teachings, customs and letters in this book (most of which had previously been published in other works) the editor has added 'Sayings' of the latter-day Koidanov *Tsaddikim*. The book contains genealogical details about the Koidanov, dynasty and about the grandson of the *Tsaddik* R. Aharon of Koidanov, the *Tsaddik* R. Hanokh-Dov Silberfarb, now in Tel Aviv, who aspires to make himself the leader of the Koidanov hasidim living in Israel and is in contact with the Koidanov study circle [*kolel*] in America.

[15] V. supr., p. 188.

[16] V. supr., p. 195.

[17] *Beth Avraham (Kuntres)*, Tract 3, pp. 37, 38, Jerusalem 1951.

[18] *Kithvei Kodesh . . . me-Rabbotheinu . . . Slonim*, published by the Slonim hasidim, Germany 1948, on the title page and p. 47.

[19] *Beth Avraham (Kuntres)*, Tract 3, on the title page of the volume ; M.B., '*Ha-Rav R. Shelomo, Aharon Admorei Slonim*,' *Baranovich, Sefer Zikkaron*, p. 267 ff.

[20] The above-mentioned Tracts 1, 2, 3 ; the book *Beth Avraham*, Jerusalem 1958, and the book *Torath Avoth*, Jerusalem 1961.

[21] V. supr., p. 192.

[22] Tsinovets, '*Le-Toledoth ha-Rabbanuth be-Kobrin*,' *Sefer Kobrin*, p. 27 ff.

[23] V. supr., p. 205.

[24] V. supr., p. 209.

[25] Gottlieb, *Oholei Shem*, p. 30.

[26] Pichenik, *op. cit.*,; Dr. G. Beigel, *Ayarathi Berezna*, p. 23 ff. This book contains details about the last representatives of the dynasty ; Y. L. Yonathan, *Nof va-Geza*, p. 10 ff., Tel Aviv 1955.

[27] V. supr., p. 211.

[28] Y.Z., '*R. Aharele Ginsburg*,' *Yizkor Kehilloth Luninyets-Kozhan-Horodok*, p. 86.

[29] *David-Horodok, Sefer Zikkaron*, p. 208 ff.; cf. supr., Chap. Five, n. 27.

A MAP OF LITHUANIAN HASIDISM

MANUSCRIPTS OF THE STOLIN *GENIZAH* AND OF THE 'COURTS' OF LAKHOVICH AND KOBRIN

The asterisk (°) indicates that a copy of the original MS. is in the present author's possession.

°Aharon the Great of Karlin, His postscripts in the Nesvizh *pinkas*.

°*Idem*; Letter to one of his hasidim about principles of hasidism.

Aharon the Second of Karlin, Proclamation on behalf of the Jewish community in the Holy Land.

°*Idem*; Proclamation after buying the prayer-house in Tiberias, which had previously been erected by R. Mendel of Vitebsk.

°*Idem*; Letter to Kozhenits hasidim.

Idem; A short prayer.

Idem; Letter to his family not to fast on *Taanith Esther*.

Idem; Letter to his hasidim about their payment to the 'court' fund.

°*Idem*; Letter to his family about doctors [in the possession of his descendants].

°*Idem*; Letter to his son-in-law R. Avraham-Yaacov [in the possession of his descendants].

Regulations of Mishnah-reading society in the town Yanovo, signed by R. Aharon the Second of Karlin (1930).

Deeds of sale relating to houses bought in R. Aharon's name in Jerusalem and Tiberias.

Letters to R. Aharon the Second of Karlin from the recipients of the *halukkah*, appointing him as the 'chief general administrator' of all the funds sent to the Holy Land and his son, R. Asher the Second of Stolin, as his assistant.

°Asher the First of Karlin, Letter to R. Yosef of Pinsk about the persecution of his followers.

°*Idem*; Proclamation on behalf of the Jewish community in the Holy Land.

°*Idem*; Letter to the *Tsaddik* R. Yisrael of Kozhenits [in original and a copy].

Idem; Letter to the salt merchants of Kremenets (Volhynia), that they should not desecrate the Sabbath.

Idem; Letter to one of his followers explaining the value of the hasidic-style prayers on *Rosh-Hashanah*.

Idem; Various letters to his son R. Aharon the Second about family affairs.

Idem; List of his books.

Idem; His lucky charms and other proved means of warding off illness.

Idem; Receipts for various sums of money sent by R. Asher to the Holy Land.

Idem; *Pinkasim* comprising testamentary and family matters.

°Asher the Second of Stolin, Letter signed by him and sent to his hasidim [in the possession of A. Ben-Ezra].

Avraham of Kalisk, Letter to R. Nahum of Chernobil about contributions of money for the Holy Land.

Avraham-Yehoshua-Heshel of Apta, Letter of New Year greetings to R. Asher the First of Karlin.

Idem; Letter about the ritual slaughterers of Olevsk (1810).

Barukh of Mezhibozh, Letter to a certain R. Yaakov-Shimon about the journey of a family to Rashkov (1810).

David Halevi of Stepan, Letter to the Jews of the town of Rokitno about their behaviour.

*Dov-Baer of Mezerich, Letter to R. Eliezer Halevi and R. Hayyim of Pinsk on behalf of R. Aharon the Great.

Hayyim Vital, Tract in manuscript, attributed to him.

Levi-Yitshak of Berdichev, Decision in the matter of a dispute between two Jews of Petrikov (1780).

Mordekhai of Chernobil, Letter to R. Shemaryahu of Olevsk about the ritual slaughterer's licence.

*Mordekhai of Kremenets, Testament.

*Mordekhai Zakheim, Letter to R. Moshe of Kobrin (1857) [in the possession of the National Library, Jerusalem].

*Moshe of Kobrin, Letter of encouragement to his hasidim during an epidemic.

*Idem; Letter to his hasidim about the principles of hasidism.

*Moshe-Yehudah-Leib of Sasov, Letter to the hasidim (1796).

Noah the First of Lakhovich, Letter to R. Moshe of Kobrin about the funds on behalf of the Jewish community in the Holy Land.

*Noah the Second of Lakhovich, Deed of betrothal [in the possession of his son Z. Bar-Noah].

*Idem; Deed of marriage [in the possession of his son Z. Bar-Noah].

Pinhas of Korets, Letter.

*Pinkas of the Kobrin Burial Society [in the present author's possession, received from M. Meirson, a Kobrin hasid closely associated with the Kobrin Tsaddikim].

*Pledge of loyalty [shetar kithkashruth] given in 1575 in Safed by disciples of R. Yitshak Luria and R. Hayyim Vital.

*Resolutions in the pinkas of the Nesvizh community (1769).

*Shelomo of Karlin, Letter to R. Aharon Segal of Vitebsk.

*Shemuel-Avigdor Tosefaah, Letter to R. Moshe of Kobrin (1857) [in the possession of the National Library, Jerusalem].

Shemuel-Avraham Shapiro of Slavuta, Reply to invitation to R. Aharon the Second of Karlin's wedding.

Yehiel-Mikhal of Zlochov, Letter.

Yehoshua-Heshel Tsoref, Sefer Ha-Tsoref [The Book of the Refiner], in manuscript.

*Op. cit.; page 61.

*Op cit.; Forewords and Postscripts by the copyists of the manuscript.

Yisrael of Kozhenits, Letter to R. Asher the First of Karlin, after the death of the latter's wife.

Yisrael of Ruzhin, friendly letter to R. Aharon the Second of Karlin (1848).

Idem; Letter to R. Aharon the Second of Karlin about the funds collected on behalf of the Jewish community in the Holy Land.

*Yisrael of Stolin, Testament to the family (1921). Copy belonged to a Stolin hasid closely associated with R. Yisrael of Stolin.

*Idem; Testament to his hasidim (1921). Copy belonged to the above-mentioned hasid.

Deeds of sale relating to houses bought in R. Yisrael's name in Jerusalem and Tiberias.

*Yohanan of Lakhovich, Document in Polish, signed by R. Yohanan [in the possession of his brother Z. Bar-Noah].

PLEDGE OF ALLEGIANCE BY THE DISCIPLES OF THE ARI AND R. HAYYIM VITAL (1575)*

'We the undersigned have pledged ourselves to form a single company to worship the Divine Name and study His Law day and night, as we shall be instructed by the perfect and divine Sage, the *Rav* and Teacher, R. Hayyim Vital (may his light shine forth !) and we shall learn with him the true wisdom and be faithful in spirit, concealing all that he shall tell us, and we shall not trouble him by pressing him too much for things that he does not wish to reveal to us, and we shall not reveal to others any secret of all that we shall hear spoken in truth by his mouth, nor of all that he taught us in the past, nor even of what he taught us in the lifetime of our Teacher, the great *Rav* R. Yitshak Luria Ashkenazi (of blessed memory) during all that time ; and even what we heard from the lips of our Teacher, the above-named *Rav* (of blessed memory) we shall not be able to reveal without his permission, since we should not understand these things if he had not explained them to us. This pledge, taken under solemn oath in the Name of the Lord, concerns our Teacher, the above-mentioned *Rav*, R. Hayyim (may his light shine forth !) ; and the duration of this pledge is from today for ten consecutive years. Today is the second day of the week, the 25th *Menahem Av*, 5335 of the creation [1575], here in Tsfath [Safed] (may it be built and established speedily in our days !) ; and all these words are clear and valid.'

*A copy of this Pledge of Allegiance was made in Stolin by the late David-Tsevi Baehlinski in 1937. The signatures were copied by him in ink on tracing paper. He reported that there were altogether about ten signatures, of which he copied only seven (see W. Z. Rabinowitsch, '*Min ha-Genizah ha-Stolinaith*,' *Zion*, Year 5, p. 123 ff., Jerusalem 1940 ; G. Sholem, *Shtar Hithkashruth shel Talmidei Ha-Ari*, *ibid.*, p. 133 ff.).

by R. Yehoshua Heshel Tsoref (born 1633, died 1700 or 1720)
Forewords by the Copyists of the Manuscript

'With God's help, the words of the first copyist. This is the *Sefer Ha-Tsoref* [The Book of the Refiner] which was found in the house of our Master, our Teacher the *Rav* Ribash [R. Yisrael Baal Shem] (of righteous and holy memory), and in which the following was written: This book was composed by the perfect and revered Sage, through whom the spirit of the Lord spoke and His word was on his lips, the Teacher R. Heshel Tsoref from the community of Krakov, who had a different spirit, as it is written: "A pure heart He has created for me," etc.; and from heaven he was vouchsafed various wondrous and awesome mysteries, for all of which(?) he provided authority, *almost every single one of them being based on a small verse in the Torah,* "*Hear, O Israel!*" When you, O reader, see them (God willing) in the original hand of the author and when you look at page 130, he [sc. you] will know from the contents of his manuscript that it is more than human intelligence. Especially as it is explained *how four volumes like these were written about the verse, Hear, O Israel!* Thus far what was written of the author. The father of the author was called R. Yosef, as explained on leaf 400, in the passage beginning with the words "You shall rule," at the end of the passage. There it is explained that the spirit of the Messiah revealed itself in him, as I was told by the talmudic scholar, the Teacher R. Shabbethai of Rashkov (may his memory be blessed!), on the authority of Ribash, in the following words: The year 1648 was the time of grace for the Lord . . . to create the soul of Messiah. And when, on account of our many iniquities, there was an accusation [sc. divine displeasure] against Israel (Heaven deliver us!), the author took upon himself to compose several books through an act of repentance that he then performed. See leaf 31 of the author's work; . . . and possibly page [?] referred to this. This book is the fourth part, as the author wrote in this book several times. The author was a refiner [i.e., goldsmith, Heb. *tsoref*], as he wrote on page 409, see there.

And the Teacher R. Shabbethai told me that the Ribash had intended to make a copy of it. The Ribash therefore gave it to him to copy out, but in the meantime the Ribash was summoned to heaven, and his son, R. Tsevi-Hirsch (of blessed memory) came and took this book from his house, until eventually this book came into the hands of the son of R. Tsevi-Hirsh, the Sage R. Aharon (may his light shine forth!). He agreed with my Teacher, R. Yeshayahu Halevi, who was a *Maggid* in the community of Dinavits [i.e., Dunayevtsy], that a copy should be made of this book, when he saw how this precious work was in danger of being lost as the pages were becoming defaced. Then I, a young man sitting at the feet of the righteous, came forward and was ordered by the Teacher R. Yeshayahu to copy it out. He also sent me written instructions to copy it out letter by letter. After the usual greetings, he informed me that, when he was in the community of Kasnitin, he had seen the *Sefer Ha-Tsoref* in the home of the learned scholar and Teacher R. Aharon, the grandson of the Besht, and had spoken with him about making a copy of that book and publishing it; also that he had mentioned there that I could copy it out; and that they had agreed that I should live in the house of R. Yeshayahu, both on Sabbaths and on weekdays. For the above-mentioned man had undertaken this in his presence gladly and most affectionately. A special room had been set aside for the writing, and if I was willing to go there, so much the better. Such were the contents of the letter written by the Teacher, the *Rav* and *Maggid*, R. Yeshayahu Halevi.

For several years from the time of R. Shabbethai of Rashkov I kept on thinking how I could succeed in carrying out this task of copying it [the book] letter by letter, as I have now done. When I saw the book, I found that it refers from leaf to leaf, so I decided to write it out leaf by leaf. Only, there was too much written on the leaf, so that it was impossible to copy it exactly leaf for leaf, and I therefore chose to transfer all the annotations on the page into the body of the text. Moreover, on every single page I marked off the annotations between two half moons, one like this (at the beginning, and one like this) at the end. And this I found yet another handwriting on the page, I marked it off from the first by a sign like this ((at the beginning, and like this)) at the end, to show that it was another handwriting. Subsequently, I discovered that *this was the handwriting of the author's son,* as is explained on leaf 230a (see there), and this writing was so old that it was almost effaced. But Heaven granted me the privilege to be its copyist, and with the help of the Lord, Whose loving kindness did not desert me or the learned author, I was given the strength and good eyesight to be able to copy it. Praise be to God who by His grace enabled me to see where mortal men cannot see, for the manuscript had been effaced by age. Also, the handwriting was very small, and without God's help it would have been impossible to copy it. But God was with me and helped me. I also make grateful mention of the Sage, R. Aharon, the grandson of the Besht, who lent me the book to take to my home. For when I saw how great the work was and that the task could not be performed in a day, I was obliged by the pressure of the times to take the book home with me, since I could not be away from my home, for without flour there is no study [i.e., a scholar must earn enough to feed himself]. Blessed be He that has helped me thus far to copy it; and may the merits of the author, together with the merits of the *Rav* Ribash and of all the righteous ones who wished to have a copy made of this book, be my support, that I may be of those that worship the Lord with love and awe, according to His will. Such are the words of the first copyist, Yehoshua, the son of the Teacher Aharon of Dinavits, resident in the community of Dinavits.

This book was also in the archives of the holy teacher and man of God, the *Rav* and *Maggid* of Chernobil (of blessed and righteous memory) to whom it was left by his father the *Tsaddik* . . . who had copied it from the text that he found written in the house of the *Tsaddik* R. Yeshayahu Halevi of Dinavits; and after his death it was divided up by lots between three of his sons, since it was bound in three parts, the middle part being as large as both the first and last together. It was agreed between them that, if one of the sons wished to have it [sc. the whole book] copied out for himself, then the other two would give him their parts to be copied. The first to have a copy made was the renowned Teacher R. Aharon (long may he live!) the son of the above-mentionod *Rav*, by the copyist Mordekhai the son of Rivkah of Kovli [Kovel]. Next came his equally saintly brother . . . R. Moshe . . . who had the good fortune to receive by lot the middle part of his late father's library; this Moshe had the first and last parts too copied out for himself, also by the above-named copyist, two being better than one. . . . And now the third holy Sage to rouse himself [to the task] was the sons' kinsman, the *Rav* and Teacher R. Aharon of Karlin, who desired to have a copy of this book made for him, also by the above-named copyist; and since he was their kith and kin, he gladly, with their [sc. the sons'] permission placed this holy book in his library at the disposal of that copyist who lives here in Chernobil. Moreover, since the middle part, as divided up by lot among the brothers (may their righteousness protect us !), contains twice as many pages as the other parts, as can be seen from its thickness, and since it is hard to carry, the copyist divided it into two—the first time in the copy of the renowned Teacher R. Aharon, and again now, making twice altogether. All the parts appear pleasingly equal in size and evoke the admiration of all beholders for the excellent work, since they are all almost the same in shape and size and all together contain the pure teaching of the Lord, for they all form parts of one whole. By the merits of the author, may it speedily be granted us to say " Behold, this is our God ! And may the reader walk in the straight path and comprehend the words aright."

Postscripts by the Copyists

The first copyist declares: Thus far the manuscript of the author, the *Gaon* and Teacher, R. Yehoshua Heshel the son of R. Yosef of Krakov, and I have copied it as I found it and as I have explained at the beginning of the transcript. Therefore this is the end of this copy, which is the second copy, on the fifth day of the week, Portion of the Law *Reeh*, the 28th of the month *Menahem Av*, in this year [5]542 [=1782], by Yehoshua, the son of the Teacher and *Rav* R. Aharon (may his light shine forth !) of Dinavits, resident in the holy community of Dinavits.

And now I, the copyist Mordekhai, the son of Rivkah, offer praise to God Who has granted me to copy this, the fourth and last part of this *Sefer Ha-Tsoref*, and has helped me to complete it. I trust that God will raise me up and again have mercy on me and speedily deliver us ; and that the merit of the author will powerfully protect us, that we may not be found wanting in anything, for this book was divided into four parts on account of its size and thickness. May the merit of the author be with us for ever, that this book may be among the books of the righteous whose names are enshrined in this book ; and we and our children and our children's children will worship the Lord and keep His commandments and laws and cleave to Him, Blessed Be He.

GENEALOGICAL TABLE OF THE OTHER HASIDIC DYNASTIES IN LITHUANIA

LEGEND : | DISCIPLE || SON, GRANDSON ||| SON-IN-LAW

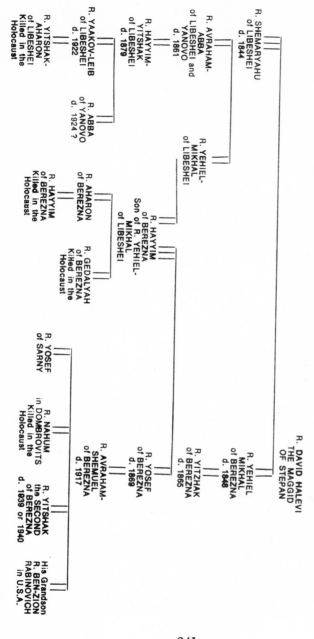

R

R. SHEMUEL HALEVI of KOSHIVKA

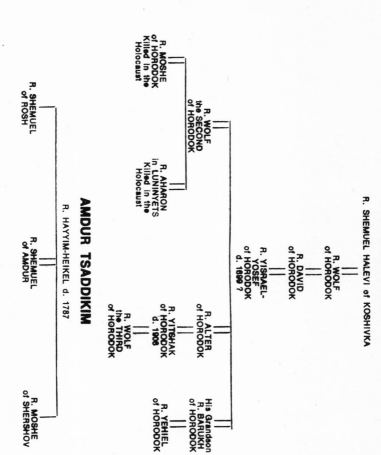

R. WOLF of HORODOK

R. DAVID of HORODOK

R. YISRAEL-YOSEF of HORODOK d. 1899 ?

R. WOLF the SECOND of HORODOK

R. MOSHE of HORODOK Killed in the Holocaust

R. AHARON in LUNINYETS Killed in the Holocaust

R. ALTER of HORODOK

R. YITSHAK of HORODOK d. 1905

R. WOLF the THIRD of HORODOK

His Grandson R. BARUKH of HORODOK

R. YEHIEL of HORODOK

AMDUR TSADDIKIM

R. HAYYIM-HEIKEL d. 1787

R. SHEMUEL of ROSH

R. SHEMUEL of AMDUR

R. MOSHE of SHERSHOV

242

ADMOR: Leader and teacher of the hasidim. See also: Tsaddik, Rebbe.

AFIKOMAN: The piece of *matsah* broken off by the head of the house from the central of the three *matsoth* used in the *Seder* service.

AGGADAH: All that part of talmudic literature which consists of edificatory stories and legends.

AM HA-ARETS: A Jew with no knowledge of Jewish matters contrasted with a talmudic scholar.

ARI: Abbreviation of Ashkenazi R. Yitshak (Luria) of Safed, leading kabbalist and mystic.

AV: Jewish month, corresponding to July-August.

AV BETH-DIN: Head of the rabbinical court of law.

AZHAROTH: Exhortations.

BAAL HA-NES: The Wonder-Worker.

BAAL SHEM: 'Master of the Name'—a man able to perform miracles through the Name of God.

BAAL SHEM TOV: 'Master of the Good Name', the name given to R. Yisrael ben Eliezer, the founder of hasidism; Besht.

BE-HAALOTHKHA: Weekly Portion of the Law, beginning with the words, 'When you set up the lamps' (Num. viii, 1).

BESHT: See Baal Shem Tov.

BETH-DIN: Rabbinical court.

BETH MIDRASH, pl., BATEI MIDRASH: House of worship and study.

CHERVONTSY: A Russian coin.

DAYYAN: Judge of rabbinical court; Jewish judge.

DEVEKUTH: Intensity of devotion.

DIVREI TORAH: Discourse on a topic of (hasidic) doctrine, usually based on a scriptural passage, which the *Tsaddik* would deliver at the communal meal with his hasidim.

DYBBUK: Evil spirit which possesses a living person.

ELUL: The month preceding the New Year and Day of Atonement. It is devoted to self-examination and soul-searching in preparation for the divine judgement. Corresponds to September-October.

ERETS YISRAEL: Palestine, 'The Land of Israel'.

GABBAI: An honorary officer of a synagogue or other communal institution who acts as treasurer; amongst the hasidim, he also assists the Rebbe.

GALUTH: The dispersion of the Jews in exile.

GAON, pl., GEONIM: Honorific title of address for any outstanding talmudic scholar; applied in particular to R. Eliyahu of Vilna.

GEMARA: That part of the *Talmud* which consists of discussions of the *Mishnah*.

GENIZAH: Depository in which Hebrew books and documents were placed for safe-keeping.

GOLAH: The Jewish Diaspora.

GOOD JEW: Designation of the *Tsaddik*.

HABAD: The hasidic movement founded by R. Shneur-Zalman of Ladi.

HAGGADAH or HAGGADAH SHEL PESAH: The book of the Passover *Seder* service.

HAGGAHOTH: Annotations.

HAKKAFOTH: Circuits made in the synagogue with the Scrolls of the Law on *Simhath Torah*.

HALAKHAH, pl., HALAKHOTH: A legal regulation prescribed by the Written and Oral Law.

HALAKHIC: Belonging to *halakhah* (q.v.).
HALUKKAH: Contributions raised from among the Jews of the diaspora and distributed as charity to the Jewish poor of the Holy Land.
HANHAGOTH YESHAROTH: Rules of Right Conduct.
HANUKKAH: The Feast of Lights, commemorating the victory of the Maccabees.
HASKALAH: The 19th century enlightenment movement for the modernisation of Jewish life.
HATSOTH: Midnight lamentation in memory of the destruction of the Temple.
HAVDALAH: Benediction recited at the close of Sabbaths and Festivals.
HAZZAN: Synagogue cantor; reader of prayers.
HAZZANUTH: Cantillation.
HEDER: (Religious) school.
HEETEK KEREKH MAFTEAH MAHSHAVOTH KESILIM: 'A copy of the volume A Key to the Thoughts of Fools.'
HEREM: Religious excommunication; social boycott.
HESHVAN: Month of Jewish year, corresponding to October-November.
HEVRA KADDISHA: Burial society.
HOSHANA RABBAH: The 7th day of *Sukkoth*, on which the willow branches of the *lulav* are stripped of their leaves.
HOVOTH HA-LEVAVOTH: 'The Heart's Duty', a book of Jewish religious philosophy.
ILANA DE-TSADDIKAYA: The Genealogical Tree of the *Tsaddikim*.
IYYAR: Month of the Jewish year, corresponding to April-May.
KABBALAH: Esoteric lore of Jewish mysticism.
KAHAL: A Jewish community and its administration.
KASHER: Ritually clean; permitted as food by the Mosaic Law.
KASHRUTH. Ritual purity; observance of dietary laws.
KAVVANAH: Intensity of mental concentration and emotional devotion in the utterance of a prayer or in the performance of a religious act; the mystical meaning of prayer.
KEHILLAH: Jewish community.
KIDDUSH: Benediction pronounced over wine on Sabbaths and Festivals.
KISLEV: Month of Jewish year, corresponding to November-December.
KITHVEI KODESH: Holy Scriptures (with reference to the Bible); holy writings.
KITTEL: Long white robe, worn on *Rosh-Hashanah* and *Yom Kippur* and on the *Seder* night; also used as cerement.
KOL NIDREI: 'All Vows'—the initial words in the solemn formula of absolution, intoned in the synagogue on the Eve of the Day of Atonement.
KOLEL: Organised division of Jewish community in Palestine for receipt of *halukkah*.
KOROBKA: (Russian) Communal tax on meat and other commodities in the Russian Jewish communities. Cf. *Pinkas Medinath Lita*, ed. Dubnow, p. 340, s.v.: *Kropkee*, Berlin 1925.
KUNTRES, pl., KUNTRESIM: Tract.
LAG BA-OMER: 33rd day of the counting of the *omer* (from the second day of Passover); a day of rejoicing.
LAHMA ANYA: Bread of affliction.
LULAV: Palm branch (Lev. xxiii, 40).
MAARIV: Evening prayer.

MAGGID: Preacher, often itinerant ; hasidic teacher.
MAHASHAVAH: Thought.
MAHAZIKEI HA-DATH.('Upholders of the Faith'.
MAROR: Bitter herbs eaten during the *Seder* service.
MASKIL: Active supporter of *haskalah* movement (q.v.).
MASORAH: Traditional Jewish way of life.
MATSAH: pl., MATSOTH: Unleavened bread eaten at Passover.
MEAH SHEARIM: Quarter of Jerusalem, occupied by ultra-Orthodox Jews.
MEDINAH, MEDINATH: Province, State.
MEKHILTA: Collection of midrashic homilies on Exodus.
MELAMMED, pl., MELAMMEDIM: Teacher of children.
MELAVVEH MALKAH: The meal taken by the hasidim after the departure of the 'Queen Sabbath', accompanied by community singing and often an address by the *Tsaddik*.
METSAREF HA-AVODAH: 'The Purifier of Religious Worship'.
MIDRASH: Allegorical exegesis of Biblical texts.
MIKRA: Bible.
MIKVEH: Ritual bath.
MINHAH: Afternoon prayer.
MINYAN: Prayer quorum of ten adult males.
MISHNAH: The earliest part of the *Talmud*.
MISNAGDIM: See Mithnagdim.
MITHNAGDIM: The opponents of hasidism.
MITHNAGED, pl., MITHNAGEDIM: See Mithnagdim.
MITHNAGGEDIM: See Mithnagdim.
MITSVAH, pl., MITSVOTH: Religious injunction.
MIZRAHI: Zionist organisation of orthodox Jews.
MOREH-TSEDEK: Rabbinical judge.
MUSAR: Moral.
NER TAMID: Perpetual light.
NIGGUN: Melody ; tune. *Ha-Niggun Ha-Kadosh :* The holy tune.
NIGLEH: The written and oral law, as codified in the *Talmud*.
NISAN: Jewish month, corresponding to March-April.
NISTAR: Hidden lore of the *Kabbalah*.
OHEL: Structure over a grave.
OMER: Sheaf taken from the first fruits and offered in the temple (Lev. xxiii, 9-14). See Lag Ba-Omer.
OR TORAH: Light of the *Torah*.
PERUSHIM: Groups of disciples of the *Gaon* R. Eliyahu of Vilna in the Holy Land.
PESAH: Passover, the spring Festival commemorating the Exodus from Egypt.
PIDYON: Redemption money, paid by the hasidim as a gift to their Rebbe.
PINKAS: Communal register ; private notes.
PINKAS VAAD HA-KEHILLOTH HA-RASHIYOTH BI-MDINATH LITA or PINKAS MEDINATH LITA: Register of the principal communities of the Province of Lithuania.
POLOZHENIYE: (Russian) Laws affecting Jews promulgated by the Russian Government.
PORITS: Gentile aristocrat and estate owner.
POSEKIM: Authors of halakhic rulings.

PURIM : Festival commemorating the deliverance of the Jews recorded in Book of Esther.
RABBI : General term for Jewish scholar.
RAV, pl., RABBANIM : Teacher of the Law ; Jewish judge, and spiritual head of the community.
REBBE : A hasidic *Tsaddik* is designated as ' Rebbe ' as distinct from the Rabbi proper or the *Rav*, who discharges the rabbinical functions as spiritual leader of the whole community.
ROSH HA-KAHAL, pl., RASHIM : Head of the community.
ROSH-HASHANAH : New Year Festival.
ROSH HODESH : New Moon.
ROSH YESHIVAH : Head of a talmudic school.
ROZEN, pl., ROZENIM : Communal leader.
SANDEK : Man who holds child on his knees during circumcision rite.
SEDER : The service commemorating the Exodus, conducted in the home on the eve of Passover.
SEFER ZIKKARON : Memorial Volume.
SHABBATH KODESH : Holy Sabbath.
SHAMASH : Caretaker and usher ; Rebbe's servant.
SHAVUOTH : ' Festival of Weeks ', commemorating the Giving of the Law and the ingathering of the first fruits.
SHEELOTH U-TESHUVOTH : ' Questions and Answers ', Responsa.
SHE-HEHEYANU : ' Who has kept us alive ', blessing recited on Jewish Festivals, and on doing anything for the first time.
SHEKHINAH : Divine Presence.
SHEMA : ' Hear O Israel ', the Jewish profession of faith, recited daily in the morning and evening prayers.
SHEVAT : Jewish month, corresponding to January-February.
SHIDDUKH : Negotiatons preliminary to marriage ; a marriage match agreement ; a match.
SHIVAH : The seven days of mourning over a close relative.
SHOFAR : Ram's horn, blown in the synagogue on *Rosh-Hashanah*.
SHOHET : Ritual slaughterer.
SHTIEBEL : Name given to hasidic prayer-house.
SHTREIMEL : Hasidic fur hat.
SHULKHAN ARUKH : Codification of halakhic law.
SHULKHEN : Small prayer-house.
SIDDUR : Prayer-book.
SIMHAH : Rejoicing ; joy ; happy occasion.
SIMHATH TORAH : ' Rejoicing of the Law '—joyous Festival on the day following *Sukkoth*.
SIVAN : Jewish month, corresponding to May-June.
SOTAH : A tractate of the *Talmud*.
SUKKAH : Booth, tabernacle.
SUKKOTH : Festival of Tabernacles, commemorating the wandering in the desert and the fruit harvest.
TAANITH ESTHER : Fast on the day before *Purim*.
TABLE : Festive communal meal of the hasidim at which the *Tsaddik* delivered an address.
TAKKANAH, pl., TAKKANOTH : Measure, enactment.
TALITH, pl., TALITHOTH : Prayer-shawl.
TALMID HAKHAM : Talmudical scholar.

GLOSSARY

TALMUD: *Mishnah* and *Gemara*.
TALMUD TORAH: Communal school.
TAMMUZ: Jewish month, corresponding to June-July.
TANNA, pl., TANNAIM: Scholar of the *Mishnah*.
TANYA: Hasidic philosophical work by R. Shneur-Zalman of Ladi.
TASHLIKH: Ceremonial purification from sin on the New Year.
TEFILLIN: Phylacteries.
TEREFAH: Ritually unclean food.
TEVETH: Jewish month, corresponding to December-January.
'THIRD MEAL': The main Sabbath meal, eaten after the *minhah* prayer and accompanied by hasidic community singing and an address by the *Tsaddik*.
TISHRI: Jewish month, corresponding to September-October.
TORAH: The Mosaic Law; the teachings of Judaism.
TOSAFOTH: Exegetical annotation to the *Talmud*.
TOSEFTA: Teachings closely related to the *Mishnah*.
TSADDIK: Head and teacher of a hasidic community.
TSADDIKISM: Personal cult of the *Tsaddik*.
TSAVVAAH: Will; testament.
TSOREF: Refiner; purifier.
VAAD HA-MEDINAH: Council of the Province.
VAAD KEHILLOTH RASHIYOTH BI-MDINATH LITA: Council of the principal communities of the Province of Lithuania.
VA-YAKHEL: Portion of the Law beginning with the words 'And Moses assembled' (Exod. xxxv, 1).
VIDDUY: Confession of sins.
VIKKUHA RABBA: 'The Great Dispute'.
YAMIM NORAIM: Penitential Days; Days of Awe.
YENUKA: Child chosen by hasidim as their future leader.
YESHIVAH, pl. YESHIVOTH: High school for study of *Talmud*.
YETSER HA-RA: Evil inclination.
YIRA: Religious awe.
YIZKOR: Memorial (Volume).
YOM KIPPUR: Day of Atonement, a day of fasting and repentance.
ZEMIROTH: Liturgical songs.
ZOHAR: 'Book of Splendour', the chief work of *Kabbalah* and of Jewish mysticism.

BIBLIOGRAPHY

In the case of books which have been published several times, the edition referred to in the Bibliography is that used in this work.

Adath Tsaddikim (A Community of Righteous Men) Lemberg 1865.

Aharon mi-Karlin: Beth Aharon (Aaron of Karlin : The House of Aaron) Brody 1875.

Akty Izdavayemyye Vilenskoyu Kommissiyeyu dla Razbora Drevnikh Aktov (Records ed. by the Vilna Commission for the Examination of Ancient Documents) Vol. XXVIII, Vilna 1901, and Vol. XXIX, Vilna 1902.

Alexander-Suesskind mi-Horodno: Tsavvaah (Alexander-Suesskind of Grodno: Testament) Lemberg 1870.

Alexander-Suesskind mi-Horodno: Yesod ve-Shoresh ha-Avodah (The Foundation and Root of Divine Worship) Warsaw 1875.

Avatihi, A.: Ha-Shosheleth ha-Bereznaith (The Berezna Dynasty) Stolin Memorial Volume, ed. by Avatihi, A. and Ben-Zakai, Y., Tel-Aviv 1952.

Avraham mi-Slonimo: Beth Avraham (Abraham of Slonim: The House of Abraham) Jerusalem 1958.

Avraham mi-Slonimo: Hesed le-Avraham (Abraham of Slonim: Graciousness to Abraham) Yuzefov 1886.

Avraham mi-Slonimo: Yesod ha-Avodah (The Basis of Worship) Warsaw 1892.

Avraham mi-Slonimo: Beer Avraham (The Well of Abraham) Warsaw 1927.

Avraham mi-Slonimo: Kithvei Kodesh (Holy Writings) published by the Hasidim of Slonim, Germany 1948.

Beigel, G.: Ayarathi Berezna (My Native Town, Berezna) Tel-Aviv 1954.

Ben-Ezra, A.: Ha-Yenuka mi-Stolin (The Yenuka of Stolin) New York 1951.

Ben-Ezra, A.: Ha-Rav Avraham Eisenstein (Rabbi Abraham Eisenstein) Drohichin Memorial Volume, ed. by D. B. Warshawski, Chicago 1958.

Benjamini, Y.: Hilluf Mishmaroth be-Hatsar ha-Rebbe (The Old Guard and the New in the Court of the Rebbe) Stolin Memorial Volume, Tel-Aviv 1952.

Ben-Porath, B.: Ha-Admur mi-Karlin (The Rebbe of Karlin) Ha-Tsofeh (daily paper), Tel-Aviv 22.6.1945.

Ben-Zakai, Y.: Ha-Kether she-Nuppats (The Crown That Was Dashed in Pieces) Or Zarua, A. Collection of Records and Pieces, ed. by Avatihi, A., and Ben-Zakai, Y., Tel-Aviv 1952.

[Y. Berger]: Eser Tsahtsahoth (Ten Splendours) Petrokov 1910.

Beth Avraham: Kuntres (The House of Abraham, a Tract) Tract No. 1, Jerusalem 1950 ; Tract No. 2, Jerusalem 1951 ; Tract No. 3, Jerusalem 1951.

Bihovski, H. A.: Ginzei Nistaroth (Hidden Treasures) Jerusalem 1924.

[Bodek, M.]: Seder ha-Doroth mi-Talmidei ha-Besht (Order of the Generations of the Besht's Disciples) no place and date of publication.

Braver, A. Y.: Al ha-Mahloketh bein R. Shneur-Zalman mi-Ladi ve-R. Avraham Hacohen mi-Kalisk (On the Dispute Between R. Shneur-Zalman of Ladi and R. Abraham Hacohen of Kalisk) Kiryath Sefer, Vol. I, Jerusalem 1921.

Brisk de-Lita (Brest-Litovsk) Memorial Volume, ed. A. Steinman, Jerusalem 1954.

Buber, M.: Tales of the Hasidim, Early Masters, New York 1966.

Buber, M.: Tales of the Hasidim, Later Masters, New York 1966.

BIBLIOGRAPHY

Bunim, M.: Ahron ha-Admorim be-Karlin (The Last of the Rebbes in Karlin) Stolin Memorial Volume, Tel-Aviv 1952.

Chemerinski, H.: Ayarathi Motele (My Native Town, Motele) Tel-Aviv 1951.

David-Horodok, Sefer Zikkaron (David-Horodok Memorial Volume) ed. Idan, Y. and others, Tel-Aviv, no date of publication.

Dinur, Benzion: Be-Mifneh ha-Doroth (At the Turning-Point of the Generations) Jerusalem 1955.

Dolinko, A.: Kakh Nehervu Kehilloth Pinsk ve-Karlin (How the Pinsk and Karlin Communities Were Destroyed) Tel-Aviv, stencil, no date of duplication.

Dov-Baer of Mezerich: Magid Devarav le-Yaakov (Proclaiming His Words unto Jacob) Lublin 1927.

Drohichin Memorial Volume, ed. D. B. Warshawski, Chicago 1958.

Dubnow, S.: Toledoth ha-Hasiduth (History of Hasidism) Tel-Aviv 1932.

Dubnow, S.: Chassidiana, Supplement to the He-Avar, Vol. II, Petrograd 1918.

Dubnow, S.: Kithvei Hithnagduth al Kath ha-Hasidim (Mithnaged Writings about the Sect of the Hasidim) Devir Vol. I, Berlin 1923.

Dubnow, S.: Vmeshatelstvo Russkovo Pravitelstva v Anti-Hasidskuyu Borbu (The Intervention of the Russian Government in the Struggle against Hasidism) Yevreýskaya Starina, Vol. III St. Petersburg 1910.

Dubnow Archives, in Yiddish Scientific Institute—YIVO, New York, manuscripts.

Dvorzhetski, M.: Yerushalayim de-Lita ba-Meri u-ba-Shoah (Jerusalem of Lithuania in the Revolt and the Holocaust) Tel-Aviv 1951.

Efron, Y.: Mayn Geburt-Stetele Amdur (My Birth-Town, Amdur) Grodner Opklangen, periodical, Vol. 5-6, Buenos Aires 1951.

Efron, Y.: Amdurer Klei-Kodesh (Religious Personages of Amdur) Grodner Opklangen, Buenos Aires 1953.

Ehrlich, M., compiler: Sihath Avoth (Sayings of the Fathers) Tel-Aviv 1963.

Eisen, A.: R. Aharon ha-Gadol (R. Aaron the Great) Ha-Modia, daily paper, Jerusalem 6.10.1954.

Eliezer Halevi: Siah ha-Sadeh (The Bush of the Field) Shklov 1787.

Eliezer Halevi: Reiah ha-Sadeh (The Perfume of the Field) Shklov 1795.

Emden, Yaakov: Sidur 'Beth Yaakov' ('House of Jacob' Prayer-Book) Warsaw 1881.

Encyclopaedia Judaica, Vol. X, s.v.: Lewin, Noach Chajim, Eschkol-Edition, Berlin 1934.

Entsiklopediyah Yisraelith (Encyclopaedia Judaica) Vol. I, Eschkol-Edition, Berlin 1929.

Eshkoli, A. Z.: Ha-Hasiduth be-Polin, Beth Yisrael be-Polin (Hasidism in Poland, The House of Israel in Poland) Pt. II, ed. Halpern, I., Jerusalem 1953.

Feingold, Y.: Gilgulo shel Niggun (The History of a Melody) Davar, daily paper, Tel-Aviv 28.12.1945.

Fishko, B.: Gilgulei Hayyim (Vicissitudes of Life) Tel-Aviv 1948.

Friedenstein, S. E.: Ir Gibborim (The Town of Heroes) Vilna 1880.

Friedkin, A.: A. B. Gottlober un Sayn Epokhe (A. B. Gottlober and His Epoch) Vilna 1925.

Friedman, M.: Amdur, Grodner Opklangen, periodical, Vol. II, Buenos Aires, no date of publication.

Frumkin, A. L.: Toledoth Hakhmei Yerushalayim (The History of the Sages of Jerusalem) additions by A. Rivlin, Jerusalem 1929.

Fuen, S. Y.: Kiryah Neemanah (The Faithful City) Vilna 1860.

Geshuri, M. S.: Niggunei Karlin u-Stolin (Melodies of Karlin and Stolin) Stolin Memorial Volume, ed. Avatihi, A., and Ben-Zakai, Y., Tel-Aviv 1952.

Gordon, Y. L.: Olam ke-Minhago, Sippur Sheni, Ahrith Simhah Tugah (The World as Usual, Second Story, Joy Ends in Sadness) Vilna 1873.

Gordon, Y. L.: Iggeroth (Letters) Vol. I, Warsaw 1895.

Gottlieb, S. N.: Oholei Shem (The Tents of Shem) Pinsk 1912.

Graetz, H.: Geschichte der Juden (History of the Jews) Vol. XI, Leipzig 1890.

Grossman, L.: Shem u-Sherith (A Name and Remnant) Tel-Aviv 1943.

Grossman, L.: Sheerith la-Sheerith, Supplement to Shem u-Sheerith (A Remnant of a Remnant) no place and date of publication.

Gruenspan, A.: R. Mordekhai mi-Lakhovich (R. Mordekhai of Lakhovich) Lakhovich Memorial Volume, ed. I. Rubin, Tel-Aviv 1949.

Gruenspan, A.: R. Noah ha-Zaken, Ben ha-Rav R. Mordekhai mi-Lakhovich (R. Noah the Elder, the Son of Mordekhai of Lakhovich) Op. cit.

Gruenspan, A.: R. Mordekhai Ben R. Moshe-Hayyim, R. Mordekhai ha-Sheni (R. Mordekhai the Son of R. Moshe-Hayyim, R. Mordekhai the Second) Opt. cit.

Gruenspan, A.: Ha-Admur R. Aharele Malovitski (The Rebbe A. Aharele Malovitski) Op. cit.

Had min Havrayya: Hithgalluth ha-Yenuka bi-Stolin (The Revelation of the Yenuka in Stolin) Ha-Shahar, Vol. VI, Vienna 1875.

Halpern, I.: Yahaso shel R. Aharon ha-Gadol mi-Karlin klapei Mishtar ha-Kehilloth (The Attitude of R. Aaron the Great of Karlin to the Kehillah System) Zion, 22nd year, Jerusalem 1957.

Halpern, I.: Havuroth la-Torah ve-la-Mitsvoth ve-ha-Hasiduth be-Hithpashtuthah (Group for the Study of the Torah and for Mitsvoth and the Spread of Hasidic Movement) Zion, 22nd year, Jerusalem 1957.

Hausman, A.: Divrei Aharon (The Words of Aaron) Jerusalem 1962.

Hayyim-Heike me-Amdur: Hayyim va-Hesed (Hayyim-Heike of Amdur: Life and Grace) Jerusalem, no date of publication.

Heilman, H. M.: Beth Rabbi (The House of the Rabbi) Berdichev 1903.

Hessen, J.: Yevreyi v Rossiyi (The Jews in Russia) St. Petersburg 1906.

Hessen, J.: Istoriya Yevreyskogo Naroda v Rossiyi (History of the Jewish People in Russia) Vol. I, Leningrad 1925.

Hilman, D. T.: Iggeroth ha-Tanya (Letters of the Author of Tanya) Jerusalem 1953.

Hok le-Yisrael (A Law Unto Israel) ed. T. Manksur, Jerusalem.

Horodets Memorial Volume, ed. Ben-Ezra, A., and Sussman, Y., New York 1949.

Horodezki, S. A.: Ha-Hasiduth ve-ha-Hasidim (Hasidism and the Hasidim) Vol. II, Tel-Aviv 1951.

Iggereth ha-Kodesh . . . mi- . . . Menahem-Mendel . . . mi-Vitebsk . . . mi- . . . Avraham mi-Kalisk . . . mi-Hayyim-Heikel mi- . . . Amdur . . . (Holy Letters . . . from . . . Menahem-Mendel . . . of Vitebsk . . . from

BIBLIOGRAPHY

. . . Abraham . . . of Kalisk . . . from Hayyim-Heikel of . . . Amdur) no place and date of publication.

Iggereth ha-Kodesh, Helek 2 mi-Sefer Likkutei Amarim . . . Menahem-Mendel mi-Vitebsk . . . Avraham . . . Kalisk . . . Hanhagoth ha-Rav ha-Kadosh mi-Lakhovich ve-Rabbi Hayyim-Heikel (The Holy Letter, Part 2 of the Book of Selected Sayings . . . by Menahem-Mendel of Vitebsk . . . Abraham . . . of Kalisk . . . Guides to Conduct by the Holy Rabbi of Lakhovich and R. Hayyim-Heikel) Lemberg 1911.

Israelit, N.: Mishpahath Israelit (The Israelit Family) in Pinkas Kletsk, Tel-Aviv 1959.

Ivenski, M.: Der Koidanover Rebbe R. Aharele (The Koidanov Rebbe R. Aharele) Koidanov Volume, New York 1955.

Jewish Encyclopedia, Vol. VII, s.v.: Kobrin.

Kehal Hasidim (Community of Hasidim) no place and date of publication.

Kehal Hasidim he-Hadash (The New ' Community of Hasidim ') Lemberg 1904.

Kempinski-Lieberman, B.: Yamav ha-Ahronim shel ha-Rebbe Moshele Perlov (The Last Days of the Rebbe Moshe Perlov) Stolin Memorial Volume, Tel-Aviv 1952.

Kerman, M.: Meine Sikhreynes (My Reminiscences) stencil, no place and date of publication, [Haifa 1953?]

Kithvei Kodesh . . . mi-Rabbotheinu . . . Slonim (Holy Writings of our Teachers . . . of Slonim) published by Slonim Hasidim, Germany 1948.

Klausner, Yisrael: Vilna bi-Tkufath ha-Gaon (Vilna in the Time of the Gaon) Jerusalem 1942.

Klausner, Yosef: R. Alexander-Suesskind mi-Horodno—he-Hasid bein ha-Mithnagdim, Sefer Asaf (R. Alexander-Suesskind of Grodno—the Hasid among the Mithnagdim, The Asaf Volume) Jerusalem 1953.

Kleinbaum, Y. M.: Shema Shelomo (The Fame of Solomon) Petrokov 1928.

Kleinman, M. H.: Mazkereth Shem ha-Gedolim (In Memory of the Great Ones) Petrokov 1908.

Kleinman, M. H.: Zikhron la-Rishonim (A Memory of the First Ones) Petrokov 1912.

Kleinman, M. H.: Or Yesharim (Light of the Upright) Petrokov 1924.

Kleinman, M. H.: La-Yesharim Tehillah (Praise to the Upright) Jerusalem 1960.

Kobrin, Sefer (Kobrin Memorial Volume) ed. Shwarz, B., and Biletski, Y. H., Tel-Aviv 1951.

Kopelovich, M: Ha-Yeshivah (The Yeshivah), Stolin Memorial Volume, Tel-Aviv 1952.

Kule, Y.: Hasidisher Shabbes in Luninyets (A Hasidic Sabbath in Luninyets) Luninyets-Kozan-Horodok Memorial Volume, Tel-Aviv 1952.

Kunde-Ginsburg, T.: Zikhronoth (Reminiscences) David-Horodok Memorial Volume, ed. Idan, Y., and others, Tel-Aviv, no date of publication.

Levin, Noah-Hayyim: Masekheth Avoth im . . . Perush (The Tractate Avoth with . . . Commentaries) Warsaw 1878.

Levin, Y.: Letter, Ha-Melits, daily paper, 1886, No. 26, pp. 544, 545.

Levinstein, Y.: Dor va-Dor ve-Dorshav (Every Generation and its Interpreters) Warsaw, no date of publication.

Lichtenstein, K.: Toledoth ha-Yishuv ha-Yehudi bi-Slonim, Pinkas Slonim

LITHUANIAN HASIDISM

(History of the Jewish Community in Slonim, in Pinkas Slonim) Vol. I, Tel-Aviv 1962.

Lieberman, H.: Hearoth Bibliografioth, Sefer ha-Yovel le-Alexander Marx (Bibliographical Notes, Alexander Marx Jubilee Volume) New York 1943.

Lifschits, Y.: Zikhron Yaakov (Memory of Jacob) Pt. I, Kovno-Slobodka 1924.

Lipson, M.: Mi-Dor Le-Dor (From Generation to Generation) Tel-Aviv 1929-1938.

Luninyets-Kozhan-Hodorok, Yizkor (Memorial Volume) ed. Zeevi, Y., and others, Tel-Aviv 1952.

Mahler, R.: Toledoth ha-Yehudim be-Polin (The History of the Jews in Poland) Merhaviah 1946.

Maimon Salomon: Lebensgeschichte, Munich 1911.

Malakhi, A. R.: Sefer she-lo Zakah liroth Or, Sefer ha-Yovel shel ha-Doar (An Unpublished Book, Ha-Doar Jubilee Volume) New York 1952.

Marek, P.: Vnutrennyaya Borba v Yevreystve v XVIII Veke (The Internal Jewish Struggle in the 18th Century) Yevrayskaya Starina, Vol. XII, Leningrad 1928.

Margoliyoth, Meir: Meir Nethivim (The Illuminator of Paths) Polonnoye 1791.

Margoliyoth, Meir: Sod Yakhin u-Boaz (The Secret of Yakhin and Boaz) Ostrog 1794.

Menahem-Mendel . . . of Vitebsk: Peri ha-Arets (The Fruit of the Land) Kapost [Kopys] 1814.

Meirim, Meir: Nir, Perush al . . . Yerushalmi (A Ploughed Field, Commentary on the Jerusalem Talmud) Warsaw 1875—Vilna 1890.

Meirson, M. M.: Ha-Shosheleth ha-Kobrinaith (The Kobrin Dynasty) Kobrin Memorial Volume, ed. Schwarz, B., and Biletski, Y. H., Tel-Aviv 1951.

Meoroth ha-Gedolim (The Great Lights) ed. Tseilingold, A., Pt. III, Bilgorai, no date of publication.

Mosesson, Y. L.: Masa be-Russiyah (A Journey in Russia) Ha-Shahar, Vol. VI, Vienna 1875.

Moshe mi-Kobrin: Amaroth Tehoroth (Moses of Kobrin: Selected Utterances) ed. Hacohen, Y. Y., Warsaw 1910.

M.B.: Ha-Rav ha-Tsaddik R. Avraham Weinberg . . . be-Baranovich (The Rav and Tsaddik R. Abraham Weinberg . . . in Baranovich) Baranovich Memorial Volume, Tel-Aviv 1953.

M.B.: Beth ha-Rav ha-Tsaddik R. Nehemyah Perlov, ha-Admur shel Hasidei Koidanov be-Baranovich (The House of the Tsaddik R. Nehemyah Perlov, the Rebbe of the Koidanov Hasidim in Baranovich) Op. cit.

Nadav, M.: Kehillath Pinsk ba-Tekufah she-mi-Gezeroth Tah-Tat ad Shalom Andruszov (1648-1667) (The Community of Pinsk from the Khmelnitski Massacres to the Peace of Andruszov [1648-1667]) Zion, 31st year, Jerusalem 1966.

Nadav, M.: Toledoth Kehillath Pinsk (History of the Community of Pinsk) in ms.

Noah-Naftali mi-Kobrin, Maamarim Tehorim (Noah-Naftali of Kobrin, Pure Sayings) Supplement to the book of Amaroth Tehoroth by R. Moshe of Kobrin, ed. Hacohen, Y. Y., Warsaw 1910.

Oppenheim, Y. A. L.: Sheloshah Sefarim Niftahim, Zemiroth shel Shabbath (Three Opened Books, Liturgical Sabbath Songs) Petrokov 1910.

BIBLIOGRAPHY

Or Zarua (A Shining Light) ed. Avatihi, A., and Ben-Zakai, Y., Tel-Aviv 1952.

Otsar Yisrael (The Treasure of Israel's *Encyclopedia*) s.v.: Halukkah, ed. Eisenstein, Y. D., London 1935.

Ovchinski, Levi: Nahlath Avoth (The Ancestral Patrimony) Vilna 1894.

Perlov: Shalom mi-Koidanov, Divrei Shalom (Shalom of Koidanov, Words of Shalom [=Peace]) Vilna, 1882.

Perlov: Mishmereth Shalom (The Keeping of Peace) Warsaw 1912.

Perlov: Atereth Shalom (The Crown of Peace) Warsaw 1895.

Perlov: Ha-Tsevi Yisrael (The Glory of Israel) supplement to the book Atereth Shalom, Warsaw 1895.

Perlov: Tikkun Lag ba-Omer (Lag ba-Omer Prayers) Jerusalem (?) 1910.

Perlov: Kuntres Dover Shalom, Tsavvaath . . . R. Shalom . . . me-Ir Brahin (The Tract of the Speaker of Peace, Testament . . . of R. Shalom . . . of the Town of Brahin) New York, no date of publication.

Perlov, Yitshak: Erez ba-Levanon (A Ceder in Lebanon) Vilna 1899.

Pichenik, A.: Ha-Shoshaloth ha-Hasidiyoth be-Vohlyn: Berezna (Hasidic Dynasties in Volhynia: Berezna) Yalkut Vohlyn, Tel-Aviv 1946.

Pinkas Medinath Lita (Minutes of the Lithuanian Provincial Assembly) ed. Dubnow, Berlin 1925.

Rabinowitsch, S. M.: Al Pinsk, Karlin ve-Yoshveihen (On Pinsk, Karlin and their Inhabitants) Talpioth, Pt. Kehilloth Yaakov, Berdichev 1895.

Rabinowitsch, W. Z.: Min ha-Genizah ha-Stolinaith (From the Stolin Genizah) Zion, 5th year, Jerusalem 1940.

Rabinowitsch, W. Z.: Al ' Sefer ha-Tsoref ' (The Book of the *Tsoref* [Purifier]) Zion, 6th year, Jerusalem 1941.

Rabinowitsch, W. Z.: 19 Kislev ve-hey Hanukkah (19th *Kislev* and 5th Day of Hanukkah) Ha-Olam, 26th year, No. 13, Jerusalem 1937.

Rabinowitsch, W. Z.: Mikkterei Bakkashah (Wish Letters) Zion, 33rd year, Jerusalem 1968.

Razi, Y.: Mamshikh ha-Shosheleth (The Heir to the Dynasty) Or Zarua, ed. Avatihi, A., and Ben-Zakai, Y., Tel-Aviv 1952.

Rivkind, Y.: Amdur, Grodner Opkangen, periodical, Buenos Aires, November, 1955.

Roysen: Avraham-Abbele mi-Makov, Birkath Avraham (Abraham-Abbele of Makov, The Blessing of Abraham) Warsaw 1895.

Rubinstein, A.: Shever Posheim le-R. David mi-Makov—Zoth Torath ha-Kanauth le-R. Yehezkel mi-Radzimin (The Book ' *Shever Posheim* ' ascribed to R. David of Makov, and ' *Zoth Torah ha-Kanauth* ' ascribed to R. Yehezkel of Radzimin) Kiryath Sefer, Vol. XXXV, Jerusalem 1960.

Rubinstein, A.: Ha-Kuntres ' Zimrath Am ha-Arets ' bi-Kthav-Yad (The ms. Tract ' *Zimrath Am ha-Arets* ') Aresheth, Vol. III, ed. Ben-Menahem, N., and Rafael, Y., Jerusalem 1961.

Schlossberg, Y.: Hasidim un Misnagdim Amol in Mein Stetel (Hasidim and Mithnagdim in the Old Days in My Town) Tog-Morgen-Jurnal, daily paper, New York 4.12.1957.

Seder Tefillath Yisrael . . . Or ha-Yashar, Nusakh . . . Rabbi . . . mi-Koidanov . . . ve-Rabbi mi-Stolin (Prayer-Book ' *Or ha-Yashar* ' . . . of Rabbi of Koidanov and of Rabbi of Stolin) Vilna 1928.

Sefer Shimon Dubnow (Simon Dubnow Memorial Volume) ed. Rawidowicz, S., Jerusalem 1954.

Shakh, A.: Yeshivath ' Beth Yisrael ' (' The House of Israel ' *Yeshivah*)

Luninyets-Kozhan-Horodok Memorial Volume, ed. Zeevi, Y., and others, Tel-Aviv 1952.

Shalom, S.: Dodi Reb Aharele, Shirim (My Uncle Rabbi Aharele, Poems) Tel-Aviv 1949.

Shapiro, A. E.: Mishnath Hakhamim (The Teaching of the Sages) Jerusalem 1934.

Shazakh, S.: Simhath R. Aharele (The Rejoicing of R. Aharele) Ha-Tsofeh, daily paper, Tel-Aviv 14.10.1951.

Shelomo mi-Helmo: Mirkeveth ha-Mishneh (Solomon of Helm, The Second Chariot) Frankfurt on the Oder 1751.

Shelomo mi-Radomsk: Tifereth Shelomo (Solomon of Radomsk: The Glory of Solomon) Petrokov 1889.

Shemuel . . . mi-Slonim . . . Hamishah Mikhtavim, Kuntres Kithvei Kodesh (Samuel of Slonim, Five Letters, Holy Writings) published by the Hasidim of Slonim, Germany 1948.

Shisha, A.: Hadarom, periodical, Vol. V-VI, New York 1958.

Shivhei ha-Besht (The Praises of the Besht) ed. Horodezki, S. A., Berlin 1922.

Shivhei ha-Rav . . . R. Shneur-Zalman (The Praises of the Rav . . . R. Shneur-Zalman) ed. Druker, Lemberg, no date of publication.

Shneur, Z.: Ha-Gaon ve-ha-Rav (The Gaon and the Rav) Tel-Aviv 1958.

Shtam, S. E.: Zekher Tsaddik (The Memory of the Righteous Man) Vilna 1905.

Sifron, Y. Y. Y., mi-Komarno: Heikhal ha-Berakhah (Sifron, Y. Y. Y., of Komarno: The Shrine of Blessing) Lemberg 1867.

Stolin, Sefer Zikkaron (Stolin Memorial Volume) ed. Avatihi, A., and Ben-Zakai, Y., Tel-Aviv 1952.

Teitelbaum, M.: Ha-Rav mi-Ladi u-Miflegeth Habad (The Rav from Ladi and the Habad Branch [of Hasidism]) Pt. I., Warsaw 1910.

Tishby, I.: Tikkunei Teshuvah shel Nathan ha-Azathi (Penitential Prayers of Nathan ha-Azathi) Tarbits, Vol. XV, Jerusalem 1944.

Tishby, I.: Ha-Raayon ha-Meshihi ve-ha-Megammoth ha-Meshihiyoth bi-Tsmihath ha-Hasiduth (The Messianic Idea and Messianic Trends in the Growth of Hasidism) Zion, 32nd year, Jerusalem 1967.

Toledoth Anshei Shem (The History of Famous Men) ed. Rand, A. Z., New York 1950.

Torath Avoth, Maamarei Kodesh . . . me-eth Shosheleth Lakhovich-Kobrin-Slonim (The Teaching of Our Forefathers, Holy Sayings . . . by the Lakhovich-Kobrin-Slonim Dynasty) Jerusalem 1961.

Toyzend Yor Pinsk (A Thousand Years of Pinsk) ed. Hofman, B., New York 1941.

Tsavvaah . . . Yad Kodesh . . . R. Aharon . . . mi-Karlin . . . ve-Hanhagoth . . . mi-Beno . . . R. Asher . . . mi-Karlin (Will Written in the Hand of R. Aaron [the Great] of Karlin and Guides to Conduct by His Son, R. Asher of Karlin) Chernovits 1855.

Tsavvaath ha-Ribash (The Will of the Ribash [R. Yisrael Baal-Shem]) Jerusalem 1948.

Tsinovets, M.: Le-Toledoth ha-Rabbanuth be-Kobrin (On the History of the Rabbinate in Kobrin) Kobrin Memorial Volume, ed. Schwarz, B., and Biletski, Y. H., Tel-Aviv 1951.

Tukchinski, Y. M.: Lakhovich mi-lifnei 70 Shanah (Lakhovich Seventy

BIBLIOGRAPHY

Years Ago) Lakhovich Memorial Volume, ed. Rubin, Y., Tel-Aviv 1949.

Uri ha-Saraf mi-Strelisk, Imrei Kadosh ha-Shalem (Uri the Seraph of Strelisk, The Complete Sayings of the Holy Man) ed. Shenblum, B. Z., Lvov, no date of publication.

Valden, A.: Shem ha-Gedolim he-Hadash (The New 'Memorial to the Great') Warsaw 1880.

Vilenski, Y. Z.: Zikhronoth (Reminiscences) Kobrin Memorial Volume, ed. Schwarz, B., and Biletski, Y. H., Tel-Aviv 1951.

Weizman-Lichtenstein, H.: Be-Tsel Korathenu (Under the Shadow of Our Roof) Tel-Aviv 1948.

Wilensky, M.: The Polemic of Rabbi David of Makov against Hasidism, Proceedings of the American Academy for Jewish Research, Vol. XXV, New York 1956.

Wilensky, M.: Teudah 'Mithnagdith' bi-Dvar Serefath 'Zemir Aritsim ve-Harvoth Tsurim' (A Mithnaged Document Concerning the Burning of 'Zemir Aritsim ve-Harvoth Tsurim') Tarbits, Vol. XXVII, Jerusalem 1958.

Wilensky, M.: Hearoth la-Pulmusim bein ha-Hasidim ve-ha-Mithnagdim (Notes on the Polemic Between the Hasidim and the Mithnagdim) Tarbits, Vol. XXX, Jerusalem 1961.

Yaakov mi-Novominsk: Shufra de-Yaakov (Jacob of Novominsk, The Best of Jacob) ed. Perlov, N. M., Jerusalem 1964.

Yahalal [Yehudah-Leib Levin], Zikkaron ba-Sefer (Memoirs) Zhitomir 1910.

Yaari, A.: Ha-Defus ha-Ivri bi-Shklov (The Hebrew Printing-Press in Shklov) Kiryath Sefer, Vol. XXII, Jerusalem 1945.

Yaari, A.: Sheluhei Erets Yisrael (Emissaries of the Land Israel) Jerusalem 1951.

Yevreyskaya Entsiklopediya, Vol. VII, s.v: Dombrovits, and Vol. XIV, s.v.: Stolinskiye Tsaddiki.

Yisrael-Leibel, Sefer ha-Vikkuah (The Book of the Dispute) quoted by Dubnow, Toledoth ha-Hasiduth, q.v.

Yitshak mi-Neskhizh: Zikhron Tov (Isaak of Neskhizh: A Good Fame) ed. Landau, Y., Petrokov 1892.

Yonathan, Y. L.: Nof va-Geza (Landscape and Genealogy) Tel-Aviv 1955.

Y. Z.: R. Aharele Ginsburg, Yizor Kehilloth Luninyets-Kozhan-Horodok (R. Aharele Ginsburg, Luninyets-Kozhan-Horodok Memorial Volume ed. Zeevi and others, Tel-Aviv 1952.

[Zak], Barukh Yosef, Birkath Yosef (The Blessing of Joseph) New York 1919.

Zeevi, Y.: Luninyetser Botei Midroshim (The Prayer- and Study-Houses in Luninyets) Luninyets-Kozhan-Horodok Memorial Volume, Tel Aviv 1952.

Zeidman, H. R.: Aharon Perlov be-Ghetto Varshah (R. Aaron Perlov in the Warsaw Ghetto) Stolin Memorial Volume, Tel-Aviv 1952.

Zemiroth le-Shabbathoth ve-Yomim Tovim (Liturgical Songs for Sabbaths and Festivals) ed. A.B., Jerusalem 1947.

Zevin, S. Y.: Sippurei Hasidim, Moadim (Tales of the Hasidim, Festivals) Tel-Aviv 1957.

Zweifel, E. T.: Shalom al Yisrael (Peace Upon Israel) Pt. II, Zhitomir 1869.

.: Gad-Asher Levin, Pinsker Stot Luah (Gad-Asher Levin in the Pinsker Year-Book) Vilna 1903/4.

S